TURKISH CINEMA

# Turkish Cinema

## Identity, Distance and Belonging

Gönül Dönmez-Colin

REAKTION BOOKS

*To my parents.*

Published by Reaktion Books Ltd
33 Great Sutton Street
London EC1V 0DX, UK
www.reaktionbooks.co.uk

First published 2008

Printed and bound in Great Britain by
CPI Antony Rowe, Chippenham, Wiltshire

All picture material is from the collection of the author.

British Library Cataloguing in Publication Data
Donmez-Colin, Gonul
    Turkish cinema : identity, distance and belonging
    1. Motion pictures - Turkey
    I. Title
    791.4'3'09561

ISBN: 978 1 86189 370 3

# Contents

# Introduction

In an old commercial Turkish movie, the heroine, with her voice quivering, declares to her lover: 'We belong to different worlds, Kemal'! What are these different worlds and why is there such an irremediable gap between the two?

Türkan Şoray, the *sultana* of Turkish cinema, plays the daughter of a fisherman in the Atıf Yılmaz classic *Kara Gözlüm / My Dark-eyed One* (1970); she is a wild beauty whose appealing voice catches the attention of the king of music halls, who wants to make her a star, but first she has to be schooled in the ways of the West. She is appointed a teacher of etiquette she calls 'Madame', an attribute for non-Muslim women. Madame's accent reveals a Christian background – probably Armenian, the minorities who live in the European section of the town and represent Western culture. In ten lessons the fisherman's daughter is to learn how to cross her legs like a modern woman when she sits ('If you show too much, it's striptease, if you show too little, it's bad manners'), to dance to Western tunes, to answer the phone with a 'bedroom voice' and to make small talk about classical music at cocktail parties. She is expected to upgrade from *à la turca* to *à la franca*, two common expressions identifying Anatolian and European cultures, respectively. For each lesson Madame informs the fisherman's daughter how it is on 'their' side, to which Şoray responds boldly, to the cheers of the audience, with how it is on 'her' side.

The terms *à la turca* and *à la franca*, part of common life from music and food to the living-room furniture, have become almost obsolete today, giving way to another polarity of identities, Muslim and secular, the Muslim identity connected with the Ottoman past and back-to-the-roots concept and the secular equated with modernity fashioned after the Western modes.

Istanbul is a booming metropolis similar to other urban centres of the East to which urbanism has arrived too fast. The city, which was the centre of cosmopolitan culture at the turn of the twentieth century, has been confronted with the challenge of sustaining the balance of East and West, as migration from rural Anatolia has transported a different culture, long alien to the elite of Istanbul, who have prided themselves in a European heritage. The 'transformation of society from traditional, rural and less developed to modern, urban, industrial and more developed, or alternatively, from feudal to capitalist', is felt deeply in Istanbul, where 'the process of social fragmentation and differentiation' has been more densified and visible.[1]

To what degree do artists respond freely to their environment and to what degree does the urban experience impose a specific vision? Istanbul is in almost every film from the traditional commercial cinema to contemporary self-reflexive *auteur* films. Lovers separate and reunite on the shores of the Bosporus, the turbulent strait that divides Europe from Asia. The lonely man draws a long puff from his cigarette cursing his fate (say poverty) for losing his beloved. The disillusioned artist/intellectual has a moment of reflection on a bench facing the Anatolian coast and perhaps begins to see the point of view of the provincial, his suppressed

The disillusioned artist/intellectual has a moment of reflection on a bench facing the Anatolian coast and perhaps begins to see the point of view of the provincial, his suppressed 'other'. *Uzak / Distant* (2002), dir. Nuri Bilge Ceylan.

'other', while the young provincial watches the cargo ships he thinks may one day change his destiny but always leave without him.

Istanbul is where cinema was born in Turkey. The grand Western invention arrived in 1896 to the cosmopolitan milieu around Pera (the Beyoğlu district of today in the European section) where most Europeans resided, and despite several facelifts over the decades, has kept this district as its axis, growing around one particular street, Yeşilçam (The Green Pine), which gave its name to a Turkish Hollywood without a studio system in the American sense.

For Yeşilçam, whose widest audience was the lower middle class or the proletariat, the West and the lifestyles it promoted was both utopia and dystopia, an object of desire that could lead to loss of innocence. The metropolis lured the innocent peasants to its clutches. The new-comers seeking a new identity and a place to call 'home' in a city reputed to be paved with gold were caught between traditional values and the daily challenges to conform. The devious prospered while the honest learned a hard lesson.

The kinetic and disorienting reality of the urban scene has been an integral part of many films. Sometimes the city is a beautiful dream, sometimes a horrific nightmare, from *Ah, Güzel Istanbul / Oh, Beautiful Istanbul* (1966) by Atıf Yılmaz (and Ömer Kavur's 1981 version bearing the same title) to Nuri Bilge Ceylan's internationally acclaimed *Uzak / Distant* (2002). In the labyrinth of the city old identities are discarded and new ones formed; as the distance between the past and the present self widens, the future and the sense of belonging becomes blurred. In several contemporary films home loses its sheltering function altogether (*Meleğin Düşüşü / Angel's Fall*, 2004, Semih Kaplanoğlu); becomes a trap or a burden (*Kasaba / The Small Town*, 1997; *Mayıs Sıkıntısı / Clouds of May*, 1999, Ceylan) or ceases to exist (*Tabutta Rövaşata / Somersault in a Coffin*, 1996, Derviş Zaim; *Masumiyet / Innocence*, 1997, Zeki Demir-kubuz; *Herkes Kendi Evinde / Away From Home*, 2001, Kaplanoğlu; *Rıza*, 2007, Tayfun Pirselimoğlu).

The connection between 'urban memory' and the city is significant, as Anthony Vidler points out. Urban memory was easy to define in the traditional city, whether antique, medieval or Renaissance, and the image of the city facilitated identification with the past and present as a political, cultural and social entity. The city provided a familiar moral and protected environment for daily life that could be called 'home'.[2] What is 'uncanny' or *unheimlich*, to use the Freudian term,[3] in global

'Home loses its sheltering function, or becomes a trap or a burden.'

*Meleğin Düşüşü / Angel's Fall* (2004), dir. Semih Kaplanoğlu.

*Mayıs Sıkıntısı / Clouds of May* (1999), dir. Nuri Bilge Ceylan.

*Kasaba / The Small Town* (1997), dir. Bilge Ceylan.

cities of today is that ethnic and social diversity and the accompanying exclusion have made it difficult to create a collective urban memory for the citizens to identify. In the vacuum, obscure identifications have led to urban discourses based on fear and insecurity, creating urban ghettos or gated communities.[4] *C Blok / Block C* (1994) by Zeki Demirkubuz, *Ağir Roman / Cholera Street* (1997) by Mustafa Altıoklar and *İki Genç Kız / Two Girls* (2005) by Kutluğ Ataman are some of the realistic explorations of lives affected by the urban maelstrom.

Literary figures such as Baudelaire and Zola had illustrated the psychological consequences when the city evolved into a metropolis in the late nineteenth and early twentieth centuries and the urban space as home became 'uncanny'. The individual felt estranged in the metropolitan mass and the uncanny manifested itself in agoraphobia and claustrophobia.[5] The complete oeuvre of Zeki Demirkubuz displays 'the feeling of not-being-at-home'.[6]

For Nobel Laureate Orhan Pamuk, who calls himself 'a writer of Istanbul', the in-between-two-cultures status of Turkey and the conflict between European and Islamic values have created confusion and loss of identity. Comparing the present republic which, over the years 'has expelled, exiled or silenced its ethnic minorities' (also illustrated in Yaşar Kemal's novel, *Fırat Suyu Kan Akıyor Baksana / Look, the Fırat River is Flowing with Blood*, 1997) to the multicultural, multi-ethnic, multi-confessional and multi-linguistic constitution of the Ottoman Empire, Pamuk finds a certain *hüzün* (melancholy) in the disposition of the city's citizens who seem in a constant search for (lost) identity. Like *Istanbul Hatıraları / Memories of Istanbul* (2005), Pamuk's personal essay on his city, Ömer Kavur's *Gizli Yüz / The Secret Face* (1991), scripted by Pamuk, carries the motif of loss and absence in the character of a young woman who searches for signs in human faces. In Nuri Bilge Ceylan's *Uzak / Distant*, one feels the *hüzün* of Orhan Pamuk in the way the country cousin takes a puff from his Samsun cigarette (the cheap national product disdained by the city cousin) looking at an empty spot, or in the city

Kutluğ Ataman's
*İki Genç Kız /
Two Girls* (2005)
explores social
diversity and the
resulting exclusion
that creates a
vacuum.

cousin's incessant sighs as he shifts from Tarkovsky to porno on the TV screen, or the way the city spreads itself under the blanket of snow, all grey without a ray of the sun. Ceylan's Istanbul is akin to Pamuk's city in *Kara Kitap / The Black Book* (1990), where prostitutes assume the identities of the Yeşilçam stars (a Türkan Şoray look-alike recites lines from Lütfi Ö. Akad's classic *Vesikalı Yarim / Licensed to Love*, 1968) and hundreds of years of history are buried under the strait of Bosporus, a 'waste land' where identities are lost or negotiated.

The bridge joining the two continents has become a metaphor, albeit somewhat of a cliché, for the identity of Turkey. Hamburg-born Fatih Akın claims his musical documentary *Crossing the Bridge: The Sound of Istanbul* (2005) grew out of a desire to explore whether Turkey is European enough for the European Union, and music seemed to be an interesting way to answer that question. While shooting the film, he realized that the situation in Turkey was much more complex. Even the music stretched from Romany orchestras to hip hop, with rock bands and traditional groups vying for space. He reached the conclusion that the West does not end at the Greek border and the East does not extend from Istanbul to China. 'These are imaginary boundaries.'[7] The bridge to be crossed in the film is a literal one joining the European side to the Asian side, but also a trope for Turkey's position, geographically, politically and culturally. In this context German musician Alexander Hacke's journey to Istanbul in the film becomes more than an exploration of the Turkish musical scene, a reference to the European Union's coveted readiness to cross over and accept Turkey.

Turkey revered Europe as a model long before the establishment of the Turkish Republic, and the reforms of Kemal Atatürk, which gave the state authority to regulate the behaviour of its citizens, from the choice of music, the language they spoke to the clothes they wore, had one aim: to make a European nation out of a country that has less than a quarter of its land in Europe. Turkey's endeavours to join the European Union have almost become legendary. Most Turks believe that joining the European Union will complete the Westernization process that started in the late nineteenth century with the Young Ottomans and the Jeunes Turcs, who were influenced by French positivist thought. Even an Islamist-oriented government – the Justice and Development Party (AK) – has been willing to compromise on many controversial issues to comply with the demands of the European Union, although sceptics hypothesize that the real issue behind Europe's hesitance to let Turkey in is not its human rights record, or its policy towards Cyprus or even the Armenian issue, but its religion: Europe is not ready to open its arms to a Muslim nation with a population of over 70 million. Many Turks have settled in European countries, particularly Germany, and those who eventually returned to the motherland transposed some of the values that they have consciously or inadvertently acquired in the West, which has changed the societal make-up of the home country irreversibly. For the European psyche, however, Muslim Turkey has always remained the 'Islamic other'.

On the other hand Turkey has been reluctant to consider itself an integral part of the Middle East with which it shares a Muslim culture and many frontiers, a mentality that may be attributed to its Ottoman background, where the thrust of political and cultural life was directed to the Balkans, Rumelia being the centre for the network of religious and juridical institutions of the Ottoman Empire.[8]

In contemporary Turkey, particularly in the urban centres of the western area, the lifestyles of the West – music, jeans, foreign brand-name sneakers, Hollywood movies, fast food chains, massive shopping malls – are easily internalized, especially by urban youth. Westerners who see Turkey as a rural country where swarthy black-moustached men pledge their lives to shield their submissive women from the threatening male gaze view sceptically a film on free-spirited urban youth, *Two Girls*, arguing that women from a Muslim country cannot be so modern, so free and so 'promiscuous'. Akın's *Crossing the Bridge* takes us to the world of punks, rockers, rappers and tattoo parlours the West could never imagine in a Muslim country. Yet in certain neighbourhoods of Istanbul a woman would feel naked without a headscarf. Perhaps there is more than one Turkey, 'one composed of educated urban and Western-looking secularist upper and middle-classes (labelled in conversation as the "white Turks") and the other faith-driven lower-middle classes (labelled the "black Turks") originating from Anatolian towns' as sociologist Nilüfer Göle points out, although 'a fall of the wall' has been observed in the last two decades, despite prevailing disaffection. The upward social mobility among the second group – access to higher education in the 1960s with emigration to urban centres, the opportunities of the free market policies of the 1980s and access to political power with the electoral victory of the AK Party – turned them into 'grey', claims Göle, and the interaction between the two faces of Turkey, despite strong disagreements, 'transformed the mutual conceptions of the Muslim and secular publics and limited the claims to hegemony of the latter', the outcome facilitating the electoral feat of a party with Islamic roots (AK Party) in the general elections of November 2002.[9]

Turkish republicanism as the nation-state ideology has been founded on an authoritative and exclusionary secularism backed by the military, and an assimilative nationalism according to Göle.[10] In the structuring of the nation-state Kemal Atatürk maintained a distance from the Muslim religion, which he considered an impediment to modernization and the reforms of Westernization. The Ottoman caliphate that ruled over all Muslims was abolished in 1924. The secular policies of the new republic, parallel to its failure to find a solution to the miserable living conditions of the majority of the population, except a few urban elite, alienated the Anatolians and the ethnic minorities such as the Kurds, who had fought along with the Turks during the War of Liberation, but could not find their place in the new order. Under the 1923 Lausanne Treaty, Turkey granted minority rights to non-Muslims, who have the right to educate their children in their own language. The Kurds and other Muslim ethnic communities that are not regarded as minorities cannot receive such benefits.

The official definition of Turkish citizenship stresses 'Turkishness' – Turkish ethnicity, Turkish language and Sunni Islam – and does not allow for the separate and public manifestation of ethnic groups; Kurds, non-Sunni Muslims or non-Turkish-speaking identities. Article 66 of the 1982 Constitution (still in effect as this book is written) asserts 'Each person bound to the Turkish state through the bond of citizenship is a Turk'. Some of the finest intellectuals of the country, world-famous writers including Yaşar Kemal, Orhan Pamuk and Elif Şafak, have been tried for insulting 'Turkishness' (a crime under the controversial Article 301 of the constitution) by speaking out about atrocities committed against ethnic and religious minorities. Yeşim Ustaoğlu, who has made two controversial films, *Güneşe Yolculuk / Journey to the Sun* (1999) about the Kurdish issue and *Bulutları Beklerken / Waiting for the Clouds* (2004) about the deportation of the Greeks, points out the irony in the fact that some of the reforms that the EU demands from Turkey for its acceptance are related to the multiple identities living on its land, the identities that the Republic has ignored in its efforts to assume a European identity.[11]

Identity has become and continues to be one of the most debated issues of the present day. When lives are in a constant flux due to social, economic and/or political oppression, foreign aggression or civil wars, the issue of identity becomes very complex. All too often, the notion of identity – personal, religious, ethnic or national – has given rise to the desire to repress and/or exterminate the 'other'.

Melissa Butcher defines identity as 'the collection of inputs and influences, including ethnic, linguistic, religious, political, social, economic, family, state, and increasingly global, that form a coherent sense of place, both geographical and temporal'[12] and claims that identity is a social phenomenon, but also 'a tool for the management of the self' as pointed out by Vytautas Kavolis, 'directing correct behaviour within the context of the social so that as a unit it can continue to function'.[13] Whereas earlier societies with a social order based firmly in tradition would provide individuals with (more or less) clearly defined roles, in modern societies individuals have to work out their roles for themselves.

Theorists such as Michel Foucault and Anthony Giddens have written about how people create a sense of self and construct identities. Identity can be considered as a conception of the self in relation to others, which is constructed in the social and historical contexts by the creation of the differences between self and other as the outcomes of their interactions. According to Derrida all identities exist within their differences from others.[14]

The geopolitical situation of Turkey is crucial in defining a national or personal identity. Different ethnic groups are dispersed throughout the country although religious diversity – with the gradual departure of the non-Muslim population – has waned. Until recently, when meganarratives have lost their currency endangering the existence of the nation-state, the question of ethnicity had been overlooked, academically as well as cinematographically.

Yeşilçam ignored the ethnic mosaic of the country in favour of the official state policy of national identity based on homogeneity regardless of the differences in religion, ethnicity or sexuality. Censorship contributed to the establishment of an escapist cinema that was removed from the social, political and economical realities of Turkey. The Kurds were not depicted on the screen with their Kurdish identity until the 1990s. (Yılmaz Güney's *Seyyit Han* aka *Toprağın Gelini / Seyyit Han* aka *The Bride of the Earth*, 1968, was chastised by the censors for the protagonist having a Kurdish name, Keje; Şerif Gören's *Yol* was censored for its Kurdish songs.) They were not necessarily shown in a depreciatory manner, but they were never part of the diegesis. The audience would

surmise that 'a character in the background who wore black *shalvar*, spoke "bad Turkish", was poor and illiterate and came from the south-east was a Kurd',[15] the ignorant dark man from the mountains, devoted to his master and willing to serve him like a slave. This devotion exonerated the audience of any guilt feelings evoking Antonio Gramsci's idea of 'spontaneous consent' or 'consensual control', whereby individuals 'voluntarily' assimilate the hegemony of the 'dominant group'.[16] The non-Muslims continue to appear as motifs to decorate the narrative. Although their 'otherness' may not be displayed pejoratively, an inferential racism is evident in imitation of their accents or mannerisms, intended as mild jokes.

In the 1980s, during the Turgut Özal years,[17] the neo-liberal policies of the government facilitated technological reforms, especially in the information and communication sectors, which eased Turkey's integration into the capitalist system. However, the new economy did not benefit all citizens equally. In an atmosphere where money became the only aim (satirized in Reha Erdem's *Kaç Para Kaç / A Run for Money*, 1999),[18] corruption and crime increased. The war against the Kurdish guerrillas has exalted the national feelings of the masses, such nationalistic outbursts

Reha Erdem's *Kaç Para Kaç / A Run for Money* (1999) satirizes the free market economy.

creating a sceptical attitude among discerning citizens regarding a collective national identity. The rapid technological developments of the new millennium, worldwide globalization and the erosion of human values in the rat race to compete in the capitalist market have alienated individuals from their own being. The multiplication of the private television channels that reached its peak in the 1990s brought all aspects of life from the mundane to the extraordinary into the living room. Poverty, wars and murders graphically displayed on the television screen have contributed to the sense of alienation felt by many citizens who find no place in society, illustrated in Zeki Demirkubuz's *Yazgı / Fate* (2001), a film about a young man indifferent to death, love, marriage and prison.

Whereas the vogue in recent years has been to revive Ottoman culture, classical Turkish music and the old Yeşilçam movies, the past is manifest only as consumable nostalgia. How many who pass through the main street of Beyoğlu (the old Pera, the new SoHo of Istanbul) know that the *rebetika* music that blasts from the shops cries out the agonies of the Anatolian Greeks who were deported *en masse* during the population exchange of the 1920s? How many of the young generation that enjoy the cafés and bars of Beyoğlu today know that the area was once the hub of cultural exchange, with non-Muslim minorities plying their trade peacefully until the ransacking of their property, churches and cemeteries on 6–7 September 1955; the 1964 deportation of those who bore a Greek passport and the mass exodus of the *Rum* (ethnic Greek) that began during the nationalist frenzy of the invasion of Cyprus in 1974, which turned their neighbourhoods into ghost towns, to be revived with the arrival of Anatolian migrants who appropriated the decaying apartments, only to be ejected and pushed to the periphery by 'modernizing' speculators anxious to gentrify the back streets? Or do they, like Meryem, the Anatolian girl in Zülfü Livaneli's novel, *Mutluluk / Bliss* (2002), living in the south-east in one of the biggest wooden houses of the town that had once belonged to an Armenian, Ohannes, think that one extraordinary day all Armenians were blown to the sky by a divine storm?[19]

Turkish cinema's conventional distance from controversial issues, generated by long years of crippling censorship regulations, extends to matters of sexuality as well. Mainstream cinema is heterosexual and masculinist. Zeki Müren, the most popular singer of several decades, whose homosexuality was not a secret, played the Romeo in heterosexual stories written for him, where he appeared as 'Zeki, the famous singer' wearing more make-up than the principal actress and wiggling his hips more (*Beklenen Şarkı / The Awaited Song*, 1953; *Berduş / Vagabond*, 1957; *Kırık Plak / The Broken Disk*, 1959; *Aşk Hırsızı / The Love Thief*, 1961; *Istanbul Kaldırımları / The Pavements of Istanbul*, 1964; *Kalbimin Sahibi / The Owner of My Heart*, 1969; *Rüya Gibi /Like a Dream*, 1971, to name a few), but the audience accepted this travesty. Women flocked to his concerts in the segregated morning matinees, competing with each other to seize the handkerchief he nonchalantly threw to the crowd. In the novel *Bliss* the intellectual character Professor İrfan Kurudal states that in Turkey sexuality is dominant in the subconscious of all layers of society. The driving force behind the society, the basic instinct that shapes its behaviour, is repressed sexuality. Most male singers in the music halls are homosexual, he points out. When one of them has an operation and becomes a woman, the veneration is amplified. Just like the *köçek* (the young male dancers of the seventeenth century), these boys twist their bodies like women to the fusion of pop music and oriental rhythms and society loves them. Kurudal declares that homosexuality was widespread among the Ottoman. Naturally, he is chastised by his colleagues for attempts at 'deciphering the sexual codes of Turkish society'.[20]

Yeşilçam endorsed traditional family values since the majority of the audience was female, or families on a Sunday outing. With the arrival of feminism the focus shifted to women and their problems, but committed studies of the lives of women and their multiple identities were rare. Atıf Yılmaz, affectionately renamed 'the director of women's films', toyed with the idea of alternative sexual preferences from lesbianism to transvestism, but the issue did not receive serious consideration until gay activist/multidisciplinary artist Kutluğ Ataman's video works, and his feature film, *Lola und Bilidikid / Lola and Bilidikid* (1998), which focused on transvestites among the Turkish community in Berlin, a group that is doubly marginalized.

Cinema's role in defining identities – national, cultural, ethnic, religious, political or sexual – and challenging their validity is very important. The case of Turkish cinema is particularly noteworthy because in the process it has also been searching for an identity of its own, and both are interlinked to Turkey's quest for an identity, or its confirmation. This book seeks to explore the representations of various identities in Turkish cinema as well as the identity of Turkish cinema itself for a better understanding of Turkish identity.

Chapter One, 'In Search of Identity', looks at the history of cinema in Turkey from its arrival in 1896, a Western invention in an Eastern Muslim country, to its present status, through its golden periods, its declines and revivals and decades-long combat against state censorship. Its evolution, which runs parallel to the evolution of national, cultural, religious and social identity, and its contribution to the formation of this identity are the focal points.

Chapter Two, 'Migration, Dis/Misplacement and Exile', examines films that reflect the social changes in Turkish society as a result of migration from the countryside to the city, focusing on rural people's search for an identity in the urban environment; the negotiation of identity in a foreign land that takes different forms with different generations and the 'exilic filmmaking' that has produced some of the landmarks of Turkish cinema during the oppressive military regimes of the 1970s and '80s.

Chapter Three, 'Denied Identities', explores Turkish cinema's stand on minority and ethnic identities and the contribution of these identities to the evolution of Turkish cinema. Films on the plight of the Kurds and non-Muslim minorities are explored in this context and the emergence of a Kurdish cinema within Turkey is illustrated with readings of the works of Kazım Öz, one of the most prominent Kurdish filmmakers working in Turkey.

Chapter Four, 'Yılmaz Güney', aims to analyse the cinema of the most celebrated filmmaker of Turkey. Some of his lesser-known (or unknown) works are included, along with his landmark films, to draw a complete portrait of an exceptional man, from his politics to his artistic achievements. This chapter could be considered as an extension of chapter Three, since the term 'denied identity' is very appropriate in describing the films, the convictions and the life of Yılmaz Güney.

Chapter Five, 'Gender, Sexuality and Morals in Transition', traces Turkish cinema's stance on gender issues from its beginnings and its presentations of sexuality and alternative sexual choices, which are tightly connected to the evolution of morals in a constantly changing society. Such evolution often gains visibility through the stories of women, since 'women are more dramatic characters', according to Atıf Yılmaz, 'and in all levels of society, they are in search of an identity'.[21] In masculinist societies such as Turkey a certain timidity precludes the public discussion of male sexuality. Works that reflect, divert or obstruct the realities of Turkey are focalized within this context.

Chapter Six, 'A Modern Identity or Identity in a Modern World', looks at the New Turkish Cinema that has emerged in the 1990s and has acquired recognition among the contemporary cinemas of the world. Its major concerns are examined through the themes of identity, distance and belonging in a modern world as manifest in the works of some of the best representatives of this movement.

The Afterword is a reflection on the new path that Turkish cinema has taken, particularly in the first decade of the new millennium when it has reclaimed its audience, not only competing with the Hollywood products but surpassing them at the box office, while a handful of filmmakers have won prestigious awards at film festivals abroad. An outstanding point is that, whether art house fare or box office hit, the themes of contemporary films are quite similar: daily struggles of identity and belonging in a complex and complicated world appearing as one of the most pressing issues.

Layers of identity are not mutually exclusive, hence the difficulty of avoiding compartmentalization of identities in dividing the book into chapters. A film like Kutluğ Ataman's *Lola and Bilidikid*, which is discussed in 'Gender, Sexuality and Morals in Transition', is also a film about 'Denied Identities' as well as an important contribution to 'exilic' cinema. *Sürü / The Herd* by Zeki Ökten, discussed under 'Yılmaz Güney', its scriptwriter, is one of the best Turkish films on migration. Cross-references have to be made to do justice to the multilayered essence of these works and the issues they raise.

This book does not aim to narrate the long history of Turkish cinema, with all its phases, genres, trends and exceptional filmmakers. A choice had to be made of filmmakers and the films, to include the most appropriate for the subjects examined: identity, distance and belonging. Naturally, outstanding works of Turkish cinema are not confined to those examined here, but having watched innumerable films innumerable times, I feel that those included in the study meet the purpose of the book.

Scholarship on Turkish cinema is rather new and the sources available in languages other than Turkish are limited. This aspect was my main motivation in venturing into a study of a film industry that offers challenges in its diversity, originality and uniqueness. It is my wish that the present study will encourage further scholarship on this much neglected subject, particularly in the light of recent positive developments, energized with the arrival of committed filmmakers who are in a more privileged position than their predecessors in combining the technology of the West with the philosophy of the East.

Yılmaz Güney pointed out: 'Turkey is a country with several nations. For this reason, considering social contradictions and national differences, we must make films of "Turkey" and not "Turkish" films.'[22] In this book the adjective 'Turkish' does not equate with the official definition of 'Turkishness', but subsumes a heterogeneity of ethnic identities. In fact, several filmmakers whose works are discussed are transnational filmmakers; neither their concerns nor the manner in which they express these concerns can be restricted within borders. Güney has been appropriated by the Turkish left as well as the *engagé* filmmakers of the world (from Argentinian Fernando Solanas to West Bengali Goutam Ghose) as a guiding light in the struggle against state oppression and social and economic injustice. At the same time he has become a symbol for the Kurds in the assertion of their identity and an inspiration for contemporary filmmakers from Kurdish Bahman Ghobadi to Turkish Yeşim Ustaoğlu. Such is the power of art that transcends boundaries.

# 1 In Search of Identity

Cinema arrived in Ottoman Turkey, via a Frenchman named Bertrand, during a period when to emulate the West, considered the symbol of modern identity, was becoming popular. His private show at the court of Sultan Abdulhamit II in the Yıldız Palace in Istanbul was followed by public screenings at the fashionable Sponeck Restaurant in Pera by Sigmund Weinberg, a Polish Jew of Romanian nationality. Weinberg, the local agent of the French company Pathé Brothers, opened the first movie theatre in 1908 in the same district and called it Cinema-Théatre Pathé Frères.

Western powers regulated the industry they introduced. French, American, German or Danish films were distributed by Western companies and shown to non-Muslims of Pera and, later, to upper-class Muslims in cinema halls with French names: Ciné Oriental, Ciné Central, Ciné Magique, etc., which were replaced by Turkish names only a decade after the founding of the Turkish Republic. Publicity was printed in French, German, Armenian or Greek, but not in Turkish. In March 1914 two Turks, Cevat Boyer and Murat Bey, opened a cinema hall but even when Muslim-Turkish distributors took over foreign films held the market and no one seemed to mind. These films showed Europe as an enviable place. The Western identity of cinema was easily appropriated along with other technological inventions from the West that represented modernity and progress. Decades had to pass before Turkish films could find their audience.

In 1896 Alexandre Promio, the Lumière brothers' cameraman, shot short films about Turks in Ottoman Istanbul and, starting in 1907, the Macedonian Manaki brothers, Yanaki and Militiades, made documentaries. In 1914 a documentary called *Aya Stefanos'taki Rus Abidesinin*

*Yıkılışı / The Demolition of the Russian Monument at St Stephan* was apparently made by a reserve officer, Fuat Uzkınay, with the sponsorship of the army. (The demolition of a monument erected by the Russians to proclaim their victory in the 1876–7 war was one of the propaganda events organized by the Union and Progress Committee to improve public opinion.) Although no evidence substantiates that this film was actually made, the official history of Turkish cinema considers it as the first national film.

Enver Pasha, a prominent *jeune turc*, and the leader of the Ottoman Empire in the Balkan Wars and the First World War, was impressed by how the allies used cinema as a tool for propaganda. He ordered the establishment of a cinema institution following the German model and appointed Sigmund Weinberg as its head. Merkez Ordu Sinema Dairesi/ MOSD (Central Army Office of Cinema) was set up in 1915. Although lack of infrastructure and qualified personnel did not permit a large output, except for a few documentaries, the move was significant in establishing a solid relationship between the army and cinema, which has manifested itself overtly or covertly over the decades.

Weinberg was granted permission to make narrative films with army equipment. The shooting of the first feature film, *Himmet Ağanın İzdivacı / The Marriage of Himmet Aga*, a free adaptation of Molière, was suspended when most actors were recruited to serve in the Dardanelles. The film was completed in 1918 by Uzkınay; the Romanian Weinberg was dismissed when war broke between Romania and the Ottoman Empire.

In 1917 another military office, Müdafaa-i Milliye Cemiyeti (Association for National Defence), was involved in cinema with Fuat Uzkınay at its head. A young journalist, Sedat Simavi, made two films, *Pençe / The Claw* and *Casus / The Spy*, the first complete narrative films of Turkish cinema.

A leading figure of theatre, Ahmet Fehim, drew controversy with *Mürebbiye / The Governess* (1919), a sex-vaudeville about a licentious French seductress called Angélique (Madame Kalitea). Adapted from an 1898 novel by Hüseyin Rahmi Gürpınar, a celebrated Turkish novelist, the film was a vindictive satire on the infatuation of the upper classes with French culture. The War Veterans Association produced this film as well as Fehim's next, *Binnaz* (1919), also adapted from a novel by Gürpınar. Shot inside the Topkapı Palace about the decadent *Lale Devri* (Tulip Era of the Ottoman Empire), and featuring the eponymous heroine as a seductress who pits one man against the other, *Binnaz* is

considered Turkey's first historical film. According to the critics of the time, the film was not as remarkable as *The Governess* but was a box office hit, rumoured to have been sold to England for £5,000.[1] *The Governess* was banned by the commandant of the occupying French forces for degrading French women. Although Fehim defended his work as the peaceful protest of an artist against the occupation, *The Governess* could not escape the fate of becoming the first Turkish film to suffer in the hands of the censors.

In 1922, when Muhsin Ertuğrul, with a theatre background, returned home from Germany where he had worked as an actor and director, a new era started for Turkish cinema, referred to as 'The Period of Theatre Men' (1923–40). Actually, Ertuğrul, who was influenced by the French and German theatres and the Soviet revolutionary cinema, was the only filmmaker during this period when cinema borrowed from the theatre and did not seek to find a language of its own. Ertuğrul's *Ateşten Gömlek / The Shirt of Fire* aka *The Ordeal* aka *The Shirt of Flame* (1923), based on a novel by a popular woman writer, Halide Edip Adıvar, was the first film to deal with the War of Independence and the first national film of the Turkish Republic. It was screened on 23 April

*Binnaz* (1919), dir. Ahmet Fehim, considered Turkey's first historical film.

1923, on the third anniversary of the founding of the Turkish Grand National Assembly in an Istanbul still occupied by foreign armies. Commensurate with the nationalistic subject matter of the film, all roles were played by Turkish Muslims, including women's roles (as stipulated by Adıvar), which were previously given to non-Muslim minorities such as Greeks, Armenians and White Russians.

Ertuğrul established the 'heroic Turkish soldier' motif with the famous epic *Bir Millet Uyanıyor / A Nation is Awakening* (1932) and other filmmakers followed in his footsteps. Most of these films were inconsequential except for Lütfi Ö. Akad's *Vurun Kahpeye / Strike the Whore* (1949), considered among the classics of national cinema but reproved by Islamists for tarnishing the reputation of *imams* (see chapter Five).

Ertuğrul was the first filmmaker to introduce sound to Turkish cinema, in 1931 with *Istanbul Sokaklarinda / In the Streets of Istanbul*, about two brothers who play the accordion on pavements and sing to receive a few coins. Shot in Egypt, Greece and the town of Bursa in Turkey with the sound effects done in Paris, the film was removed from the realities of Turkish life, where the busker culture did not exist. Nonetheless, it was instrumental in the formation of the biggest studio of the country, İpek Film. Apart from being the first talkie, the film is also the first co-production of Turkey (Greece and Egypt).

In 1934 Ertuğrul participated in the second Venice Film Festival with *Leblebici Horhor Ağa / Horhor Aga, the Chickpea Seller* (1934),[2] which received an honorary mention, the first international award for a

Muhsin Ertuğrul's *Ateşten Gömlek / The Shirt of Fire* aka *The Ordeal* aka *The Shirt of Flame* (1923), the first film to deal with the War of Independence and the first national film of the Turkish Republic.

Lütfi Ö. Akad's *Vurun Kahpeye / Strike the Whore* (1949), exalting the image of the 'new woman of the Republic', received the ire of the Islamists.

Turkish film. Ertuğrul was also the first to focus on village life with *Batakli Damın Kızı Aysel / The Girl from the Marshes* (1934), a film with overt influences of Soviet cinema that was adapted from Selma Lagerlöf's novel, *Töser fran Stormytorpet*.[3]

As the only filmmaker of the early years Ertuğrul has a significant place in the film history of the country, although he was often criticized for imitating the West instead of contributing to the emergence of a national cinema inspired by the local culture. Gülseren Güçhan claims that his stand was in accordance with the cultural policy of the state, which aimed to sever all ties with the Ottoman past and to rebuild on the foundations of Western civilization. The hat 'reforms' (banning of the fez), balls, social mixing of the opposite sexes, *à la franca* music instead of *à la turca* were all Western elements that Turkish people were trying to assimilate and the cinema of Ertuğrul was doing the same thing.[4] The identity that Ertuğrul gave to his women characters – liberated and equal to men in love and business, living the lives they chose to live – was an echo of the social reforms envisioned by Atatürk, who considered the emancipation of women a priority, and the bourgeoisie presented in these films was the class Atatürk wanted to establish economically and socially.[5]

'The Period of Theatre Men' with the hegemony of Muhsin Ertuğrul is comparable to the one-party system of the early years of the Republic, its governing policy and its perception of society. The period that followed, which is referred to as 'The Period of Transition' (1940–50), was a transition period for Turkish politics as well. With the change in the municipality tax laws in 1948, a boost was given to the industry when the tax on national films was reduced to 25 per cent; film studios were established; organizations were formed and the first film festival held, but exceptional works were rare. Cinema continued to imitate the West and did not seek a new idiom or a particular identity.

With the founding of the Turkish Republic and the drastic changes in education, law and religion through the reforms of Atatürk, culture and art gained importance, and fine arts academies and conservatories were established, but cinema was somewhat neglected, although Atatürk often praised it and stressed its importance. The Ottoman past and the religious belief that forbids images might have been among the reasons for the reticence of society as a whole to embrace the new invention. More likely, the Western cultural identity of the invention was appealing only to those who could dream of achieving this identity one day, the elite. For the rest of the public, it was as alien as the felt hat the 'hat reform' obliged them to wear. French cinema remained dominant at least until the Second World War and even the American films that began to infiltrate by the 1930s were dubbed into French or shown with French and Turkish subtitles. National products were only poor imitations of foreign models.

Turkey's celebrated poet, Nazım Hikmet, who wrote several scripts under a pseudonym during his long years in prison for charges of communism, wrote in 1946 that the stagnation of the film industry, social reasons aside, was not due to a lack of technique, competent actors or filmmakers, or capital. The producers and filmmakers saw American, British and French films as models and failed to see that they could make films using the technical possibilities, talents and money available to them and attract an audience who would not have to compare their works to foreign films; the genre would be completely different.

> We always make the same mistake. We imitate the films of the others, films that depend on big technique, baby doll actresses, extravagant decor . . . but we do not have these facilities, so the result is a catastrophe . . . Since we do not have the possibilities of the American films to dazzle the audience, we should give up dazzling and do our work with sincerity and expertise and maybe then the audiences will come to see our films as if they are something they have never seen before.[6]

But cinema was a Western invention. Not only the technical equipment but also the genres were imported from the West, just like the modernity that Turkey was trying to adapt. Atatürk had said: 'If our borders are in the East, our mentality is oriented towards the West.'

The government change in 1950 brought a different cultural policy, which tried to reverse the historical, societal and cultural moves that were geared towards modernization and Western civilization. The Democrat Party (DP) that came to power advocated populism and the rule of the people. Farmers were given easy loans; the prices of their crops were inflated; imported tractors were sold to growers on credit; and highways and new roads were constructed as far as the remotest villages. (Landless peasant Şivan in *Sürü / The Herd* aka *The Flock*, Zeki Ökten, 1978, admits that he votes for the Democrat Party: 'they are the only ones to take care of us'.)

Engin Ayça claims that the period of Democrat Party rule could be identified as the establishment of the rural Anatolian capital enforcing its own culture, the 'monopoly of one-party state capitalism' giving way to the 'hybrid peasant-*comprador* capitalism'.[7] The populism of the governing policies had repercussions on the entertainment industry, and the commercial Yeşilçam cinema that was born in this period reflects such tendencies. Until the 1950s going to the cinema was a social event for the elite class, just like other cultural activities (theatre, concerts, opera) adopted from the West. They would arrive in evening gowns holding beautifully printed invitations. With increased internal migration, scripts began to be chosen for the masses rather than an elite audience. The *nouveau riche* that emerged with the move to capitalism was quite different from the bourgeoisie that frequented the cinemas, theatres and concert halls. Not only would they be uncomfortable in smoking and evening gowns, but they would fall asleep at Western classical concerts (as caricaturized in several Yeşilçam movies). 'It was a source of myth to cinema audiences that the *nouveaux riches* could not bring off refined activities such as theatre-and-opera-going; this was only natural, since nothing in their backgrounds had prepared them for it.'[8]

The industry found a profitable market in Anatolia. For the producers, cinema was not a tool for art and culture but a means for entertainment with no other aim than financial profit. In the absence of a model to meet the growing audience demand, time to reflect or capital to invest, the industry was moulded according to the wishes of the spectator, who wanted the values of the accustomed folk culture to be preserved with its common heroes and common values. The balance /imbalance/return-to-balance sequence of the narrative was cathartic. The public went to the movies with their traditional identity and what they wanted from the bards, the troubadours and the storytellers of yesterday, they expected from the cinema today. The producers did not question history, society or politics, and the directors and actors followed suit during a period when the Cold War experienced internationally was having its repercussions in Turkey with laws being created to curb different expressions or tendencies, individual or collective. Although the visual storytelling was developed along the lines of the oral tradition of storytelling, as an art form that could reach the masses, cinema was not exempt from government scrutiny. Yeşilçam abstracted itself from the realities of daily life from the start and hid behind legendary stories where the space, time, characters and story were not topical, and in this manner avoided taking a definite stand or displaying open criticism.[9]

Within the codes and restrictions of such a system, and the policies of a government that waged war against intellectuals, a number of talented filmmakers such as Lütfi Ö. Akad, Atıf Yılmaz (Batıbeki), Metin Erksan and Memduh Ün entered the industry, starting a new era called 'The Period of Cinema Men'. Lütfi Ö. Akad deserves to be identified as the first true *cinéaste* of Turkish cinema. Under the influence of French poetic realism (the pessimism of Marcel Carné or Jean Renoir), which he denies, and the visual style of the American *film noir*, which he accepts, Akad created a personal film language with *Kanun Namına / In the Name of the Law* (1952). Despite its reliance on melodrama and the usual good/bad dichotomies, the film is a milestone in terms of the character portrayals, the location shooting, the shifting camera angles, the high-contrast and occasionally low-key lighting, deep shadows and oblique angles that bring a new sense of reality to Yeşilçam-style filmmaking. Based on a true story about a theft that took place in the Galata district of Istanbul, the breathtaking chase scenes carry the audience from one historical quarter to the other as the hero jumps into trucks and barges or hides in trams. The city of Istanbul becomes an important part of the diegesis foreshadowing another film, Nuri Bilge Ceylan's *Distant*, although the latter is in a different genre.

The trend for 'village films' initiated by Muhsin Ertuğrul found a medium in literature during this period with Mahmut Makal's *Bizim Köy / Our Village* (1950), a village boy's account of his life, and other works by talented authors such as Yaşar Kemal, Orhan Kemal and Necati Cumalı. However, cinematic versions were contrived and condescending. The rural scenes were customarily shot in the empty fields around Istanbul, with actors who never set foot in a village. Makal would lament in *Our Village*: 'Where are our artists? . . . What masterpieces might be born of this sweat that runs in torrents. Those who still think of the Turkish village in terms of "The shepherd plays upon his pipe, how romantic is his life," do not know this country'.[10] Akad's *Beyaz Mendil / White Handkerchief* (1955), based on a Yaşar Kemal story, is the first significant film in this genre, a film with a realistic approach to the socio-cultural aspect of rural life. To prepare his role, the main actor Fikret Hakan lived for a year with the local people of the Black Sea village where the film was to be shot and the background music was authentic.

The state was lenient to 'village literature' but very harsh to its equivalent in cinema, as in most countries with a low literacy rate. Atıf Yılmaz (his family name is Batıbeki, which is rarely used) combined comedy with local legends and folklore to thwart censorship in depicting village reality and made memorable films, often using parables and allegory, the only means of political expression in repressive regimes (as evidenced in the cinemas of the former Iron Curtain countries during the USSR period). Akad, on the other hand, was blacklisted as a communist and continued his profession under very difficult circumstances.

Yeşilçam cinema, which had its golden years in the 1950s and '60s, followed the classical 'boy meets girl' narrative tradition of Hollywood. Events were arranged chronologically in accordance with the cause–effect principle. Destiny, rather than one's struggles, was the determining factor in overcoming obstacles and reaching the goal. In contrast to Western melodrama that routinely takes off from a conflict in the family and then concentrates on the individual, Yeşilçam was closer to the Eastern melodrama that focuses on the family. The dissolution of the family or the separation of the couple were typical motifs for the conflict, which was perpetuated by false accusations, misunderstandings, infidelity, revenge, honour or class differences. Seduction, a frequent motif of Arab (particularly Egyptian) as well as South Asian melodrama, was an integral part of most Yeşilçam melodramas. The main conflict was between the 'good' and the 'bad'. True to tradition, resolution was possible through a male authority figure.

Muhsin Ertuğrul is justly credited for introducing the genre of melodrama to Turkish cinema with *Istanbul'da Bir Facia-i Aşk / A Love Tragedy in Istanbul* (1922), which recounts the misfortunes of men who fall prey to a smart seductress (played by white Russian Anna Mariyevich). *The Girl from the Marshes* applied the genre to the rural milieu in the story of a deceived and deserted young maiden and set the precedent for countless similar films. The success of this film may be attributed to the skilful voyeurism of Ertuğrul in depicting village life, but also to Cahide Sonku, a former theatre actor, who played the leading female role. The film is significant for creating the first woman star of Turkish cinema. Sonku was adopted by republican intellectuals as the Turkish Greta Garbo, her blonde hair and aloof disposition identifying her with the West. 'She was the star of the republican ideology, whose adherents were by choice occidentalized, unaware of all things that they had to repress in order to become westernised.'[11] However, the rural audience, which began to increase with internal migration, had to wait for dark-eyed, dark-haired Türkan Şoray with a modest heart (and a round figure) to crown their *sultana* (a term referring to the wife of the Ottoman emperor) in their hearts.

A popular Anatolian personality, Muharrem Gürses, played an important role in the establishment of the village melodrama. Usually adapted from his novels, the 'Gürses melodramas' juxtaposed the good/bad, rich/poor, pretty/ugly binaries through inflated love stories; the positive values always triumphed and the audience got what they came to see: The Happy Ending.[12]

The reason for the extensive popularity of melodramas lay in audience identification. They knew the end from the beginning; nonetheless, they watched them as stories resembling their lives. Some filmmakers who started with this genre were soon forgotten while others made their mark: Atıf Yılmaz entered the industry with a strong melodrama, *Kanlı Feryat / Bloody Scream* (1951), but created some of the landmarks of Turkish cinema such as *Selvi Boylum, Al Yazmalım / The Girl with the Red Scarf* (1977); Lütfi Ö. Akad is another accomplished filmmaker who used the genre with success in films such as *Yalnızlar Rıhtımı / The Quay of the Lonely Ones* (1959).

Christine Gledhill asserts that Hollywood transformed melodrama by negating the 'class opposition' of European melodrama.[13] Since the struggle between the aristocracy and the bourgeoisie was not the issue within the socio-political system of American culture, class oppositions were transformed into rural/urban and rich/poor dichotomies, which was also the backbone of Turkish melodrama. Yeşilçam equated the lower class/rural with the East/local culture and upper class/urban with the West/foreign culture. The upper class was the object of desire but also the source of moral corruption, displayed via American cars, blonde women in provocative dresses, cocktail parties, whisky and gambling. Rural/lower-class women were chaste and loyal. They dressed modestly, respected their elders and never contradicted their men.

Although the 'othering' of the West was an important element in melodramas, Yeşilçam's position was rather ambivalent. The social class that represented the West (usually the Istanbulites) was shown as the ultimate object of desire, but also fear. When the heroes wanted to declare their honesty, all they had to say was 'we are rural people'. The rich were shallow, but they lived in luxury. At the end the lower-class hero with a heart of gold would win, but not before giving a moral lesson to the corrupt rich. It is remarkable that so many apolitical films were made about class differences in a period when the official policy stressed the concept that Turkey was a classless society of equal opportunities.[14]

In *Rüyalar Gerçek Olsa / If Dreams Could Come True* (Hulki Saner, 1972) the society girl tries to snub the daughter of the laundry woman. 'Dance, music, table manners, stylish dressing – you know nothing.' Her response is, 'Do you know humanity? A broken-heart? You only know make-up, dance . . .'. However, when the poor girl receives the love of the rich boy, she takes etiquette lessons, how to sit, walk straight (the Hollywood cliché of training with a pile of books on her head), accept a cigarette, dance without stepping on her partner's toe and not to click her fingers 'like in Turkish folklore' while she does the disco. She must flirt, which, she is told, 'is common in these circles'.

When Madame Bulbulyan (an Armenian representing Western culture) sings an operatic piece, the camera moves from the cocktail party upstairs to the servants' quarters downstairs where it is heard as some incomprehensible cacophony (in fast-forward). The daughter of the laundry woman announces to the distinguished guests: 'I love our *à la turca* . . . I'll sing one of our songs' and begins a popular folk song. Ironically, at this stage, she looks conspicuously European with her blonde hair and low-cut long evening gown, but she is also *à la turca* (the ideal Turkish identity endorsed by the state and promoted by Yeşilçam). When she finally gets the rich boy, *à la turca* music is heard, *Rüyalar Gerçek Olsa / If Dreams Could Come True* sung by a popular star of the period, Emel Sayın. The society boy has to cross over to the other side of town to retrieve his beloved from the old wood house where she lives. (All the poor of Yeşilçam somehow live in these historical wood houses around the neighbourhood of Süleymaniye, almost non-existent today.)

The message that the East will come together with the West only on its own terms is prevalent in the films, and also implies that to facilitate acceptance by the West, one must first resemble it. While imposing the cultural values attached to national identity, Yeşilçam implies that conforming to the values of the West for the moment would lead to reaching the West in the future.

A typical Yeşilçam movie would set the binaries as 'here' and 'there': 'Here' was the innocent young man from the country who came to the big city to improve his lot. He was poor but honest. He lived on the outskirts of the town with people like himself who preserved the good old values (his mother, or some traditional female figure, such as a wise landlady). 'There' was Beyoğlu (the old Pera at the heart of the

European Istanbul), the cradle of evil, home to the degenerate with slippery values, a trap for innocent country boys (and naïve young women without male protection). While the good young man earned his living working from dawn to dusk, in Beyoğlu life began after dark, in the sinuous back streets where the only law was that of hard muscle and guns. A stereotypical merchant from cotton-rich Adana would warn his son going to Istanbul: 'men have three enemies – gambling, alcohol and woman'. The biggest threat to a man's integrity was the woman. She could destroy a man. A rare film that rises above the cliché by its *mise-en-scène* and the moving acting of the famous duo, Türkan Şoray and Kadir İnanır, is *Licensed to Love* by Akad, a classic of Turkish cinema.

Another fascination of Yeşilçam, integral to most Eastern melodramas, was mistaken identity. A poor Anatolian boy would fall for a rich city girl thinking she was the maid. This device was necessary to prove that he was not interested in money. She would step down to his side and almost apologize for her social status. But before all that could happen, mutually hostile stereotyping between the educated urban bourgeois and the agrarian peasant or proletariat would prepare the audience. In one film, when a poor boy finds out that his girlfriend is very rich, he slaps her at her birthday party in front of her rich (modern) friends for playing with his honour. The girl tells him he is right (to slap her). The poor triumph over the rich, satisfying the sense of justice of the audience, made up of the lower middle class or the lower class.

One could argue that historical film as a genre has been rather neglected in Turkish cinema. Several films with nationalistic sentiments,

The famous duo, Türkan Şoray and Kadir İnanır, in *Vesikalı Yarim / Licensed to Love* (1968), dir. Lütfi Ö. Akad.

glorifying the achievements of the army, such as *Kore'de Türk Kahramanları / Turkish Heroes in Korea* (1951) by Seyfi Havaeri, appeared when Turkey as a NATO ally sent troops to Korea. Cyprus films were also established in this period, but intensified after the invasion of the island in 1974. The popularity of these films encouraged producers to invest in the genre, covering diverse periods including the Ottoman era and the War of Independence. Between the 1950s and 1980s almost all filmmakers made such films.[15] One characteristic of these 'historical films' was that the stories remained constant. The past was evoked through charismatic heroes who came from the Altai Mountains and Central Asia and fought imaginary wars winning victories over the bad Byzantines, Chinese or Hungarians and created history by showing Europe who they were. The battle scenes were grandly choreographed to reinforce a sense of national unity. It is interesting that the official Turkish history written with the approval of Kemal Atatürk glorifies the Ottoman period up to and including the reign of Suleiman the Magnificent, lionizing his conquests. The emperors who followed him are presented as womanizers, traitors, bad characters or imbeciles. The feats of the Ottoman are measured only through the success of the army.[16]

Yeşilçam presented superheroes in the style of cartoon characters in 'historical fantasies' and cast the same actors for similar roles to facilitate audience identification. Malkoçoğlu (a sixteenth-century war hero), Kara Murat (a loyal fighter in the court of Sultan Mehmet the Conqueror) and Battal Gazi (veteran Battal, a legendary folk character of the eighth century reputed to have led the Arab forces in their attempt to conquer Constantinople) were all played by Cüneyt Arkın, and Tarkan (created in 1967 and not placed in a particular period) and Karaoğlan were played by Kartal Tibet.[17] They fought unknown enemies with fascistic chauvinism, not unlike the Polat Alemdar character of the controversial *Kurtlar Vadisi / Valley of the Wolves* television series and the movie *Kurtlar Vadisi Irak / Valley of the Wolves: Iraq* (2005) by Serdar Akar. And, just as in the contemporary version, violence was justified by the initial aggression of the enemy: massacre, torture, rape or insult to honour. Such films fuse three ideologies: nationalism, conservatism and Islamism. In *Valley of the Wolves: Iraq* Polat Alemdar and his men represent the nationalist conservative line and the Kerkuk Turkmenians the Islamist. The most important characteristic of the enemy is that they wound 'our' honour and insult 'our' flag.

*Kurtlar Vadisi Irak / Valley of the Wolves, Iraq* (2005), dir. Serdar Akar.

In modern Turkey, where nationalism is on the rise, particularly manifest in soccer games, celebrations of national holidays and 'going to do military service' festivities, 'historical fantasies' have become cult films, predominantly favoured by guideless adolescents (many from middle-class homes) who identify with the characters. *Valley of the Wolves: Terror* (2007) had to be taken off the air for inciting the young to violence after several incidents where the perpetrators admitted they were inspired by the actions of Polat Alemdar.

Blatantly nationalistic combat movies are not unique to Turkish cinema. In fact, Hollywood has mastered the genre. However, the army's role in political, public and private life is significant in Turkey. 'Her Türk Asker Doğar' (every Turk is born a soldier) is a familiar precept. To serve the army makes men out of boys but, more importantly, pays the 'debt' every Turkish man owes to his country. The army, which easily accommodates the themes of war, absence and loss and destiny, is a suitable subject for melodrama: the lovers cannot unite because the girl is given to another man while her fiancé serves his country; the beloved son does not return; or the virtuous wife becomes a fallen woman when her husband is martyred and she is left without male protection. The army as an institution, however, is never reproached. *Ezo Gelin*, which was made three times (Orhan Elmas, 1955; Orhan Elmas, 1968; Feyzi Tuna, 1973), tells the story of a young woman forced to marry her young brother-in-law when her husband does not return from the Korean War.[18] Although the film criticizes feudal customs, it does not challenge the futility of war or the presence of the Turkish army in a land so far away from home. Deaths or separations are usually attributed to *kader* (destiny) and cinema endorses the state ideology in glorifying the army.

In the 1960s a new kind of cinema emerged that was influenced by social and political changes in the country, particularly the *coup d'état* of 27 May 1960 and the establishment of a progressive constitution in 1961, which brought a more relaxed atmosphere that nourished arts. More books were published and more films were made. Translations of diverse ideologies including Marxism-Leninism became available, giving the impression that the oppressions of the ousted Democrat Party, particularly censorship, would disappear.

Commercial films continued their dominance, but some filmmakers, encouraged by the new constitution, experimented with 'social realism'. *Karanlıkta Uyananlar / Those Awakening in the Dark* (Ertem Göreç, 1964) was the first Turkish film to deal with the social consequences of the workers' strike; *Gurbet Kuşları / The Birds of Nostalgia* (Halit Refiğ, 1964) was first to examine the phenomenon of migration from rural areas to urban centres; *Yılanların Öcü / The Revenge of the Serpents* (Metin Erksan, 1962) recounted one man's fight against rural traditions (and was heavily censured for alleged communist propaganda); *Susuz Yaz / A Dry Summer*, also by Erksan, foregrounding the problematic of single women (without a male protector/owner) in the rural milieu, opened the path of Turkish cinema to the world, receiving the Golden Bear in 1964 in Berlin; Yılmaz Güney drew attention with *At, Avrat, Silah / Horse, Woman, Gun* (1966), his first film; and Lütfi Ö. Akad's *Hudutların Kanunu / The Law of the Borders* (1966), from a script by Akad and Güney, with Güney in the lead role, was declared by critics the most important film up to that time, earning invitations to Berlin and Venice film festivals, although the Central Film Control Commission prevented its participation in foreign events, dashing once more hopes for a censor-free cinema. In fact, the film is one of the most censored films of Turkish cinema; it was shown a year later only after several scenes were changed.

Turkish social realism was less based on solid social and artistic grounds than Italian social realism, according to film scholar Aslı Daldal, since it lacked the social unification of the anti-Fascist war and the rich literary tradition of Italy. In film it almost 'naively' reflected the artistic and political objectives of a 'new intelligentsia, trying to harmonize its traditional Ottoman heritage with the universal penchant of neo-Kemalism' and displayed the earnest attempts of the filmmakers trying to develop a 'national film language' and personal styles.[19]

*Otobüs Yolcuları / The Bus Passengers* (1961) by Ertem Göreç, based on a script by Marxist intellectual Vedat Türkali, is one of the first examples of social realism in Turkish cinema. Interweaving a love story with an actual story of corruption in a co-operative, the film was a box-office success. The hero, bus driver Kemal, is a handsome and intelligent young man whose education is disrupted by financial problems. He works for the municipality, loves literature and writes poetry but does not hesitate to use brute force to fight injustices; in other words, his identity is worker, intellectual and brave in that order. He falls in love with Nevin, the daughter of the rich bad man. 'When I got worried, I read; the more I read, the more worried I got', he tells her, which suggests he has political consciousness. It is as if the strength of all those who resist ugliness is amalgamated in him. The arena must not be left to inequality, exploitation or capitalism. At the end, the good proletariat who live by the sweat of their brow triumph over the bad living plentiful yet meaningless lives. The film carries the *naïveté* of many social realist films that aspire to transmit a clear message to the masses. However, it raises a crucial issue: customarily the oppressed do not unite, a theme that Yılmaz Güney would develop a decade later.

'People Who Unite Do Not Lose' is the slogan of *Those Awakening in the Dark*, also made by the duo of Ertem Göreç and Vedat Türkali on the subject of strike, a novelty in Turkish cinema but not in real life. A year before the film was released the first Union of Cinema Workers (Sine-İş) was founded under the leadership of Metin Erksan and soon after the set workers went on strike. Although they were unable to achieve a contract, they sowed the seeds for action.[20]

The title of the film, referring to the workers who wake up before dawn, metaphorizes their political awakening. The paint industry, which exploits both the workers and the financial resources of the state, is the main target. The director and scriptwriter researched for several months the logistics of the industry, the raw material used to make the paint, where it was obtained, the cost, the state's relations with those who produced the paint and similar technical and bureaucratic aspects. The film has a dark tone, but what gives some relief is the action taken by the workers for a strike.

Unlike *The Bus Passengers*, in *Those Awakening in the Dark* characters are not all good or bad, but multifaceted. The son of the factory owner who is also the childhood friend of the welder hero is a modest chap. However, when his father dies, he takes power and sacrifices the workers for profit. His inexperience and ignorance place him in the position of the despised capitalist character. On the other hand, the brave welder who has achieved class awareness can become aggressive and degenerate. At the end the rich man returns to his agreeable old self and the welder sees his mistakes and joins the good co-workers.

For the intellectuals of the 1960s, *Those Awakening in the Dark* was a source of pride. But the film had a long struggle with censorship. Furthermore, the sympathizers of the governing party threatened the audience that came to see the film. After it received the Third Best Film and Best Script awards at the national film festival in Antalya, the censorship board recalled the film, to be released for distribution only after the Minister of the Interior approved it. Turkish cinema soon realized that the newly found freedom was only relative. The Constitution Court revived the censorship regulations established in 1939 in the wake of the outbreak of the Second World War, arguing that they were not anti-constitutional. During this period, which Yılmaz Güney would later define as the McCarthy years, a small detail, a dialogue, the colour of a garment or even a name could easily receive the stamp of 'separatist aims' or 'threat to national wholeness and togetherness' and result in the rejection of a script.

Although social realism was a short experiment during the middle-class rule between 1960 and 1965, it reflected the search for identity in a period of rapid transition from traditionalism to modernism. Committed filmmakers were united with a strong anti-bourgeois and anti-capitalist agenda. They also tried to find a new film language by experimenting with depth of field, multiple camera angles and location shooting. But the movement itself remained eclectic. A mixture of modernist cultural avant-gardism and Marxism was displayed in different ways by different filmmakers. Due to financial restraints a populist tendency had to be employed (to the chagrin of the intellectuals) to entertain the masses while educating them.

The debate about national identity in Turkish cinema intensified in the mid-1960s. Intellectuals involved in the film journal *Yeni Sinema / New Cinema* founded the Turkish cinematheque in 1965 with help from Henri Langlois. They argued that Yeşilçam's escapist and exploitative stand and its plagiarism and cliché formulas were incompatible with a national cinema that should adhere to international standards. Publishing interviews with celebrated filmmakers such as Godard and Antonioni, screening masterpieces of European art cinema along with examples of Soviet Revolutionary Cinema and organizing discussions on the French *nouvelle vague*, Italian neo-realism and Brazilian 'cinema novo', the group endeavoured to establish resistance against Yeşilçam like the resistance of European art cinema to Hollywood. They also criticized the new social realist movement for lacking a theoretical basis and artistic maturity. Cinema clubs that began in the large cities in the 1960s and joined under a confederation in the beginning of the 1970s also contributed to the emergence of a culture of alternative cinema.

However, by the end of the 1960s Halit Refiğ was advocating that Yeşilçam was the true national cinema. It was not possible to reach Turkish people using Western forms. Several filmmakers refused to collaborate with the cinematheque and its publication *New Cinema* for their 'hostility' towards Turkish cinema.[21] Instead, they proposed what was called *Asya Tipi Üretim Tarzı-ATÜT* (Asian Style of Production). Refiğ published his articles on the issue in *Ulusal Sinema Kavgası / National Cinema Dispute* (1971), which drew attention to the anti-imperialist role of cinema similar to what the theoreticians of Third Cinema promulgated, and stressed the importance of promoting cultural heritage. His *Haremde Dört Kadın / Four Women in the Harem* (1965) and *Bir Türk'e Gönül Verdim / I Fell in Love with a Turk* (1969) are examples of the trend.

New Cinema was perceived as modelled after the art cinema of the West. The aim was to create. The *auteur* policy and the alternative modes of production were its trademarks. The target audience was the film festivals. Yeşilçam, the domestic popular cinema, was modelled on Hollywood. To produce was the principal aim. The star system, the capitalistic mode of production, distribution and exhibition were its trademarks. Yılmaz Güney was a rare artist whose commercially successful populist films were also praised by the New Cinema group, which extolled *Umut / The Hope* (1970) as a turning point in Turkish cinema.

Heated polemic that had started as early as the 1960s intensified when two trends challenged each other: while *ulusal sinema*, a cinema with nationalist ambitions, emphasized the behaviour of all Turkish people through a common history and a heritage of traditional, cultural and social life experiences, *milli sinema* focused on the identity of Turks within the Islam–Turk culture since leaving Central Asia and stressed the degeneration caused by Westernization.[22] *Ulusal* and *milli* both mean 'national', but *milli* is an Ottoman word. According to some critics, both trends were Ottomanist and *milli sinema* was in fact Islamist cinema, but could not openly be claimed as such since Item 163 of the constitution forbade using religion for such a purpose.[23]

Yücel Çakmaklı (*Kızım Ayşe / My Daughter, Ayşe*, 1974, discussed in chapter Five) was the forerunner of the *milli sinema* trend that focused on national stories built within the framework of commercial considerations, but always with a religious message. The aim was to regain the audience alienated by cheap sex on one side and militant politics on the other.

For Yılmaz Güney, who stressed that cinema was not outside the field of the class struggle, such movements had to be examined as counter-developments against the revolutionary democratic movement. There could not be a film or filmmaker without political ideology. The ideological and political convictions of those who advocated *milli* (national) cinema would draw light on their concept of 'national'. For Güney to be national was to be anti-imperialist. 'What is called "Islamic cinema" is nothing but the manifestation of a reactionary attitude', he claimed, 'In many corners of the world, Muslim people struggle for their liberation. Cinema that narrates the revolutionary struggles of the Muslim people is not Islamic cinema but revolutionary cinema. Instead of the geographical or religious angles, we must evaluate the problem from the angle of class.'[24]

In the socio-economic atmosphere of the 1950s and '60s, when capitalism was glorified, peasants suffering poor agricultural conditions saw migration to metropolitan centres (or abroad) as the only way to benefit from industrialization and the opening of the market. The 'in-between' position of the urban peasants inspired noteworthy films discussed in chapter Two.

One cultural outcome of the migration phenomenon was *arabesk* (arabesque), which began as a music genre with an Arabic flavour and quickly infiltrated into cinema. Arabesque conveyed the sense of nostalgia felt by the alienated urban Anatolian for the old traditions, transferring folk culture and its attributes of impossible love and fatalism into modern space through the tribulations of the male hero. Clearly masculinist and mostly sung by men, *arabesk* idealized the rural home left behind and lamented the impossibility of return, offering the alternative of imposing the rural culture to the modern urban life. In the 1960s, banking on his success in arabesque music, Orhan Gencebay started the arabesque films rage. Anatolian İbrahim Tatlıses, who entered the music scene at a very early age as little İbo with a wailing voice, was the hero of several of these films.

Arabesque was derided by both secular and Islamist Turks. Güney defined the ideology behind arabesque as an ideology to lure people away from the hardships of daily life rather than encourage them to solve their problems. (In 1989 Ertem Eğilmez parodied the genre with a very popular comedy called *Arabesk / Arabesque.*)

Despite a ban on TV and radio, arabesque reached the public with the growing cassette industry and was regularly heard in the collective minibuses that serviced shanty-town settlements. One reason for its unprecedented success was perhaps its ability to provide a temporary (albeit artificial) relief for the liminal man when cultures were in transition.

The arrival of television in 1968 was detrimental to Yeşilçam, which did not have a robust infrastructure.[25] According to Türkali, Yeşilçam and its representation of human relations mirrored the socio-economic structure of the country. The dependence on foreign elements rather than national resources and the lack of a firm stand resulted in an impasse at the micro level for cinema and the macro level for the country. Every change of government, every military intervention, every renewed law had its repercussions on the cinema sector, which never managed to be an industry, but always stayed in the hands of the middleman and the importer. The producers were exploited by the distributors and the theatre owners had to resort to the star system to stay solvent. Since the money earned from films was not reinvested in the industry, no capital was accumulated.[26] The gradual multiplication of free channels, the availability of cheap videos, a political climate that rendered the streets unsafe and the dilapidated condition of cinema halls all contributed to the decline of the commercial film industry that at its prime was producing close to 300 films a year. With the total demise of Yeşilçam at the end of the 1970s the industry returned almost to its beginnings. Foreign films, this time not European, but American, took over, the hegemony of Hollywood leaving little room for a national cinema to develop. Many film companies began to churn out cheap sex and kung-fu films to win back audiences, alienating the family and especially women, who had constituted the largest audience.

The politically charged 1970s were not beneficial to Turkish cinema. Under the pressure to take a stand, several filmmakers made *engagé* films to appear militant. Others tried to benefit from the attention social realist films from the developing countries were receiving in the West. Many mediocre films were made that blended surface realism with local colour and stereotyped exoticism without aesthetic dimensions. According to local critics, it was not clear whether they were marketing films or kilims.[27]

A handful of exceptional films were made despite the economic limitations, the political atmosphere and the heavy hand of censorship, and these received international accolades, for instance *The Herd*, scripted by Yılmaz Güney while in prison and directed by Zeki Ökten (see chapter Four). Süreyya Duru's 'village films' *Bedrana* and *Kara Çarşaflı Gelin / The Bride in Black Chadoor* (1975) were praised by the critics and successful at the box office, although *The Bride in Black Chadoor* suffered from the censors like his urban film, *Güneşli Bataklık / The Sunny Marsh* (1977), rejected on the grounds that it promoted separatism, endorsed murder and anarchism and insulted the police. (The decision was reversed after two years.)

At the end of the 1970s Turkish cinema began to gain international visibility with the arrival of young filmmakers trained under Yılmaz Güney or simply influenced by his *engagé* cinema. Their works represent the transition to a more personal *cinéma d'auteur*. Erden Kıral, whose humanist portrayals of rural life were often compared to Erksan, Akad and Güney, won the Silver Bear at the Berlin Film Festival with *Hakkaride Bir Mevsim / A Season in Hakkari* (1983), about an exiled intellectual who finds his true self in a remote village in south-east Anatolia. Ali Özgentürk's *Hazal* (1979), about tradition on the eve of change, and *At / The Horse* (1982), about migration to urban centres and the resulting clash of two faces of Turkey, are the best examples of this period.

The military intervention of 12 September 1980, which plunged the country into the dark ages by closing the parties and syndicates and banning politics, burning books and films and arresting thousands of militants of both the right- and the left-wing factions, paradoxically benefited cinema. In this period of depoliticization intellectuals began to look within themselves to evaluate the past. The absence of pressure to be politically engaged liberated artists from the thematic impositions of the 1970s, and the urban problems of the individual came to the foreground.

A new generation of filmmakers with urban backgrounds appeared. Paris-educated Ömer Kavur, who received his training with Bryan Forbes and Alain Robbe-Grillet, established the concept of *auteur* in modern Turkish cinema. The distinct characteristic of Kavur's cinema is that each film recounts a journey. This journey may stretch over kilometres, as in *Amansız Yol / The Merciless Road* (1985); may involve a *voyage intérieur* as in *Anayurt Oteli / Motherland Hotel* (1987); or may explore the spatial division between abstract space (*chora*) and concrete space (*topos*), as in *The Secret Face*, which carries *Sufi* overtones.

The opening of film schools during this period ended the apprentice–master tradition of Yeşilçam. The new generation brought new ideologies and the older generation began to try out new ideas. Established writers – Yaşar Kemal, Furüzan and Selim Ileri – took an active part in the film industry, contributing scripts with real characters that eliminated the typecasting of Yeşilçam. Attention began to be paid to space and narrative structure. More importantly, focus shifted from men to women, coinciding with women joining the workforce and the (late) arrival of feminism. Foreign soap operas brought contemporary urban life styles to a society shaped by rural–traditional ideologies and opened the way for addressing some taboos and sexuality, although issues of sexual identity are still not discussed realistically and openly.

The move from the 'village films' to urban middle-class lifestyles was not welcomed by all viewers. The average local audience was alienated again, this time with existential stories that offered them little identification, whereas foreign critics expecting films with picturesque and exotic landscapes depicting harsh economic realities of Third World daily life were disappointed. Urban *angst* stories were pushed aside paternalistically by Europeans attending the Istanbul International Film Festival of 1992, who argued that if they wanted to see *nouvelle vague* they should stay at home.

Foreign critics were not entirely wrong in displaying impatience with narratives removed from the realities experienced by ordinary citizens: inflation, rapid Westernization and subsequent demoralization, not to mention the bloody civil war raging in the south-east. They wondered why no one cared or dared to pick up the burning daily issues, political, social or even personal. Hence began another crisis of identity in Turkish cinema. Meanwhile, the American major studios took the opportunity to strengthen their hegemony. Following changes in foreign

A Film by SİNAN ÇETİN

# BERLIN IN BERLIN

HÜLYA AVŞAR • CEM ÖZER • ARMİN BLOCK • ALİYE RONA • EŞREF KOLÇAK

*In someone else's city, behind the door, between love and death...*

Director, Producer: SİNAN ÇETİN • Director of Photography: REBEKKA HAAS • Music: NEZİH ÜNEN • Screenplay: SİNAN ÇETİN, ÜMİT ÜNAL
Lighting Supervisor: MARTİNA RADWAN • Sound: TOM NEUBAUER • Art Direction: ZEYNEP TERCAN • Executive Producer: CEMALETTİN ÇETİN
Editing: ÖMER SEVİNÇ

PLATO

capital laws, in 1987 Warner Bros and in 1989 United International Pictures (UIP), which distributed Universal, Paramount and Touchstone, entered the film and video market.

In the early 1990s national film production was reduced to not more than ten films annually, with sporadic success at international film festivals and practically no home audience. To save the industry from collapsing, some filmmakers, such as Şerif Gören, decided to follow the box-office formula of Hollywood. In skilful hands, this succeeded in luring some of the audience to the national cinema. Gören's *Amerikalı / The American* (1993) was a big box-office success in addition to gaining the Public Jury Award of the national film festival in Antalya. Sinan Çetin, who started his career with socially committed films, defended the notion that to win the audience back filmmakers should stop taking Godard or Fellini as models but instead emulate Spielberg or Polanski. He also argued that the Ministry of Culture should support successful films rather than the so-called art films with no audience. His *Berlin in Berlin* (1993), a thriller about a Turkish family living in the Kreutzberg

A combination of commercially viable qualities with those of a good film led to national and international success.

Sinan Çetin's *Berlin in Berlin* (1993).

Sinan Çetin's *Propaganda / Propaganda* (1999).

*Eşkıya / The Bandit* (1997), dir. Yavuz Turgul.

ethnic neighbourhood of Berlin, had a remarkable box-office success, received favourable reviews from foreign critics and won international awards. *Propaganda / Propaganda* (1999), a satire on border politics, also did well at the box office and received eleven international awards.

*Eşkıya / The Bandit* (1997) by Yavuz Turgul combined commercially viable qualities (action, melodrama, romance, star actors and technical superiority) with those of a good film (made by an experienced film-maker who knew his craft) and achieved unprecedented national and international success, setting a precedent for several other films of the next decade that were audience favourites also praised by the critics.

In the early 1990s, with the rise of fundamentalism, religious cinema was revived. Discovering the power of the media, with the immense success of *Minyeli Abdullah / Abdullah of Minye* (1989) by Çakmaklı, which competed with American blockbusters (530,000 viewers), the Islamists began to use cinema as a platform. In a symposium organized by the Islamic Research Fund a decision was taken to 'Islamize' news-papers, cinema, television and theatre, and to call on the industrialists who had been building mosques to invest in the arts. It was declared that 'with art began the alienation of our people, with art it will be annihilated'.[28]

The new trend came to be known as *beyaz sinema* (white cinema) as defined by Abdurrahman Şen, an Islamist journalist. *Sürgün / The Exile* (1992) by industrialist Mehmet Tanrısever, the story of a teacher whose destiny is to be forever an exile in the world of 'infidels', garnered some awards abroad despite its naïve narrative and faulty editing. In dramatized flashbacks the film expresses anti-Kemalist sentiments as it tries to give the 'suppressed' history of devoted Muslims following the founding of the secular state.

Mesut Uçakan, an advocate of Islamist cinema, does not shy away from blatant religious propaganda. His *Yalnız Değilsiniz / You Are not Alone* (1990), about the banning of the headscarf in universities, was a box-office success with its appeal to young women experiencing a crisis of identity. *İskilipli Atıf Hoca – Kelebekler Sonsuza Uçar / Atıf Hoca of İskilip – Butterflies Fly to Eternity* (1993) challenged the official history of the Turkish Republic with the story of a learned man, Atıf Hodja, who was hanged for his beliefs (his opposition to the Hat Reform of Kemal Atatürk) by the Liberation Trials that were established after the founding of the Republic. Uçakan explained that with this film he

*Minyeli Abdullah /*
*Abdullah of Minye*
(1989), dir. Yücel
Çakmaklı, drew
530,000 spectators.

aimed to exonerate Atıf Hodja and to set a precedent for similar cases, which he claimed have remained taboo.[29]

Like most contemporary Islamic movements in Turkey, such films have been oriented towards reclaiming the Muslim self, which was perceived as having been robbed of its authenticity and heritage. Initially they attracted a large audience, mostly the Anatolian poor with rural backgrounds who face alienation in an urban environment. However, 'white cinema' did not establish itself as a genre, mainly because the films lacked artistic quality. Their melodramatic and sentimental content, soap-opera style, stereotypical characters and the propagandistic and didactic approach could not keep the interest of the young, who constitute the larger part of the audience. The trend was also criticized within its own sector, one of the weekly Islamist magazines declaring *Minyeli Abdullah* not worthy to be called a work of cinema and another leading Islamist magazine denouncing this new culture as 'Islamist Arabesque'. Perhaps the initial success of these films was not sustained because they 'tried to bring a solution to the complex problems and value judgments of a rapidly changing society with fossilized religious and moral understandings',[30] although filmmakers like Uçakan have continued with sporadic works in the genre. Gradually, the newspapers, journals, television stations and websites owned or subsidized by rich Islamist industrialists/businessmen inside and outside Turkey have replaced 'white cinema' to carry on the struggle to re-image Islamist political identity.

Severe censorship laws, inspired by Mussolini's *Codice di censura*, were established in Turkey in 1939 during the tense atmosphere of the antici-

Mesut Uçakan's *Yalnız Değilsiniz / You Are Not Alone* (1990) appealed to young women experiencing a crisis of identity.

pated war, and a censorship board connected to the Ministry of Interior was created. A commission whose members were from the state departments, including the police and the military, scrutinized the script as well as the final product, and in some cases artists who did not conform were sent to prison or exile.

Yeşilçam, which dominated the screens for almost three decades, showed the world through rose-tinted glasses. The censorship board ensured that films that would be harmful to the undividable wholeness of the state – that would affect national independence, general morality, health and politics in a negative manner and insult national feelings, or have qualities not commensurate with the national culture, customs and traditions of the country – would not be approved for distribution.[31] During the worst political crisis, while closing its eyes to the marketing of sexploitation films, censorship was very harsh on anything remotely resembling political or social awareness. Doctors, lawyers and especially the police force and the army were immune from scrutiny in films. Yeşim Ustaoğlu's first film, *Iz / Traces* (1994), is perhaps the first film to show a policeman with a human face, as someone struggling with his identity.

The reasons for banning some works were absurd. For instance, Metin Erksan's first film, *Aşık Veysel'in Hayatı aka Karanlık Dünya / The Dark World* (1953), a realistic account of the life of the bard Veysel shot in his native village, was censured for showing the crops in Anatolia undersized. His *Susuz Yaz / A Dry Summer* (1963), which won the Golden Bear at the Berlin Film Festival, almost failed to get there as it was banned for showing a woman marrying her dead husband's brother, which would give a negative impression of Turkey to foreigners. *Şafak Bekçileri / Guardians of Dawn* (1963) by Halit Refiğ was censored for showing a Turkish plane fall and for a scene in which Yeşilçam heart-throb Göksel Arsoy kisses his girlfriend while he is in uniform (improper behaviour for a pilot of the Turkish army).[32]

In 1986 the censorship board was moved from the Ministry of Interior to the Ministry of Culture and Tourism, and pre-scrutiny of the scripts from the centre was abolished in practicality, although the authority of local administrations to ban films was retained. During this period *Su da Yanar / Water Also Burns* (1987) by Ali Özgentürk, about the anguish of a filmmaker trying to make a film about Nazım Hikmet, the banished poet of Turkey, was banned in more than fifty provinces, which meant that Özgentürk was obliged to appear in court in each province to win his case.[33]

Censorship was officially abolished in 1998, although it still plays a crucial role in Turkish cinema's stand on controversial issues through more subtle forms of government control and financial pressures (difficulties in obtaining funds and entering the distribution/exhibition network), which often lead to self-censorship on the part of filmmakers. 'Some of the barriers have been overcome, but other forms of censorship have appeared', explains archivist and historian Agah Özgüç, 'The theatres are reluctant to show *risqué* films fearing repercussions. The political situation is the determinant.'[34]

The 'untouchable' status of the army has been challenged in the new millennium with a number of films including Mustafa Altıoklar's popular *O Şimdi Asker / He Is in the Army Now* (2002), the story of men of different ages from different backgrounds who come together (a metaphor for the country) during short-term paid military service and learn to deal with life and personal problems. With humour, the film slates the severity of the military structure, but the institution itself is beyond reproach. The army is presented as the equalizer of discordant elements. Each character leaves the army as a more mature and self-confident individual. The rigid military hierarchy that at first seems oppressive to the protagonists is finally displayed as an environment that fosters familial ties and even obliterates class differences.[35] The film, which received aid from the army, including loan of uniforms and real soldiers acting as extras, garnered 589,586 admissions during its first ten days.

Özgüç points out:

> an unbreakable law exists regarding the army or the police force. The soldiers can do as they please and no one can question their actions. They have immunity almost akin to the immunity of the MPs. In a remarkable scene in *Yol* (Şerif Gören, 1981), the gendarme stops the minibus to search the passengers and the brutality of the army is inferred through small details. No matter how brave you are, certain immunities cannot be destroyed. Regulations are clear. A film against the military service can never be made.[36]

In the relatively more relaxed atmosphere post-1998, several attempts were made to approach sensitive subjects such as the military terror of the 1980 *coup d'état*, which has left a deep wound in the national psyche. Not only have the perpetrators never been brought to justice but the constitution established during that period was also still in effect. *Gülün Bittiği Yer / Where the Rose Wilted* (1998) by İsmail Güneş, a right-wing Islamist filmmaker, was the first film to show torture by the police graphically through the story of a young man taken into custody for alleged political involvement. The opening scenes of the film corroborate Turkish society as violent and denounce the traditional Turkish method of educating by brute force; parents beat their children at home and teachers beat the students at school. The original title refers to the Turkish proverb 'A rose would bloom where a parent/teacher hits'. Abused children become

Mustafa Altıoklar's very popular *O Şimdi Asker / He Is in the Army Now* (2002) poked gentle fun at the compulsory military service.

abusive adults. Torture scenes in the film were found damaging to the reputation of the police by the authorities and Güneş was advised to declare in the final credits that the policemen involved were finally brought to justice. Since this was not the case, Güneş refused and the film could not be distributed.[37] Charges were brought against filmmakers Kazım Öz and Handan İpekçi, in 1999 and 2001 respectively (discussed in chapter Three) for violating the integrity of the state under the infamous Article 301, punishable by up to three years in prison. Tayfun Pirselimoğlu's *Hiçbiryerde / Innowhereland* (2002), about a woman searching for her son, was refused a permit by the Supervisory Council of Cinema, Video and Music Productions after its screening at the Istanbul International Film Festival, and sent to the State Council (composed of seven members, four from the National Security Council General Secretary, Ministry of Interior and the Ministry of Culture and three from the film sector) and finally granted a permit (see chapter Four). What is noteworthy is the double standard employed regarding inspection of the films participating in festivals in Turkey; foreign films are exempt of any scrutiny, but national films to be shown in such festivals must have a distribution licence.[38]

Self-censorship has become a serious threat to contemporary Turkish cinema. Çağan Irmak's *Babam ve Oğlum / My Father and My Son* (2005), a tear-jerker melodrama about an estranged activist of the left who returns to his parental home with his son when he realizes that the sickness he has been suffering since his prison days is terminal, received accolades from film critics and a large number of audiences, both rightists and leftists. Despite the political nature of the subject, Irmak stated that his concern was to narrate a story, not to make a political statement. Film scholar Hilmi Maktav points out that the film illustrated the futility of risking the breakup of families for political ideals since real happiness could be found only within the confines of the family. By placing family above ideologies Irmak was depoliticizing the audience and therefore making a very strong political statement, which was commensurate with the ambitions of the 'generals' – a depoliticized Turkey. 'The most applauded film about the 1980 coup does not even name the coup or its leaders.'[39]

The 2007 cinema season began with several films dealing with the 1980 military intervention. *Suna* by veteran Engin Ayça focused on relationships that were thwarted in the atmosphere of the terror, which was continuously alluded to but never identified; *Fikret Bey* by newcomer Selma Köksal was about the reminiscences of an old man, who made

Self-censorship has become a serious threat to Turkish cinema. Çağan Irmak's *Babam ve Oğlum / My Father and My Son* (2005).

obscure references to all atrocities of modern history from the ransacking of the properties of non-Muslims on 6–7 September 1955 to the three military interventions, without taking time to dwell on any of them. *Beynelmilel / International*, the first feature of Sırrı Süreyya Önder and Muharrem Gülmez, dealt with military atrocities with subtle irony and black humour and succeeded in terms of filmic language, acting and directing, but once again the political context was shrouded. The culprit behind so much suffering was never identified. *Eve Dönüş / Coming Home* (2006) by Ömer Uğur was a more courageous indictment of the 1980 coup with scenes of graphic torture inflicted on an innocent man. Although the script won an award a decade ago, Uğur could not make the film until the relative easing of censorship pressure.

The interest in these films was short-lived, mainly because the subject has lost its immediacy according to Özgüç, giving way to the pressing issue of honour killings and violence against women,[40] which was evidenced in no less than three films that competed at the 44th Antalya Golden Orange (National) Film Festival: *Mutluluk / Bliss* by Abdullah Oğuz, *Saklı Yüzler / Hidden Faces* by Handan İpekçi and *Janjan* by Aydın Sayman.

A new energy has been discernible in Turkish cinema since the second half of the 1990s. The opening of several film schools, global advancements in technology and communications, financial initiatives available to filmmakers – European funds or government loans – and the relaxation of censorship regulations could be cited as contributing factors. The new generation of filmmakers, who have grown up during the years

The script of *Eve Dönüş / Coming Home* (2006), dir. Ömer Uğur, had to wait a decade before it could be filmed.

of modernization, have acquired a new set of values and approaches to life and cinema. Recognized in the West as well as at home, these film-makers search for a new language to mirror a society that has the privileged position, if it chooses to do so, of benefiting from the possi-bilities of a rich tradition and the advantages of modernity. Nuri Bilge Ceylan brought attention to this new movement with *Distant*, which won the Grand Jury and the best male actor awards (shared by Mehmet Emin Toprak and Muzaffer Özdemir) at the Cannes Film Festival in 2003, the first time a Turkish film won at Cannes since *Yol* (Şerif Gören) shared the Palme d'Or with *Missing* by Costa Gavras in 1982.

The concept of cinema as an art form was introduced to Asia from the West, although as Robert Stam points out, proto-cinematic or pre-cinematic cultural forms and aesthetic philosophies pre-date the birth of cinema.[41] Throughout Asia, cultural phenomena that originated cen-turies before the arrival of movies such as the shadow puppet (the Turkish version of which is *Karagöz*) display cinematic qualities.[42] Asian cinemas have faced the dichotomy between 'the imported nature of the medium and the unyielding will to bend it in the service of exploring indigenous experiences and culturally sanctioned values, beliefs, and lifeways', as a result of which the question of 'cultural identity' has gained importance, particularly with the 'process of internalization, with its overt and covert threats to indigenous culture'.[43] Opinions differ on the need for a sense of

Military atrocities are dealt with subtle irony and black humour, but the culprit behind so much suffering is never identified.

*Beynelmilel / International*, dir. Sırrı Süreyya Önder and Muharrem Gülmez (2006).

cultural identity, as Dissanayake points out, which may be 'brush[ed] aside as misplaced patriotism, a gratuitous anachronism' or an ideal to be pursued; the process of internationalization may be perceived as detrimental to indigenous cinemas or a phenomenon with 'a great potential for invigorating, creative growth'. Asian masters Yasujiro Ozu and Satyajit Ray were able to convert cinema, the Western invention, 'into a more indigenous instrument of communication by drawing on the strengths and vitality of traditional culture', one important focus being 'the clash of tradition and modernity', which is perhaps 'the single most dominant theme in Asian cinema', according to Wimal Dissanayake, for whom all good film directors project a vision of the world and society they inhabit and all good films possess the quality of universality.[44]

Cinema in Turkey has experienced diverse periods: the domination of one man, Muhsin Ertuğrul, in the early days, the hegemony of Yeşilçam in the 1950s and '60s, experiments with social realism and neo-realism in the 1970s, *auteur* cinema in the 1980s, a serious decline in the early 1990s and a new movement of independent art cinema on the one hand and a revival of commercial cinema on the other. Questions of how 'national' is the national cinema, is there a 'national cinema' in Turkey, or should there be a 'national cinema', have been subjects of sporadic discussion. One of the systematic criticisms remains, as the celebrated poet Nazım Hikmet pointed out sixty years ago. Unlike the Asian masters such as Ozu and Ray, who were able to use cinema, the Western tool, to create a cinema that fed on the national culture, Turkish cinema in general has chosen a mimetic relationship with the West, following Western modes without attempting a synthesis.

Corresponding to the geopolitics of the country, Turkish cinema has turned its head towards the West while its feet are grounded on the soil of the East. Within that context, there have been individual signatures, such as Lütfi Ö. Akad, Metin Erksan, Atıf Yılmaz, Yılmaz Güney, Erden Kıral, Ali Özgentürk and Ömer Kavur, and more recently Yeşim Ustaoğlu, Nuri Bilge Ceylan, Zeki Demirkubuz, Semih Kaplanoğlu and Tayfun Pirselimoğlu, each harbouring a unique style and language as well as a creative vision and intellectual quest that transcend borders.

# 2 Migration, Dis/Misplacement and Exile

We'll start life from a place that does not exist, the children that arrive with migration are lost and ask the police the way home, my mother will make an address amulet and pin it to our pockets. We are too old to forget the silent fields and too young for Istanbul . . .[1]

They say that when one leaves one's country behind one has to be ready to sacrifice at least one part of himself. If this were the case, Ömer knew what he sacrificed: his dots! . . . For the bearer of the name to assimilate better to this country, to be on the inside, the dots of his name were left outside . . . Some things are certain to disappear during the process of adaptation of the names to foreign countries – sometimes a dot, sometimes a letter or the accent . . . The first condition of living in a foreign land is to become a stranger to the thing one is the most familiar with, one's name.[2]

Migration, dis/misplacement and exile have been an integral part of social, economic and political evolution in Turkey. Urbanization did not run parallel to industrialization but was an outcome of the increase in population, lack of infrastructure in the rural milieu, lack of possibilities for a better income and unemployment. Modernization of agriculture as a policy of the Democrat Party (DP) rule (the arrival of the tractor and mechanization of the farm sector) did not benefit the landless peasants. After 1950, during the transition to a market economy, industrial centres were established in the peripheries of the large cities of the west and migration from the east intensified. The city was also the symbol of a better life for rural people who had limited resources in terms of education, health care and entertainment. However, the rate of migration was higher than the rate of industrialization, which resulted in unemployment and housing shortages as the city population increased. With no assistance from the state, the migrants themselves began to seek solutions to their problems. They built makeshift houses on the outskirts of cities such as Istanbul, and these came to be known as *gecekondu*, literally, 'placed during the night'. The urban peasants worked in unfamiliar jobs such as superintendents in apartment buildings and itinerant vegetable vendors, but preserved their accustomed lifestyles in these ghettos.

Cinema began to approach the subject of migration only in the 1960s. Serious studies about the reasons for migration, the trauma of displacement, anxiety concerning loss of identity and the conflicts between rural migrants and urban dwellers had been absent from Turkish cinema. *Gurbet Kuşları / The Birds of Nostalgia* aka *Migrating Birds*, aka *Birds of Exile* (1964) by Halit Refiğ was the first film to problematize the migration issue, and along with *Bitmeyen Yol / The Never Ending Road* (1965) by Duygu Sağıroğlu is considered the best work on migration to be produced in the 1960s.

In *The Birds of Nostalgia* the narrative follows a family which leaves its home in Maraş (a southern town) due to economic difficulties and to give the youngest son a university education. The film begins at Haydarpaşa, a train station on the Asian side of Bosporus, a threshold for the Anatolians metaphorized in several migration films. This is where they see their first glimpse of Istanbul. The family embarks on the ferry along with others like them and shows their amazement at the magnificent palaces, mosques, towers and modern buildings. 'Whore Istanbul! I come to conquer you,' one character shouts, 'I'll be your king!' But for some the river to be crossed is like Acheron, the river of sadness. The film ends in the same location when the family returns home the way it came, with some members missing – the daughter threw herself off the roof of a building when chased by her brother who caught her prostituting herself and the youngest son remained behind to marry a city girl. As they leave, a new family arrives, with the same actors repeating the same lines. Migration continues.

*The Birds of Nostalgia* has been compared to Luchino Visconti's *Rocco e i suoi fratelli / Rocco and His Brothers* (1960). Both films start at a major train station with a family arriving from the provinces, but

Refiğ claims there are essential differences: Visconti's epic foregrounds the class struggles in an industrialized society, whereas Refiğ draws attention to such struggles in a society not yet industrialized. Furthermore, the migrants in his film arrive in Istanbul with a conqueror mentality. Visconti's modest family does not have such aspirations.[3] According to Sağıroğlu, however, *The Birds of Nostalgia* is valid for Italy but not Turkey, where families do not migrate together, but the males arrive first. They find refuge with a family already settled and ask for their help.[4]

*The Birds of Nostalgia* shows the duality of a city that is both traditional and Westernized, where people with different social status may exist side by side without forming a whole. A bar woman lives in the same uptown neighbourhood as a bureaucrat family and the decor of her apartment is not much different from theirs. In the traditional section of the town, where the migrant family settle, neighbours share similar lifestyles facilitating adaptation. It is only when they try to compare their lives with those living uptown that the trauma of alienation settles in.[5]

The family's misadventures in the city are prosaic. The older boys chase women and squander the family income; the youngest, Kemal the university student, lies about his background to his upper-class girlfriend and the daughter Fatma is lured into prostitution by a bad neighbour. What sets the film apart is the universal film language Refiğ employs, with skilful depth of field and triangular spatial arrangements, with which he had already experimented in *Şehirdeki Yabancı / A Stranger in Town* (1962). However, *The Birds of Nostalgia* has been polemicized on two grounds: first, Refiğ looks for private reasons behind the social and economic failure of the family rather than evaluating social inequalities within the context of class relationships, advocating hard work and patience. His stance is commensurate with the *Yön* movement, which he joined after the 1960 military intervention, which sought a socialist method of development in Turkey with emphasis on nationalism and the work ethic. Second, Refiğ's position on migration corresponds to the anti-migration and anti-Western theories he developed later concerning 'national cinema' (see chapter One). At the end of the film Kemal refuses to emigrate to the United States, choosing to do his social and national duty to his country, and the family go back to Maraş to improve conditions in their town.[6]

The Anatolia trilogy of Lütfi Ö. Akad, *Gelin / The Bride* (1973), *Düğün / The Wedding* (1974) and *Diyet / The Blood Money* (1975), is one

In the city, even in the shanty towns, women can break the chains of feudal masculinist oppression. *Gelin / The Bride* (1973), dir. Lütfi Ö. Akad.

of the most important works on migration, and *The Bride* is among the classics of Turkish cinema. It is the story of a displaced family from Yozgat (central Anatolia) who try to build new roots in the city through economic advancements. The family is not poor but their mentality is feudal and patriarchal. The motivation of the uprooted men is to make money as fast as they can and the duty of the women is to obey men unconditionally. When Meryem's son is sick the family refuse to pay for a doctor; they save the money to open a better shop uptown. Symbolically, the son dies on the day of the *Kurban Bayramı*, the religious festival when a sheep is sacrificed by devout Muslims. Meryem leaves the family to work in a factory, defying patriarchal convention. Her husband does not kill her, as his father demands, but joins her to start a new life.

The family in the film is an apposite trope for the changes in Turkish society in the 1970s, triggered by the exodus from the east to the large cities of the west. As much as economic reasons, dreams of social climbing and quick riches were often behind the exodus. The head of the family, Hacı İlyas, represents the pain of transition from feudal underdevelopment to capitalism that Turkey experienced after the 1950s. The decor inside the house illustrates the in-between status of the family, the traditional – the wall-carpet, the coffer, the dining table on the floor, the Qur'an – and the modern: the radio, the alarm clock, standing side by side. The family preserve the old values; they respect the elders and celebrate religious holidays, but these values are emptied of their essence. Women are ignored by men and do not receive support from each other.

The older daughter-in-law with two healthy children uses her privileged status as a weapon against Meryem, whose son is sick.

The title of the film refers to Meryem, the daughter-in-law who leaves her family behind to move in with her in-laws. The word *gelin* carries a dual meaning in Turkish: the bride and the daughter-in-law. Within the feudal system, she is the most exploited person in the family without recourse to rebellion. The film uses her liminality as a metaphor for the in-between position of displaced migrants in a society experiencing an unhealthy progress. Akad's Meryem, however, is not a weeping willow. She represents the new rural woman that migration to the city has created; she has the chance to decide her fate and at the same time to be a binding force for the family with her maternal instincts.[7] To stress her pivotal position in the narrative the camera follows her everywhere; in the crowd scenes the attention is continually drawn to her.

The husband's position is also in between. He feels the pain of the injustices toward his wife, but, within the feudal structure, is incapable of opposing his elders. (A similar situation is presented in *The Herd*, discussed in chapter Four: Şivan is helpless when his father, the old patriarch, insults his wife, Berivan.) Only after the tragedy of his son's death is he able to take a stand. Little Osman, who dies on the day of the sacrificial holiday, stands for all the sacrifices Turkey has made – human values, love and respect – in the race to embrace capitalism.

In *The Wedding* (1973) Halil leaves Urfa, a south-eastern town, with his brothers and sisters to seek employment and, just like the family in *The Bride*, they settle in the shanty towns of Istanbul. They choose Istanbul because an uncle has already settled there. Most migrants rely on a relative to find employment. If this fails, they search door to door, but do not consider the unemployment office. (In *Uzak / Distant* by Nuri Bilge Ceylan, made about thirty years later, the country cousin follows the same pattern. He arrives at the door of the older cousin already settled in Istanbul and when he receives no help, starts knocking on doors, but never goes to the unemployment office.)

Halil, as the oldest male, assumes the responsibility for the family, doing marginal and transitory jobs to earn the capital for a small business, the dream of most migrants, who are cautious about working for someone else. He marries off his sister Cemile for money and the husband makes her work as a cleaning woman until the debt is paid. The second sister, Habibe, in love with the young partner of the local butcher, is married off to a rich widower, again for money. During a fight with street vendors the two older brothers wound a man, but the younger assumes the guilt and goes to jail, which does not bother Halil, since this is a practical solution that will not exacerbate their financial situation. He does not consider the lost dreams of the boy who wants to be educated. Only one sister reacts to Halil's materialistic practicality, the oldest, Zelha, who has made several sacrifices for her siblings, including leaving the man she loved behind in Urfa. The fate of the woman is unchanged as long as the values of the feudal and capitalist systems prevail, Akad asserts. The slums around Istanbul look more like Anatolia.

The opening shots of *The Wedding* pan on shops without customers, street vendors selling nothing and idle men sitting against walls or under trees. Suddenly the scene shifts to a crowded square in Istanbul, where shoe-shiners and porters ply their trade zealously and vendors are busy selling everything from bagels to brooms. The energy emanating from the crowd and the animated action of buying and selling make the city attractive to the newcomers. The documentary style establishing shots that Akad employs was exploited effectively in later films such as *Güneşe Yolculuk / Journey to the Sun* (1999) by Yeşim Ustaoğlu, which starts with a similar scene in the same locale at the foot of the Galata Bridge, but they were rare in the 1970s, except for *Umut / The Hope* by Yılmaz Güney, which opens with the camera meticulously surveying the daily routine of the Adana train station.

*The Wedding* is in a sense the continuation of *The Bride*. The family agrees that there is no return to Urfa. Halil is ready to do anything, including selling his sisters (except working in the factory), to find the capital to start his own business to secure the future of the family. His obsession leads to the disintegration of family ties, although Akad's viewpoint is not pessimistic. Zelha's boyfriend Ferhat arrives from Urfa and finds a job in a factory. The end is not clear, yet there is a ray of hope that the two may unite, but sacrifices were made here as in *The Bride*: the sisters are forced to marry men they do not love and the youngest brother loses his adolescence to a jail sentence for a crime he did not commit.

*The Blood Money* begins where *The Bride* ends. The protagonists are Anatolian new arrivals in Istanbul who choose to work rather than scheme for quick riches. Meryem/Hacer is now a factory worker. She lives with her father, Yunus Dede, and her two children. When a worker named Mustafa has an accident, the foreman gives his job to his countryman, Hasan. Hacer eventually marries Hasan, and both work overtime for minimum wage, but Hacer begins to question things.

Akad presents the problems of the migrants from two angles: Yunus Dede is nostalgic about the home he left behind, the village and its values, where everyone knows each other and elders receive respect; he cannot adapt to city life. He is obliged to sell balloons on the street until death saves him. The other angle is that of the worker who does not miss the backward conditions of the village and looks to a future where his work will be rewarded.

In the beginning the audience assumes that the conflict is between the man and the machine; technology destroys human values and alienates man from himself. Soon attention is drawn to those who hold the power. The boss is a remnant of feudalism; he employs migrant workers at low rates without union protection. His son looks more modern and human but in reality is not much different and the foreman turns against his people for personal benefit.

Akad's message is: 'to be strong, we must unite'. To this purpose, he chooses characters from different echelons of political awareness. Those who believe in the union are only a handful. Initially, Hacer does not see a chance to rise against exploitation, but has an intuitive sense of it. Hasan, however, tries to ingratiate himself with the administrators by squealing on his co-workers. In the dramatic finale, when the boss divides those who are unionized from those who are not, Hasan stays with the non-unionized, but Hacer, after a moment of hesitation, joins the unionized workers. The blood money is paid when Hasan loses his arm. Hacer attacks the machines but soon realizes that those without political consciousness are the real culprits. Akad's way of illustrating the evolution of the characters to political awareness is more effective than delivering sermons through those who have already acquired this awareness.

The trilogy underscores the unionization and politicization process that began in the 1960s and reached its peak in the 1970s. Unlike Refiğ's *The Birds of Nostalgia*, which promulgates nostalgia for provincialism and conservative values, particularly with its ending, which sends the family to 'where they belong', Akad's trilogy demonstrates that in the modern context culture is not static: it can transform and liberate people, even shanty-town dwellers.

All three films are attempts at realistic narrative with detailed exploration of customs and traditions. At the centre is the woman as Mother, the backbone of the family. She is also the one who takes action. This role is played in all three by Hülya Koçyiğit. Meryem revolts against her father-in-law and finds work in the factory; Zelha protects her sisters and brothers from being further sacrificed; and Hacer is the first to achieve political awareness. Akad underlines that in the city, even in the shanty towns, women can break the chains of feudal masculinist oppression, although liberation outside the home does not always equate with liberation inside, where she is still expected to adhere to traditional roles. A decade later Atıf Yılmaz adds sexual liberation to the economic and political liberation of the shanty-town woman in *Bir Yudum Sevgi / A Taste of Love* (1984), where Aygül finds work in the factory, gets rid of her financially and sexually inadequate husband, and finds herself a new man.[8]

The essential point in all migration films is that whether they move upwards in the social scale (rare) or not, the migrants never remain the same. Those who migrate must change. The change is painful, and it erodes human values. Migrants are often forced to compete with friends and relatives, oppress or even sacrifice them for personal survival. In acquiring a new identity they risk erasing part of themselves, and hence become distant from their past. The desperate desire to belong creates characters alienated from those nearest to them and eventually from themselves, as in Ceylan's *Distant* (2002), where the assimilated city cousin and the newcomer country cousin, although essentially alike, are unable to find a meeting point.

*Bir Yudum Sevgi / A Taste of Love* (1984), dir. Atıf Yılmaz, adds sexual liberation to the economic and political liberation of the shanty-town woman.

BIR YUDUM SEVGI

A conversation in *The Blood Money* sums up the lives of the migrants: 'If you pull out a tree from its earth, no matter what you do, it does not work. We did not know. We thought human kind would survive without the roots', says Yunus Dede. His friend answers: 'those who know how to grow roots, do so, Yunus. The problem is not that. We peasants are used to till the land and leave the rest to God. Our lives are dependent on God. It is not like that here'.

The differences between *The Birds of Nostalgia* from the 1960s and films from the 1970s and '80s shed light on the changes in the identity of the metropolis and the strategies of the migrants for survival. The shanty towns are not part of the narrative in *The Birds of Nostalgia*. They appear once in a long shot from the vantage point of Kemal and his urban girlfriend as a picture alien to their lives. On the other hand, in the films that follow, the rural migrants sleep in transitory spaces (in cafés, roadhouses or construction sites) as well as the shanty towns. By 1980s even the shanty towns become a luxury for the poor. The family in Muammer Özer's *Bir Avuç Cennet / A Handful of Paradise* (1985) can make their home only inside a decrepit bus: even that would be begrudged by the apartment dwellers.

The migrants remain unskilled workers who hope to improve their life in the city. However, the identity of the city as a traditional but also Westernized space is slowly transformed as the old neighbourhoods disappear under the new (often corrupt) construction schemes. The earlier films present Istanbul as an attractive space with its historical and cultural identity, an identity at odds with the one that the migrants transport from the rural Anatolia. The inhabitants wear fashionable clothes and listen to modern music. Everything functions, trams, boats, cars . . . The opulent *yalı* (waterside Ottoman mansions) of the Bosporus are the background for romance and intrigue.[9] The city is the utopia of the rural, but also the dystopia, or utopia turns into dystopia as in *The Birds of Nostalgia*.

In the migration films of the 1970s and '80s the Western cultural identity of the city is negligible. Instead, the space occupied by the migrants gains prominence, as in Ali Özgentürk's *At / The Horse* (1981). University student Kemal in *The Birds of Nostalgia* hides his provincial identity and searches for a new one, which is characteristic of the 1960s migration films. In the later films intense migration from Anatolia has transformed the texture of the city; the differences have become blurred and the 'old Istanbulite' has become a myth. However, the invasion of

the city by its periphery has not diminished the stigmatization of the Anatolian peasant, aptly documented in *The Horse*. Ironically, the ones who stigmatize are often the ones who were stigmatized once themselves.

The aspirations of the migrants also change in parallel to socio-economical changes in society. In *The Birds of Nostalgia*, the family wants to educate the youngest son to guarantee a better future. The peasant father in *The Horse* also wants to educate his son, but his role models are adjusted to the value system of the 1980s. When he is reprimanded by a rich man for scratching his fancy car with the vegetable cart, the father does not fantasize about his son growing up and defending him against the socially and economically powerful; instead, he imagines his son in the role of the rich man bullying a poor vegetable vendor.[10]

In *Distant* the climatic confrontation between Mahmut, who has settled in the city, and his country cousin Yusuf, who also wants to benefit from what the city offers, focalizes a crucial malaise in contemporary Turkey. Both cousins are provincial, but the reasons for their arrival reflect the social and political circumstances of different periods. Yusuf is the product of the President Turgut Özal policies of development of the 1980s, when culture and intellectualism became a matter of disdain in the race to social climbing through money. In one sentence he explains his motivation for coming to Istanbul: 'The most important thing is to make money.' He wants to work in the ships because he will be paid in dollars. 'If there is a crisis, the dollar goes up.' When this plan fails he asks Mahmut for a job in his company. Mahmut vents his anger on Yusuf:

> M: You think there is no crisis here. What are you gonna do? Plant beans? . . . I've never asked for anything for myself. There is something called pride.
> Y: You people are like that. This place has changed you . . . if it were me, I would have asked.
> M: You understand nothing . . . you people come from the province and you don't think of acquiring a skill. All you do is search for someone to pull the string – an uncle, a minister, an MP . . . you want everything to fall into your lap. When I started, no one helped me. I arrived in Istanbul with no money in my pocket, not even for a hotel room. You come here without learning shit and you are left on the street. There is something called pride.

*At / The Horse*
(1981), dir. Ali
Özgentürk

But Yusuf has pride. The next day the key to the apartment is hanging on the hook and his bed is neatly made. Yusuf is gone. Whether Yusuf returns to his village, or is lost among the millions of unemployed, unskilled and alienated with no place to call home, is left to the spectator.

Just as migration to the bigger centres of western Turkey from the east has created important cultural and economical changes in society, migration to other countries, especially Germany, has also produced irreversible changes, repercussions of which are still felt. Cultural theorists such as Edward Said look at displacement from the 'Third' to the 'First' worlds, born of economic necessities, as the effect of a newly developed relationship between the West and the non-West, asserting the need for an active politics of self-location in situations where cultural and national affiliations are hybrid but slanted towards the West.[11] Displacement in the post-colonial or Third World always has a material base. After the Second World War, when Germany was short of labour, workers from underdeveloped countries were invited as *gastarbeiter* (guest workers). Some overstayed their welcome and settled in Germany without forgetting to visit home every religious holiday and building a house in the village for the return one day. For many immigrants, 'homeland' has become a space of resistance to subordination imposed by the adopted country and the option of return, even though it may never materialize, is a survival skill in the struggle for belonging, to provide them with the privilege of an imaginary space to negotiate their identity.[12] The guest workers could be Germans to Turks in Turkey ('Alamancı') and Turks to Germans in Germany, which could be used to advantage to endorse a unique identity by creating a certain distance from both Turkish and German identities. For the second and third generations, however, the return is often the dream of the parents and grandparents. Many Turks are active in the German economy, culture and politics despite persistent discrimination and the revival of anti-immigrant sentiments, which often backfire as ultra-nationalism among the immigrant communities, who try to establish their territory on foreign ground through diverse means from ghettos and enclaves to arabesque music that bursts out from their cars.

Orhan Pamuk in his essay 'My First Passport: What Does It Mean to Belong to a Country?' recounts that thirty years after receiving his first passport as a seven-year-old boy, he noticed a mistake: someone got his eye colour wrong, which taught him that a passport is not a document that tells us who we are but a document that shows what other people think of us. In the furnished apartment that the family rented in

Switzerland, young Pamuk associated 'living in another country with sitting at tables where others had sat before; another country was a country that belonged to other people'. Visiting Germany many years later as an established author, he associated his passport with a sort of 'identity crisis'. Pamuk asks: 'how much do we belong to the country of our first passport and how much do we belong to the "other countries" that it allows us to enter?'[13]

The first wave of films made by filmmakers such as Tunç Okan (*Otobüs / The Bus*, 1974) and Tevfik Başer (*40m² Deutschland / 40m² of Germany*, 1986) reflects the trauma of 'sitting at alien tables' in a country that belongs to 'other' people. The struggles for literal and metaphorical space, the culture shock, the isolation, the racism and the identity dilemmas experienced by the new immigrants are the burning issues of these films that illustrate the loss of 'cultural knowledge' in the temporal and spatial movement between homeland and the new country, which deprives the immigrant, refugee or exile of a local vernacular that would have helped them convey their culture, feelings and thoughts.[14]

The new generation, several of them born in their family's adopted country, are successful in drawing a synthesis between the two cultures of which they are a part. Still connected to the Turkish culture, they continue to deal with the issues of identity, distance and belonging through the problems of discrimination or the dichotomy of living in between two cultures and two languages, but as Fatih Akın, one of the most successful German Turkish filmmakers underlines, they no longer tell their stories from the margins, but rather from the centre of society.[15]

For Hamid Naficy, the politically enervating aspects of displacement are less interesting than the processes and products of the displaced imagination since 'journeys are not limited to those that take exilic and diasporic subjects physically, psychologically or metaphorically out of home countries and deliver them elsewhere or return them to their point of origin'. There are also 'journeys of identity' that displaced people face in the new lands. Regardless of their status as exiles, refugees or illegals, they go through a 'transformation, or their transformation is hindered, by the legal status with which they enter the new country and by the work they do there, the activities they undertake, the associations they form, and the media they produce and consume, as well as by the host society's historical perception and current reception of them'.[16]

Most films about displacement establish the protagonist's identity and its destabilization through attempts at, and failures of, self-location.

In that sense the use of space/place becomes very important. Tunç Okan's *Otobüs / The Bus* (1974) was one of the first films to foreground the external migration phenomenon. Turks who wanted to go to Germany did not receive support from an organized government programme (although the money they sent home once they had found jobs contributed to the economy). Potential workers followed in the steps of their relatives and friends, but for the first emigrants the only avenue was to trust someone who promised to get them there. Many naïve peasants were victims of schemes that robbed them of their limited resources. *The Bus* is one such story.

Several peasants (all men) are put in a run-down bus for Germany, where they are told they will have jobs. Through a foggy country landscape that blurs the vision and augments the disorientation and anxiety experienced by the travellers, the bus follows a route pre-planned by a German mafia in Hamburg, worse crooks than the Turkish driver who will confiscate all the money and the passports and leave the bus parked in the main square in Stockholm. The unwary peasants pull the curtains and start waiting. At night, when they slip out for natural needs, they see a world nefariously different. They stumble upon a man and a woman having sex in a telephone booth; an addict wants to buy drugs from them in the toilet (a *clin d'oeil* to the West's stereotyping of all Eastern men as dealers). One of them freezes to death, falling into an icy pool, and the response of a passer-by is 'filthy foreign bum'. Another follows a gay man mistaking his advances for friendship. At a party that reeks with affluent decadence, a playboy contest is held, based on the cars the men drive. Porno movies are watched with appetite as the orgy commences, but when the hungry peasant starts to devour all the available food, he is thrown out for bad manners, and killed for the colour of his skin and his dark moustache. Inside the bus is the village, where everyone knows each other. Outside are merciless strangers. Those who stay together are safer than those who stray. In that sense the bus serves as a trope for the ghettos built in the peripheries of industrial centres (like the shanty towns around Istanbul) where people with the same roots stay together in solidarity and live in conformity with their customs and traditions. In *The Bride* patriarch Hacı İlyas declares: 'inside the walls of this house is Yozgat, Istanbul is outside'. Inside the bus parked in the square in Stockholm is Turkey.

Unlike the standard immigration films of the period, *The Bus* is not about the problems of integration. The originality of the film is that the Turkish 'fugitives' (no papers, no vocabulary, no existence) are lost in

Stockholm as soon as they arrive, before they face the usual problems of adaptation and integration, which renders the 'well-organized' social system of Sweden irrelevant. At the end the bus is confiscated and the peasants arrested without having a chance to benefit from the abundance of Swedish society.[17]

In an interview he gave to French journalists Okan claimed that more than a film on immigration, *The Bus* was about the impossibility of dialogue between two different cultures, one a materialist society (capitalist or communist) and the other a typical Third World. The film was also about the gap between the underdeveloped countries of the southern hemisphere and the developed countries of the northern. To accentuate the lack of communication between the emigrants and the Swedish, Okan chose not to have any dialogue between the two groups. The film does not blame the developed countries, he pointed out, but questions if the development model of the consumer society of the West, copied by the whole world, even the communist, is a solution for happiness. For Okan the driver represents the *petite bourgeoisie* of the underdeveloped countries who try to become Western as soon as possible, ready to accept all values of the West, cultural, social and technological, but still cannot find their place in the society that they admire. The West is not only about money, sex and development, as the driver imagines, it is also culturally developed with a tradition of thinkers and a system of values.[18]

The driver is a typical example of the migrant with the mentality 'money is the key to all doors'. At Hamburg airport he expects respect because his valise is full of banknotes. Instead, he is eyed suspiciously and penetrated with rubber gloves. With his black moustache and dark skin he is the 'other', no matter how much money he brings. Civilized people don't carry their cash in a suitcase and what is this useless currency called the Turkish lira? Those who employ him dine in an expensive restaurant but would not invite him to sit down. All he can achieve is hiring two pathetic prostitutes in a decrepit hotel, who disappear as soon as he passes out, taking the rest of his money with them.

The scenes in Stockholm are caricatured representations of the West, but viewed from the angle of the newcomers they are realistic first impressions. The juxtaposition of lives, such as the Salvation Army singing hymns for peace and charity to the Christmas shoppers unaware of a busload of peasants starving in their midst, is very effective and the phantasmagorical ending is a strong message to what has come to be known in recent years as 'fortress Europe'.

*The Bus* became an event when it was internationally screened, winning several important awards despite repercussions from the Turkish officials, a large number of critics and expatriates who considered the film an exploitative disgrace. The government censored the film as 'anti-Turkish' for showing Turks eating stale bread and onions, not obeying the traffic rules and urinating in a group while standing, contrary to Turkish custom, and it was refused by a national festival.

*40m² of Germany* (1986) by Tevfik Başer is about immigrant worker Dursun and his young bride Turna, whom he is determined to protect at all costs from the 'evil influences' of the Western world. Just as *The Bus* serves as a place of refuge where one can cling to traditional values, a tiny apartment in *40m² of Germany* serves the same purpose. Turna is brought up to obey men, especially one's husband. She can only protest silently by cutting her hair and by withdrawing into herself. When she has the key to the door she does not escape. The sudden death of her husband ends her captivity but she does not know what to do with her freedom. In a sense, her captivity is a trope for the condition of all women from patriarchal societies who may not be literally locked in by their husbands, but are nonetheless captives of customs and traditions that force them to accept secondary status.

Turkish communities abroad were alarmed that *40m² of Germany* was kindling the image they had been fighting to erase. The Anatolian woman as 'victim' had been explored a decade earlier by German filmmakers such as Helma Sanders-Brahms, whose *Shirins Hochzeit / The Wedding of Şirin* (1975) was about a young Turkish woman who becomes a prostitute in Cologne and is killed by her pimp.[19] But Başer's was perhaps the first Turkish/German film that focused on the plight of the immigrant woman. For Başer the woman's captivity was a symbol. 'Even if the woman went outside, she would not be part of the society with her headscarf, her walk behind her husband, her inability to talk to strangers and especially men. The woman is forced to accept her secondary status since childhood. When living inside Western societies this image becomes more striking.'[20]

Başer's second feature, the equally successful *Abschied vom Falschen Paradies / Farewell to False Paradise* (1989), is also about women in confined spaces. The protagonist Elif is in a sense an extension of Turna. Having freed herself from the clutches of a brute husband by killing him, she is locked in a German prison where she gradually sheds the 'veil' developing her intellect and individuality among German friends. The only threat comes from the Turkish relatives (the guardians of feudal customs and traditions) who try to pull her back to the age of darkness, and her only fear is to be sent back to Turkey where darkness (feudalism) prevails.

For Deniz Göktürk, *Farewell to a False Paradise* 'is a good illustration of cinematic imprisonment of immigrants within the parameters of well-meaning multiculturalism feeding on binary oppositions and integrationist desires'. Filmmakers from immigrant or minority communities who seek funding 'have been almost driven to represent the "other" culture in terms of common assumptions and popular misconceptions. In consequence, a kind of ghetto culture emerged which was at great pains to promote politics of integration, but rarely achieved much popularity.'[21]

When Başer tried to move away from the 'guest worker' theme and shoot some films in Turkey, he found it difficult to raise funds in his adopted country. German companies were not willing to subsidize a project that would not interest or benefit Germany. 'The producers want to lead you in one direction', comments Seyhan Derin, the director of the

*Abschied vom Falschen Paradies / Farewell to False Paradise* (1989), dir. Tevfik Başer.

documentary, *Ich bin Tochter meiner Mutter / Ben Annemin Kızıyım / I am My Mother's Daughter* (1996). 'If the story involves an old woman, she has to wear a scarf. Young men beat their siblings and most young women are unhappy. The television is worse, particularly the private television, which is not able to forego the clichés that have become tiresome for our young actors and filmmakers.'[22]

When the young generation of filmmakers of Turkish origin (Fatih Akın, Yüksel Yavuz, Thomas Arslan, etc.) began to tell the story of four decades of immigration, first with short films and then features, the German media initially marketed their works like an ethnic package. However, these films showed marked distinction from the films of the Başer generation. Not only was the 'victim' literature absent, 'not knowing where to belong' was not a disadvantage any more; in fact, having multiple identities has become a virtue.[23]

Fatih Akın, born in Hamburg to Turkish parents, is the most celebrated young German filmmaker of Turkish origin. He achieved success with his first short film *Sensin! / Du bist es! / You're the One!* (1995), a slick comedy about a Turkish punk in Germany who searches for a soul mate, but she has to be Turkish! Akın's first feature, *Kurz und Schmerzlos / Short Sharp Shock* (1998), brought together a multi-ethnic trio – Gabriel the Turk, Bobby the Serbian and Costa the Greek – in a street gang. The uniting element was their alienation from their roots while growing up between two contrasting worlds.

Akın's *Gegen die Wand / Head-on* won the Golden Bear at the Berlin Film Festival in 2004 as a German production. Focusing on two Turkish-German marginals and their quest for visibility, or a 'third space' as Homi Bhabha would put it, the film eschews the typical identity problems of the second-generation Turks in Germany and focuses on atypical characters whose fight is against themselves. Sibel had her nose broken by her brother when she was seen with a boy, but her family is not the typical Muslim family, as Akın has pointed out in several interviews. The mother is quite modern (and does not support the headscarf). They want the best for her. Yet she is too full of life to be restricted. As for the self-destructive Cahit, he has his devils. They are both misplaced characters; whether their uprootedness plays a role in this or not is not the concern of the film. Among other marginals like themselves, be they Germans or other Europeans, they feel more at home than among Turks who do not approve their lifestyles; a bus driver who kicks them out for 'bad behaviour' is a Turk.

Akın avoids passing judgement on his characters. Sibel, who equates
freedom with sexual freedom, looks for a husband to escape from her
conservative home; she chooses a Turk to please her parents, but not the
kind that would put reins on her. Ironically, after hitting the bottom,
she finds shelter in a conservative home like her parents', a husband
who brings home the bread, a child and a middle-class apartment. Cahit's
self-destruction is also presented without commentary. But despite the
chaos surrounding the couple, a certain aura of romanticism follows
their misadventures. Even their dingy apartment in Germany has a
Fassbinderian appeal in its abjectness.

*Head-on* possesses the usual elements of Turkish melodrama from
*kara sevda* (dark passion) and rape to honour. The episodes with the
Turkish musicians playing classical Turkish music on the shores of the
Golden Horn with a towering mosque in the background – a Brechtian
intervention as Akın admits – bookend the chapters, but also reveal a
postcard kitsch quality, presenting Turkey as a dreamland. The fact that
the two characters, whose problems are with society in general, not with
German society in particular, end up in Turkey is somewhat problematic.

migration, dis/misplacement and exile | 75

Does Akın suggest a 'return to roots' as a solution? He has stated on several occasions that the geographical space was not important; he wanted to create 'an imaginary space' for his Turkish-German characters to escape. That 'imaginary space' happens to be Turkey, the homeland of their parents, but in that homeland Akın positions his characters in impersonal and transitory spaces (hotels, airports and bus stations), places for someone passing through as a tourist. According to scholar Filiz Çiçek, the ending of *Head-On* denies redemption to the German-Turkish characters in either country and 'offers no realistic alternative for [a] third space of existence. This feeds into the German-media's focus on the "hyphenated" identity of the Turks, which stresses the national and religious identities at the expense of other forms of identification.'[24]

Akın's *Auf der anderen Seite* (2007), meaning 'on the other side' but entitled *The Edge of Heaven* in English, is the second part of the love (*Head-on*), death and the devil trilogy. The film is about six characters in search of an identity and a place to belong. Nejat (Baki Davrat, who played Murat in Kutluğ Ataman's *Lola and Bilidikid*) is a well-integrated second-generation Turk who teaches German literature in a Hamburg university; he is also a dutiful son who likes to spend time with his retired but unruly father Ali, whose appetite for women and *rakı* (the Turkish national drink) does not seem to diminish with age. Ali is lonely but not exactly nostalgic for his homeland. He feels at home growing tomatoes in the garden of his modest home in Bremen and betting on horses with his son. Yeter, a middle-aged widow, prostitutes in Bremen to pay for her daughter's education. Threatened by two fundamentalists, she accepts Ali's offer to live with him and serve him for a 'salary' equivalent to what she earns in the brothel. She is killed by Ali, who serves a sentence in a German jail, after which he goes back to his home village to spend his old age fishing. Nejat gives up his profession and takes over a German bookshop in downtown Istanbul. Ayten, a student activist in Istanbul, thinks her mother Yeter works in a shoe shop in Bremen. When chased by the police, she goes to Germany and meets Lotte, a middle-class young German woman who befriends her to the chagrin of her mother Susanne (Hanna Schygulla), a middle-aged ex-hippie. Lotte has discovered her true self during a trip to India while realizing that she has been following the path of her mother, who had hitchhiked to India in her youth. Following Ayten back to Turkey, where she is imprisoned, Lotte dies in a haphazard incident.

Akın's *Auf Der Anderen Seite / The Edge of Heaven / Yaşamın Kıyısında* (2007).

*The Edge* starts in Turkey on the day of the sacrificial holiday, *Kurban Bayramı*, with Nejat driving towards a Black Sea town to see his father and ends with a repetition of the sequence. In between these two episodes, two coffins cross each other at Istanbul airport, Yeter's and Lotte's. Coincidence and death are integral to the film. Characters miss one another (Ayten never sees the pictures of her mother Nejat pasted on the walls; Nejat looks for Ayten who is seen sleeping in the amphitheatre where he lectures about Goethe) and die suddenly from a single blow (Yeter) or a single shot (Lotte). Death becomes a part of life. Susanne finds her former self after losing Lotte and discovers a surrogate daughter in Ayten, while Nejat finds a surrogate mother in Susanne.

The film stresses the importance of education. Nejat gives his father a book to read. His opinion of Yeter is changed when he finds out that she is prostituting to educate her daughter. After Yeter's death he searches for Ayten to pay for her education. Other issues are brought up, but not developed, such as military interventions, the threat of terrorism, cold-blooded activists, the Vietnam war, the oil crisis, the migration, the nationalist revival (demonstrators brandishing flags in Beyoğlu), police brutality, the overcrowded women's prison, the bureaucratic German asylum system and the mind-boggling Turkish legal apparatus. Fundamentalist Turks harass Yeter for prostituting, but not her customer. Yeter is from Maraş, probably a Kurd; her husband was killed in 1978, suggesting PKK (Kurdistan Workers' Party) involvement.

Susanne and Lotte as Germans represent the European Union, and Ayten and Yeter Turkey, according to Akın.[25] The events in the film stand for the relation between these two systems. The conversation in Susanne's kitchen between Susanne and Ayten about the EU is ironic, although not far from reality. Ayten claims that they are fighting for simple human rights, including the right to education, which, for the moment, is the privilege of those with money. 'Maybe things will get better once you join the European Union', Susanne repeats to the chagrin of Ayten, who retorts 'Fuck the European Union!', a sentiment increasingly shared with other Turkish people.

Unlike *Head-on*, in *The Edge of Heaven* Turkey is no longer an 'imaginary space'. Nejat gives up his prestigious job in Germany to settle in Istanbul and his father returns to his village on the Black Sea. 'Belonging to the homeland' is significant in the film, although this is not about waving the Turkish flag but about simple comforts such as returning home to spend one's retirement fishing.

According to Turkish critic Vecdi Sayar, the film is moulded in the kind of 'humanist' ideology that the audiences in the West would like to see. Akın defends the notion that the East and the West can understand each other and help each other. For this purpose he does not hesitate to use the clichés of the West. Although he also tries to turn the clichés upside down, his main concern is to reach the masses, and clichés are easily understood. For Sayar, the French title of the film, *De l'autre côté*, meaning 'from/to the other side', is more appropriate, since for both the Germans and the Turks the issue is the 'other side'. When Akın looks at Turkey he looks 'from the other side'. He presents a rather schematic panorama of Turkey: a widow forced to go to Germany to prostitute herself, a 'revolutionary' obliged to escape abroad, a macho Turk who would choose himself a woman from the brothel and his son, an accomplished professor in a German university (a role blatantly created to counteract the clichés). 'The 1 May clashes with the police, the posters of Abdullah Öcalan (the imprisoned PKK leader) and 'a "revolutionary"' who tries to defend her position with slogans that evoke Yılmaz Güney's film, *Arkadaş / The Friend*, who becomes a lesbian quite unexpectedly . . . may look interesting to the Westerners but I must say not a bit credible for us . . . The naïve European image presented by Hanna Schygulla and her daughter is also one of the well-known clichés of the cinema of the West.' Sayar feels that the film is crafted to appeal to the guilt complexes of the Western intellectual.[26]

The concerns of Yılmaz Arslan, born in Turkey but growing up in Germany, where he went with his parents for health reasons, are more tangible. The wound (sometimes physical and graphically displayed and at other times so deep that it manifests itself in unexpected ways) is the principal motif of Arslan's films. He first drew attention with *Langer Gang / Passages* (1992), an autobiographical feature about the tragic existence of disabled youngsters, particularly those of ethnic backgrounds in special facilities in Germany, where their vital needs are met but human needs ignored. His second film, *Yara / Seelenschmerz / The Wound* (1998), was about the emotional scars that haunt the lives of the young and the displaced through the story of an integrated young Turkish woman who is sent back to Turkey as protection against 'bad influences'. His third film, *Brudermord / Fratricide* (2005), focuses on misplaced youth in a foreign land through the story of ethnic hostility among immigrants in Germany.

*Fratricide* begins with a car speeding through arid eastern Turkey. Now and then, the driver, who is out of the frame, stops to ask the address of the Karaman family. An old woman tells him to drive until

*Brudermord / Fratricide* (2005), dir. Yılmaz Arslan.

he sees a fig tree, then he has to take a right and look for the third yew tree. That is where Azad would be found. Young Azad is summoned by his older brother Semo to join him in Germany. Elsewhere a grandfather sacrifices a lamb and with its blood instructs his eleven-year-old grandson Ibo, whose parents were killed by the Turkish army, to be a man and to take destiny in his own hands. This is how two young Kurds take the road to Germany and settle in a hostel for Kurdish immigrants without papers, where they meet. Because the subsistence money given by the German government is not enough, Azad works as a barber in the toilet of a *döner kebab* stand and asks little Ibo to hold the mirror for the customers. One night, in the subway, they are insulted by two punk Turks with a ferocious bulldog, unemployed and alienated youth whose frustration at not belonging manifests itself in petty crime. Azad and Ibo escape but the sign Azad makes with his fist through the closed doors will determine his fate. One day, as Azad is arguing on the street with his brother who earns his living pimping East European women, he is recognized by one of the punks, who lets his dog loose on him. During the struggle Semo knifes one of the punks and the feud results in the death of everyone except Ibo.

Arslan intersperses the legend of the Kurds through the narrative, often like a Greek tragedy (including a chorus of old women), and the film succeeds in keeping the audience in a limbo between the cruel reality (violence in the streets of Germany) and the fantasy (the legendary land of Anatolia), while the animation sequences attached to the Ibo character give a magical atmosphere, which Arslan explains is 'a visionary flight towards a childhood that was stolen from him'.[27]

The focus of the film is the children of the workers who went to Germany in the 1950s, 'the money dreamers' as Arslan calls them, and the emptiness that the second generation feels. Ibo's opening voiceover warns the viewer of the fate of the 'money dreamers' who leave home to seek their fortune elsewhere only to lose their souls in the process, a familiar theme aptly illustrated in internal migration films of the 1960s to 1980s, from Refiğ's *Birds of Nostalgia* to Akad's Anatolia Trilogy. The paradox that Arslan chooses not to comment on is that often the lives of the ones left behind depend on the cash these 'money dreamers' send home.

The film challenges simplistic judgements regarding the concept of 'homeland', particularly for the Kurdish diaspora. It also sends a message to the Kurdish community-in-exile who should be helping refugees instead of promoting their otherness by insisting on their victimization. Some viewers may think *Fratricide* is a film that defends the Kurds against the Turks. A scene when the Turkish punk rapes young Ibo violently reinforces this point of view. However, the parents of the punks are ordinary Anatolian peasants, a quiet family who run a grocer's shop, and they are hurt by the behaviour of their sons.

Arslan stresses that those who went to Germany to work have been perceived as workers and their identity as human beings forgotten; the situation has worsened in the last ten years. He is an angry young man. His heroes, when they lose their cultural/personal identity, go mad (*The Wound*) or resort to violence (*Fratricide*).

Born in Canada to Turkish and Greek parents, Phyllis Katrapani explores the meaning of 'home' for her generation with a trilogy: *Ithaque / Ithaca* (1997), *Home* (2002) and *Within Reach / Elimizin Altında* (2006). The trilogy is also an interrogation of existing or imaginary ties and a settling of accounts with one's roots for the filmmaker and others like her who try to attribute meaning to their special identity. *Ithaca* is an allegory on the return of Ulysses to his native island. In black and white and without dialogue, the film presents images of the countryside from the window of a train as it crosses Europe, heading towards Greece, while the protagonist, the filmmaker's father, recites Constantine P. Cavafy's poem *Ithaca* (1911) in Greek. In the poem Ulysses is urged to take his time, not to hurry his return and to acquire as many experiences as possible along the way, the voyage being the destination and Ithaca the reason he set forth. The film tries to define the meaning of 'home', the place we return to, perhaps only in thoughts.

*Home* investigates the complex relationship between home, identity and belonging, exploring the hidden longing that those born in a different place from their parents feel for something never experienced, a nostalgia for the places that were part of their parents' history, something that cannot be shared with their parents. In this film Katrapani creates a fictional character, a male alter ego, torn between the two worlds, and intercuts the narrative with interviews with people like her to juxtapose fiction with reality. The past is reflected figuratively through the images of abandoned villages in Kayaköy in western Turkey (a thriving Greek village called Karmylassos until 1924, when the 25,000 Greek inhabitants, along with more than a million other Greeks living throughout Turkey, were repatriated to Greece through a massive government mandated population exchange between the two countries). Although this event precedes the departure of her parents by four decades, it is a striking trope for the turbulent history of the two communities and it explains the desire of her Greek father and Turkish mother to find a 'third space' to start their life together.

The diegetic present involves a fictional young couple, whose intimacy is interrupted at times by the self-reflexive ponderings of Alex regarding his identity. His partner, Marie, Canadian by 'ancestral rights', is grounded in the present and perhaps the future (her wish for a baby) and cannot share his sentiments, which she thinks draw a curtain between them. The actual interviews with several mid-1930s exiles and *émigrés* of different backgrounds living in Montreal not only add a universal voice to the individual one, but also are comforting to Alex (and the filmmaker). Through their personal stories he and others like him are able to understand the 'privilege' of belonging to two different cultures, through which they are able to construct their own special identity and their own past as new memories slowly accumulate and home becomes a corner of one's own where one feels 'at home'.

Katrapani's poetic documentary-essay *Within Reach* (2006) through the intimacy of first-person narrative focuses on objects that exiles or the dis/misplaced bring along with them; as Naficy points out, 'a small, insignificant object taken into exile (such as a key to the house) becomes a powerful synecdoche for the lost house and the unreachable home, feeding the memories of the past and the narratives of exile'.[28] In seven parts the film explores the relationship between people, objects and memory, and the artist. A house one moves into carries the traces of a family friend who is no more; a little child navigates her way in a big world by trial and error, tirelessly trying to button her jacket; exiles, *émigrés* or immigrants in search of a different life in a new country carry objects from home as if memory is not reliable – a ring, an alumni book, few grains of earth – and uprooted people gaze at the camera lens without speaking a word. The film explores distance and the different measures of distance distinctively in each chapter through the notion of filiations: relationships between the filmmaker and her daughters, her daughter and her grandmother and herself and her father, as well as through explorations of the distance between homeland and the adopted land, direct and indirect proximity, which is the feeling of closeness one experiences through objects from 'there'.[29]

Language is important in the film with its dual role of defining or obscuring identity. In the chapter called 'Belongings' Katrapani reflects on her use of English and French: 'I count in English, swear in English, love in French.' She returns to language in 'Indirect Objects' as her mother, deliberately out of focus, teaches a few words to her grand-daughter in her own language, Turkish. Then, in the last chapter, 'Other Tongue', she reintroduces her voice, now off-screen and in French, a language she has adopted to align herself with her environment in the French-speaking province of Québec in Canada. The split identity of Canada as manifest in the ongoing discussions about the two official languages of the country has an echo in the filmmaker's slight confusion (despite her self-assured mastery of the two languages) as to which to employ for which sentiments, which in turn echoes the confusions of her parents as Greek and Turkish immigrants with a mastery of English arriving in Canada to a milieu that turns out to be French, not to mention that the father is a *Rum*, a Greek from Turkey, who left Turkey in 1964, a time when notices were prominent in public places: 'Citizen, speak Turkish!' Perhaps this is the meaning of the last chapter, where

she comes to the conclusion: 'I am what I am', then adds: 'or rather what I think.'

*Hakkaride Bir Mevsim / A Season in Hakkari (1983), dir. Erden Kıral, was banned for five years.*

Over long years of economic and political turmoil Turkey has forced many of its citizens into exile. Some filmmakers chose self-imposed exile when they could no longer make films in their country. The leitmotiv of 'exile' is no stranger to Erden Kıral, who left Turkey in the 1980s when two of his films, *Bereketli Topraklar Üzerinde / On Fertile Lands* (1980) and *Hakkaride Bir Mevsim / A Season in Hakkari* (1983), were banned for five years.

In *A Season in Hakkari* an urban intellectual, in self-imposed or forced exile, arrives in a remote Anatolian village, overcomes his culture shock and discovers his real self while discovering others. *Mavi Sürgün / The Blue Exile* (1993), which Kıral made after his return from Germany, is based on the autobiography of Turkish journalist and intellectual Cevat Şakir (1890–1973) who arrives home from Oxford during the social and political upheaval of post-Liberation Turkey. In those turbulent times he publishes a story about deserters in the First World War who

were shot without trial, *How Do Those Condemned to Death, Facing their Fate, Walk to the Gallows?* and is exiled to Halicarnassus (today's Bodrum) for three years. Parallel to an actual journey from Ankara to Bodrum that takes months by train, the film traces the psychological journey of the exile as he tries to come to terms with his past.[30] When he arrives in Bodrum he tries to unload his burden by giving himself to nature. He even marries a local girl. From then on he is the Fisherman of Halicarnassus. 'The act of exile not only leads to a settling of accounts with oneself but also with the society one grew up and lived in', comments Kıral. 'This is unavoidable because the exile learns to look at himself and his society with a distance.'[31]

The subject of the Liberation Courts, formed during the first years of the Turkish Republic, and their repressive practices was taboo until the 1990s. *Butterflies Fly to Eternity*, released the same year as *The Blue Exile* (mentioned in chapter One in the context of Islamist cinema), takes an anti-Kemalist stand. *The Blue Exile*'s departure point is an actual event that took place during that period, but neither *Butterflies* nor *The Blue Exile* attempts to open a dialogue about the Liberation

Kıral's *Yolda / On the Way* (2005).

Courts. Kıral chooses to create the oppressive atmosphere of the period after the establishment of the Republic in a 'subtle' way. His focus is the life of the exile rather than the reasons for exile. This discretion, which may be motivated by auto-censorship, leaves holes in the narrative of a visually captivating work.

Kıral's *Yolda / On the Way* (2005), made twelve years after *The Blue Exile* and twenty-two years after *A Season in Hakkari*, is the story of another banished intellectual, the most celebrated filmmaker of the country who spent the best years of his life in prison and died in exile. The narrative is based on an actual event. While Yılmaz Güney was in jail, *Yol* was directed by Şerif Gören, one of his apprentices, with detailed instructions from the master. Originally this job was entrusted to Erden Kıral but after looking at some of the rushes, Güney unexpectedly stopped the shooting and changed directors. Traumatized by the event, Kıral wrote a long letter to Güney, which he never sent. Had he sent that letter, explains Kıral, he would not have made this film.

A coming to terms with a problematic past event? Self-introspection of an artist carrying the deep wound of rejection? Homage to a revered master? *On the Way* is all of these and more. The basic themes are similar to *A Season in Hakkari* and *The Blue Exile*: exile, home, homelessness, displacement and the diverse aspects of freedom and imprisonment, physical as well as spiritual and metaphorical. The alienation of the intellectual in an industrialized society and a long journey that runs parallel to an interior journey of settling of accounts with the heavy burden of memories are also familiar Kıral themes. Whereas in *Hakkari* the journey ends in a world that is entirely opposite to the world of the intellectual but nevertheless a mirror of his soul, and the journey in *The Blue Exile* culminates in the writer/intellectual becoming one with nature, in *On the Way* the journey of the filmmaker/ intellectual is endless, effectively drawn in the scene when the protagonist and his guards drive in circles in the heavy fog trying to find the prison that will incarcerate one of the most important artists of Turkey – novelist, screenwriter, actor and director Yılmaz Güney.

*On the Way* is not a documentary but a fictionalized account of a very important event in the career of Güney, and also Kıral. The year is 1981. The military regime that took over with the coup of 12 September 1980 is in power. The curfew is on. The legendary filmmaker (played by Halil Ergün) is transferred to yet another prison for inciting prisoners to riot. During the long journey his wife, an ex-prison inmate and a young filmmaker named Sedat follow him in a car. Güney is troubled by health problems, the plans for his imminent escape and the shooting of *Yol*, which is called *Bayram* (a Muslim religious holiday when prisoners are often granted a short leave to visit their families) at that point. The young filmmaker is torn with dual emotions: to stifle his creative urges, follow his master's instructions and hence create a work of art that is not his, or to give free reign to his talent and create his own work, thus alienating his master to whom he is deeply attached. Güney is also aware of the risk involved in trusting his projects to younger talents: 'My dreams are captive in the hands of others', he laments, 'this is imprisonment.' Kıral explains: 'the relationship between the master and the apprentice is a complicated one. One cannot create without feeling admiration for the great masters and their works, but admiration slows down the thinking process. You can become a master only by killing the master.'[32]

To transmit these complex emotions the film employs a multi-layered discourse. The gaze is at the core; considering most dialogue takes place in front of two policemen, this is more than essential. Feelings and thoughts are often transmitted through eye movements (a homage to

Güney's style of filmmaking that gives importance to the language of the gaze). During the scenes where the conflict reaches its climax, the image is distorted, merging the real with the imagined. The fog that obscures the view serves as an effective trope for the psychological state of the characters. The steam on the glass blurs the view but also draws attention to the blurred emotions of Güney as he hears a passing train and thinks another person has just walked out of his life.

Sandwiched between the two police officers in the back seat of a car, with his hands cuffed, Güney looks thoughtful and troubled but in control. Having spent a large part of his life behind bars, he has learned to play the prison game. It seems as if he is the puppet-master, pulling the strings of the policemen who are effectively prisoners themselves. Güney was (is) their legend as well but the loyalty to duty forces them to act otherwise. Only the gendarme, who stops the car for inspection, an Anatolian boy with a pure heart, expresses true emotions: 'The way you looked at us in your last film, *abi* (older brother), broke our hearts!'[33]

Soon after the period focalized in the film, Yılmaz Güney escaped from prison. When he reappeared in Cannes to receive the Palme d'Or for *Yol* he was a filmmaker in exile. During interviews he expressed the dilemmas of a filmmaker cut from his roots – his background, his own stories, his own people – and his feeling of not belonging.

> The dough of my art consisted of the images of my people, with their feelings and the accumulated experience of my land and its soil. Today, I am relatively free but there is no public I can relate to, no characters I want to describe . . . you have the weapon of freedom in your hand but no ammunition to communicate . . . I have to find a new path, create a new audience. But this audience can be nothing like the one it took us years to shape in Turkey . . . You can't reassemble Turkey abroad and make films that explain Turkey from abroad.[34]

Güney's sentiments are not unfamiliar to artists severed from their roots, who try to find a new language to express the emotions and the conflicts that arise out of the new conditions they face, whether forced or voluntary. The works above, as diverse as the circumstances of the filmmakers, reflect the dynamics of movement and change in the modern world from an insightful and humanistic point of view.

# 3  Denied Identities

To be a minority . . . a difficult craft[1]

Sing me a song in your language
No matter whose it is
So long as the wail is yours
I may not understand it
But let it be in your language[2]

The concept of the nation is derived from the state in Turkey. Mustafa Kemal Atatürk, founder of the Turkish Republic, amalgamated varied identities to create a nation-state. However, the assimilation policies were only partially successful in integrating diverse ethnic, religious and national groups into Turkish society. The power of the modern nation-state to control the lives of its citizens has often forced individuals to play conflicting roles that have fragmented their identity. The banning of the Kurdish language, Kurdish proper names, even Kurdish songs, has had repercussions in politicizing Kurdish consciousness, particularly in the rural areas of the south-east where remnants of feudalism and dismal living conditions have thwarted development.

The nation is conceived as a concrete community sharing the same past, present and future, 'an imagined community', as Benedict Anderson points out: 'the members of even the smallest nation will never know most of their fellow members, meet them, or even hear of them, yet in the minds of each lives the image of their communion . . . regardless of the actual inequality and exploitation that may prevail in each, the nation is always conceived as a deep, horizontal comradeship.'[3] Continual flagging of nationhood is part of life in modern Turkey as in any established nation, from reciting the maxims of Kemal Atatürk in schools and the ritual of singing the national anthem en masse to patriotic outbursts at football matches, as illustrated in several films of the new generation from Nuri Bilge Ceylan to Yeşim Ustaoğlu. These manifestations are ways of ensuring a sense of belonging to the national community by 'imagined linkage', and creating a sense of continuity with the past. The singing of the national anthem gives us 'an experience of simultaneity', Anderson asserts, 'no matter how banal the words and mediocre the tunes'. 'At precisely such moments, people wholly unknown to each other utter the same verses to the same melody . . . If we are aware that others are singing these songs precisely when and as we are, we have no idea who they may be, or even where, out of earshot, they are singing. Nothing connects us all but imagined sound.'[4] The mass media affirm the sense of belonging to the national community by ensuring that the whole nation is watching (reading) the same news at the same time, which even extends over the borders to imagined transnational communities such as the immigrant enclaves in Germany.

The metonymic image of banal nationalism, however, is not the flag the hooligans wave at the football matches to the chants of 'Türkiyem! Türkiyem!' (My Turkey! My Turkey!), or the patriotic paradigms children parrot at schools, but the flag hanging nonchalantly on public buildings, the picture of Kemal Atatürk and his celebrated declaration, 'How happy is the one who says I am a Turk!', on the walls of every establishment (regardless of political orientation) and the news media's (again regardless of political orientation) endorsement of nationalism through inflated accounts of the feats of Turks around the world – from politicians to sports celebrities. Any internal (civil war in the south-east) or external (Europe's probing into violation of human rights, or the genocide of the Armenians) strife is repudiated with the long-established adage, 'Enemy inside, enemy outside'.

Several ethnic and religious minorities (Albanians, Armenians, Assyrians, Azeris, Bosnians, Circassians, Georgians, Greeks, Jews, Kurds, Laz, Pomaks, Tatars, Yoruks, etc.) constitute important parts of the country's population. However, the official ideology for the Turkish 'imagined community' is one nation, one state, one religion and one language, though Islamic Prime Minister Tayyip Erdoğan, to pacify the unrest in the south-east, has stated that all citizens of Turkey are united under the primary identity of a citizen of the Turkish Republic, but all Turks have 'sub-identities' and 'a Kurd can say I am a Kurd'.

In a 2007 article entitled 'Are Turks Racist?', columnist Gündüz Vassaf comments: 'We live in a country where even fictional heroes are brought to justice for "insulting Turkishness". Among those who are obliged to defend themselves against this charge are prominent writers of various newspapers and world-famous literary personalities.[5] From the issue of the Armenian genocide and the 6–7 September 1955 attacks on the properties of the Greeks to the denial of the mother tongue of the Kurds until recently, a strong feeling of enmity against 'the other' exists in Turkey, according to Vassaf.

> Not only our attitude against the minorities or the Kurds, but also our traditional stand against the Alevis is also exclusionist. When we say 'we', we do not include them despite all their efforts not to be different. They are 'othered' and considered as the agents of foreign forces that threaten our state and our unity and oppose our religious one-ness.[6]

The Kurdish issue and the war in the south-east have been thorny subjects for Turkish cinema, which, until the 1990s, showed the Kurds as Turks. The Kurds were the poor illiterate easterners from the mountains. They were identified by their black *shalvar* (loose pants), their poverty and their lack of proper discourse in the official language. The oppressive conditions of their lives were attributed to centuries-old customs and traditions, and to feudalism, but never to the lack of effective government policies to improve their lot. Commercial cinema used the Kurdish characters and the geography of their homeland without giving a name or language, but rather with an orientalizing gaze.

A serious study of the beginnings of Kurdish cinema within the borders of Turkey, Turkish films about the Kurds and the presentation of Kurdish identity in Turkish cinema has not been made. Yılmaz Güney showed both Kurds and Turks as human beings suffering under state oppression. Due to heavy censorship, which regularly condemned several of his films for 'leftist' inclinations, he was obliged to deliver the Kurdish identity of his characters through circumlocution. *Seyyit Han* aka *Toprağın Gelini / Seyyit Han* aka *The Bride of the Earth* (1968) can be considered the first film to present Kurdish characters. Although it was shot in the town of Yenice, in Adana, where Güney was born, the name of the woman is Keje, which is Kurdish, and one can read Seyyit Han's struggles against the local landlord as the struggle of the oppressed against the oppressor and draw a parallel to the plight of the Kurds in Turkey, but this aspect is so subtle that even the censors could not decipher it.

*Umut* / *The Hope* (1970) and *Endişe* / *The Anxiety* (1974) are both about the Kurdish people. *Yol* / *The Way* is about the suffering of the Kurds, but if the Kurdish language were used all those who took part in the film would have been punished by prison sentences, according to Güney. *Yol* takes place in Diyarbakır, Urfa and Siirt, areas heavily populated by Kurds, but Kurdish is not spoken. Güney tried to create a Kurdish atmosphere by the use of local elegies. Nonetheless, the film was banned for seventeen years. In interviews he gave from exile, Güney often said that in all the films that he made in Turkey, he was never able to express his thoughts in a manner he would have liked, in style or in spirit, let alone to express a serious matter like the Kurdish question, or the question of the working class. Even basic societal questions of justice and injustice had to be dealt with indirectly. The dominant common element in these works was that they were compromises.

A film that shows the harsh living conditions of the Kurds without ever mentioning the word Kurd is Şerif Gören's *Katırcılar* / *The Muleteers* (1987), a forerunner to Bahman Ghobadi's *Zamani baraye masti asbha* / *A Time For Drunken Horses* (2000). *The Muleteers* is about three smugglers who conduct business for local merchants in a border village. Someone grasses on them and they are caught by soldiers who have orders to take them to town for a trial. Although the smugglers are given Turkish names, from the way they are dressed and their interaction with the authorities there is no doubt that they are Kurds. Some of the dialogue during their interrogation by the commandant is tongue in cheek. To the question why they carry guns, they answer: 'There are bandits, wolves, "the anarchists"' (referring to Kurdish guerrillas). In return, the commandant asks if they get involved in 'anarchy-*manarchy*', knowing he will not receive an honest answer.

Daringly shot in the extreme weather conditions of the Bingöl Mountains (with clear references to *Yol*), the film bets the Kurdish smugglers, poor landless peasants forgotten by the state, struggling for survival, against the pretentious, corrupt and hypocritical bureaucrats and local merchants. The soldiers, sent to the area during their compulsory military service, seem to be caught between the two elements. Although brainwashed to follow orders even if it means to kill, they seem to be in constant struggle with their consciences. One of them is from Diyarbakır, a Kurd no doubt. On a three-day journey in the blizzard, a woman reporter from Istanbul who accompanies them to town to concoct a sensational story foregoes her journalistic ambitions and serves as a catalyst to bring out the human nature of both the soldiers with the guns and the handcuffed smugglers.

The most popular film of the 1990s (with more than two million viewers), *Eşkıya / The Bandit* by Yavuz Turgul, presents three characters with Kurdish names: the protagonist Baran, the antagonist Berfo and the woman they both love, Keje, but the word Kurd is never mentioned. They come from an unknown village in the south, which is under water for some unknown reason (a reference to the building of the dam that caused the relocation of many flooded Kurdish villages). The bandit wears a black *shalvar* and supports the *poshu* (the traditional scarf that also connotes liberation of the Kurds from the oppression of the Turkish state), but his Kurdish identity is irrelevant to the narrative. The tragedy of Baran does not originate from his oppressed existence as a Kurd, but from his inability to keep pace with the times; modernity has turned the traditional man into a fossil, a phenomenon that affects Kurds and Turks alike.

A popular film, seen by more than three million people, *Vizontele* (2001) by Yılmaz Erdoğan and Ömer Faruk Sorak is about the arrival of television in a Kurdish village in 1974. Most characters in the film are naïve Kurdish peasants, which contributes to the antics and buffoonery found offensive by some Kurdish communities, although Erdoğan claimed that he based the story on his childhood memories.

> All characters in the film think in Kurdish and speak in Turkish and the script reflects this reality. The film is not about the Kurdish problem, neither does it show the Kurds, ignorant, oppressed and pitiful, as is often the case in Turkish cinema. To illustrate how a real political stand should be, I chose an apolitical stand. In the film, one sentence is significant: 'If you love this place, then it is the most beautiful place on earth'. I do not consider inserting a Kurdish dialogue as a political stand or bravery. I use a Kurdish elegy when the son of the family dies during the Cyprus Peace Operation. I narrate a problem, which language I use for this purpose is irrelevant.[7]

According to Kazım Öz, the most prominent Kurdish filmmaker living and working in Turkey, a 'literature of the other' exists in Turkey that often 'approaches the issue of the "other" as a commodity – Assyrians and Alevis on one side, Kurds and the Gypsies on the other'.[8] 'If a film has nothing to do with the Alevis, why exploit their culture to decorate the background?', Öz asks.[9]

Öz also points to an ideological revival of feudalism in recent years through television series that depict the East's previous characteristics: landlords living in opulent palaces, honour killings and archaic man–woman relations:

> The palaces have been destroyed long ago with the war and the migration. New relations have replaced the old ones and the power relations have also changed. The woman has evolved; she is in a struggle for self-assertion. Diyarbakır is quite different from the way it is presented in these series. The dimension of violence still exists, but serious changes have also taken place. I believe the attempts to revive the past are linked to the state's refusal to accept this evolution. Turkish intellectuals still maintain an antiquated mentality regarding the Kurds. If they do not understand the issue of underdevelopment, they cannot form a proper relationship.[10]

The issue of underdevelopment, although not confined to the Kurdish population, is doubtless one of the fundamental reasons behind the unrest in the south-east, where the 'economic capital' (material wealth), 'cultural capital' (knowledge, skills, educational or technical qualifications) and 'symbolic capital' (accumulated prestige or honour), to use Pierre Bourdieu's terms,[11] have not been readily available to all citizens, and in the case of minorities like the Kurds, opportunities have been far more limited. As for cinema, 'Turkish cinema has been doing to the Kurds what Hollywood has done to the American Indians. They have drawn a curtain of nationalism', claims Öz. 'Even the filmmakers and the actors who had worked with Yılmaz Güney and gained their identity with him still do not accept that he was a Kurd.'[12]

*Işıklar Sönmesin / Let There Be Light* (1996) by Reis Çelik is perhaps the first Turkish film to show a Kurd with a political identity. Despite a schematic structure and didactic ending, Çelik's work is remarkable, not only for the spectacular photography of the mountains (accomplished under very unfavourable conditions), but also, more significantly, for approaching a previously taboo subject. A humanist story that brings face to face a rebel and a policeman, the film was appreciated neither by the Turks nor by the Kurds. What was too much for one was not enough for the other.

*Let There Be Light* opens with a candle flickering in the wind, and two pairs of hands appear and save the candle from extinguishing. The two protagonists, the guerrilla Seydo belonging to the PKK (Kurdistan Workers' Party) and Captain Murat of the Turkish Armed Forces are symbolically trapped in the mountains in extreme weather conditions. The PKK (referred to as the 'organization' throughout) has just killed a *korumacı* (village guard) travelling on a bus, and Captain Murat and his men have been sent to stop them from crossing the border. They catch up with the guerrillas, but when a soldier fires, the fighting starts. Just then, an avalanche kills almost everyone. The survivors Captain Murat and Seydo have no choice but to tolerate each other. Although Captain Murat is not unsympathetic to the Kurdish cause, as a soldier he has to follow the official line – there is only one Turkey. Representing the inseparableness of the land and the nation, he reprimands Seydo, who claims they are fighting for their identity: 'Trying to separate a state built by two people who have lived together for hundreds of years, cannot be a cause.' When the guerrillas ask him to shoot them, he reminds them that this is not his job. 'You will answer for your crime in front of the law. Do you equate guerrilla law with the law of the state?'

For Öz, the film does not show the Kurds in their proper identity. 'The characters are typecast in the tradition of Yeşilçam. The Kurdish fighters are not like the Kurdish fighters we know. Naturally, the director could not delve into the matter more realistically because of censorship. The fact that the subject is tackled is already a very good step.'[13] Çelik explains that he tried to shoot the film illegally because the area was forbidden to the cameras. Then some of the crew became suspicious that they might be making a film for the PKK. 'In 1996, when the film was made, one could be shot for pronouncing the K of "Kurd" let alone make a film about it. The civil war was raging and spreading to the cities, but art documented none of it.'[14] For Çelik the reason behind the backwardness in Anatolia is not only oppression. The problem is the system and the system has to be criticized. With this film, rather than taking sides he wanted to place a question mark in the middle, but also tried to make a film that he would be able to show in cinemas, which was essential for raising consciousness. He was aware that this would mean compromises. Even so, when the film was completed he was ordered by the censorship board to take out several scenes, which explains the gaps in the narrative.

*Let There Be Light* was chastised 'by the right, the left, the state and everyone else', reminisces Çelik.

The PKK thought the character of the soldier was too civilized because he says, '*Please*, show your identity'. I had to be cautious to avoid censorship, but those who could decipher cues would understand that the soldier also was a Kurd. The PKK did not get the message, but the army did. They opposed the soldier showing respect at the grave of the guerrilla, which was one of the accusations that I had to face at the trial. 'Where are you from?' asks the guerrilla. The soldier: 'Ardahan'. 'You are a Kurd, too?' 'What difference would it make if I were.' The army understood this very well. The film is on the edge of the knife, neither for the guerrilla, nor for the state. I did not approach the problem from the national perspective. If today, there is a country called Kurdistan, would this be the end of hunger, oppression and exploitation? Ten years later, the conditions are more favourable for approaching political subjects. Had I made the film today, I would use the Kurdish language more, and since I would not be obliged to give secret messages to thwart censorship, I would employ characters that would need less deciphering.[15]

Yeşim Ustaoğlu's first feature *İz / Traces* (1994) is a psychological thriller about the inner voyage of a police officer tormented by feelings of guilt.

Yeşim Ustaoğlu's second feature, *Güneşe Yolculuk / Journey to the Sun* (1999), went further in depicting the realities under oppressive regimes, which can turn life into prison for all citizens, as Yılmaz Güney had once said. An architect by training, Ustaoğlu had already shown her determination to 'touch the untouchable' with her first feature, *İz / Traces* (1994), a psychological thriller about the inner voyage of a disillusioned police officer tormented by feelings of guilt and loss of integrity. To depict a policeman in any role other than the protector of peace had long been taboo in Turkey. She defined the film as 'the product of ten years of feeling guilt for living in this society and keeping silent'.[16]

*Journey to the Sun* won several prestigious awards abroad before it was shown in Turkey. Although state censorship was not the issue, distributors were not willing to take a chance with a 'risky' film. Turkish audiences were at last able to see the film a year after its international success. Several local journalists and critics hailed Ustaoğlu as the new Yılmaz Güney and *Journey* as 'the best film of the last ten years'. Columnist Oral Çalışlar pointed out that the film was the mirror of the 'war and migration' that Turkey has been experiencing for the last fifteen

*Günese Yolculuk / Journey to the Sun* (1999) by Yeşim Ustaoğlu, 'a silent protest against tens of films that do not see, do not want to see the fire and the human being in the middle of the jungle.'

years, which have become part of urban life as well. As for the late arrival of the film in Turkey, 'As a society we are not in the habit of coming to terms with our realities', commented Çalışlar, who considered *Journey to the Sun* 'a journey to our history and our reality and a silent scream emanating from the pain of losing thousands of our people and uprooting millions'.[17] Senior critic Sungu Çapan called Ustaoğlu 'the Ken Loach of Turkey' and *Journey* 'a human landscape of lives from 1990s Turkey', a milestone for Turkish cinema just like Güney's *The Hope*.[18] For political author and editor Berat Günçıkan, *Journey* was 'a silent protest against tens of films of the last fifteen years that do not see, do not want to see the fire and the human being in the middle of the jungle',[19] although there were some who thought the film exaggerated the problems of Turkey in order to receive financial support from Europe.

*Journey* narrates the story of two young men, Turkish Mehmet and Kurdish Berzan, Anatolians misplaced in the big metropolis. Mehmet comes from Tire, a town in the Aegean part of Turkey; Berzan's village is in the south-east, near the Iraqi border. They meet in the urban jungle of Istanbul where Mehmet works for the water department and Berzan earns his living selling music cassettes under the Galata Bridge. Mehmet is in love with Arzu, a free-spirited girl who had lived in Germany with her 'guest worker' parents and now works in a launderette. Berzan carries the photo of the sweetheart he left behind in his remote village. Mehmet's hopes for a new life are dashed abruptly when he is arrested in error as a terrorist suspect. A package containing a gun is found next to him on the minibus. His dark complexion raises suspicions that he might be a Kurd, and therefore a terrorist. The fact that he is carrying a cassette of Kurdish music (a gift from Berzan) does not help. Tortured in police custody, he returns to the dingy hole he shares with other workers only to be discarded as a suspect. He loses his job for the same reason. Wherever he goes, a red cross follows him, painted on his door during the night. He is sheltered by Berzan, who lives in the shanty towns, and starts working as a scavenger on the municipal rubbish dump. Tragedy strikes when Berzan is found dead following his arrest for attending a demonstration to support the hunger strikes in the prisons. A new journey begins for Mehmet, who takes Berzan's coffin to his remote village, Zorduç, in ecologically ravaged and ethnically strife-torn southeast Anatolia. Travelling from west to east (a symbolic migration in reverse), Mehmet discovers a new world of abandoned villages with the now familiar red cross painted on the doors; army tanks occupying a town square (documentary footage Ustaoğlu obtained from the police using alternative means); illegal newspapers distributed via children and people who do not speak his language. When Mehmet begins to understand Berzan's world, death loses its importance. At the end Berzan returns to his village even though in a coffin. 'As the coffin slides on the water with the birds above, Mehmet stands on his two feet. There is hope in sadness', Ustaoğlu explains.[20]

Without obtrusive directorial commentary, Ustaoğlu lets the plot unfold through images. Water is a crucial element, laden with spiritual connotations embedded in the regional culture and, more significantly, as a trope for life. Each character is linked to water: Mehmet listens to the water pipes to detect leaks; Arzu works in a launderette and Berzan makes his last journey on the water. The film starts with a long shot of the reflection of Mehmet in the water carrying Berzan's coffin and returns to the image at the end. Mehmet lets Berzan's coffin float on the water, where the reflection of a minaret becomes visible. He begins to count the seagulls that fly over the rooftops and the electric pylons. In front of the fiery setting sun, an army post surrounded by barbed wire enters the frame.

Istanbul has a strange beauty in the film: a cold indifferent beauty that denies the sense of belonging to those who are different. As Mehmet crosses the bridge to the Anatolian side, driving the pick-up truck with Berzan's coffin, the sun is rising and the chanting of the *muezzin* is heard in the distance calling the devout to prayer. He continues his journey towards the east towards the sun: hence the title of the film. The interior scenes – the walls, the clothes people wear – are imbued with a reddish yellow that gives a warm tone, 'which suggests that although the film ends in tragedy, the friendship between the two young man of different ethnic backgrounds gives a sense of hope', explains Ustaoğlu.[21]

Another important element in the film is that the characters are in a constant state of movement, a perpetual search for identity, which perhaps stems from the liminality of their situations. Ustaoğlu explains:

> People of Turkey have been living this dynamism for centuries. We are part of a rich culture but we still ask ourselves 'Who are we?' All social explosions, including the Islamist fundamentalism, the Kurdish identity, the Turkish identity and the problems of the third-generation Turks in Germany are based on this question.

Everyone is asking this question and finding an open door to say I am this or that, and defending it.[22]

When Mehmet's black hair and dark skin interfere with his wish to have a peaceful life, as an act of defiance he sprays his hair yellow with a spray can he finds in a rubbish heap. (Ironically, his family name is Kara, which means black in Turkish.) After stepping to the other side and experiencing the world of Berzan, however, he denies his identity and assumes the personality of someone from Zorduç, just like Berzan, a Kurd.

A first for Turkish cinema is that Kurdish is spoken in the film. However, although Berzan is a Kurd and the village under water is a Kurdish village, the film does not mention Kurdistan. Ustaoğlu explains that this is a matter for the politicians. Her aim was to give a global dimension and human characteristics to the local events. What is in the foreground is the humanist aspect of *Journey* and what is exhibited in the background is the realities of the country.[23] These realities include torture and disappearances. Miraculously, such scenes did not cause problems with the censors. The shooting was stopped once when 90 per cent was already done, but resumed few months later.

The humanist message of *Journey to the Sun* is universal: friendship between two opposing factions is possible; the politicians are at war, not the individuals. The issue of migration to big cities, be it the result of political or economic crises, or the oppression of a minority culture by a more powerful one, is transnational. However, the script, which was inspired by newspaper articles on Kurdish villages that have been marked, burned and evacuated in the south-east, is deeply rooted in the political realities of the country. The film starts after a soccer game when the ultra-nationalist sentiments are at their peak, hooligans waving the Turkish flag and vandalizing cars. Paradoxically, a Turk and a Kurd find each other amidst this kind of mob, a clear warning that fascist nationalism will hurt Kurds and Turks alike.

The film was not only daring for 1990s Turkey, but its subject was also practically taboo. 'Newspapers write about police brutalities everyday,' points out defiant Ustaoğlu, 'and the police know what they are doing. How can one say torture does not exist in Turkey? This is on the agenda and it is a shame. I did not create a scene on something that does not exist.'[24]

Handan İpekçi is another woman filmmaker who took a political stand, beginning with her first feature, *Babam Askerde / Dad is in the*

*Army* (1994), which delved into the period of the coup of 12 September 1980, when terror had free reign: ordinary citizens were taken away from their homes in the dark or arrested on their way home from work and kept in police custody without trial or they simply 'disappeared'; citizens burned their books in fear of incrimination. The story is told from the point of view of three children from different social and economic backgrounds who have one thing in common: a father in prison. Mothers tell their children that the father has gone to the army; the children observe silently and know intuitively. Although the film was not autobiographical, there was a substantial amount of the filmmaker in the film, since İpekçi also had to tell her son that his father was 'in the army'. Following the release of the film, she said that the contradictions that Turkey has plunged into ever since the '12 September' period were deeper. 'On the one hand, any subject is openly discussed in panels on television; on the other hand, many intellectuals are behind bars for speaking or writing what they think.'[25]

İpekçi's second feature, *Büyük Adam, Küçük Aşk*, aka *Hejar / Big Man, Small Love*, aka *Hejar* (2001), is about an unusual friendship between a retired judge of principles and a five-year-old Kurdish orphan. Hejar loses her family during an attack on her village and is brought to the house of a relative in the city, where she survives a bloody raid by the police looking for two Kurdish rebels. The next-door neighbour, a retired judge, takes her in, but the mutual mistrust is very strong. The help of the housekeeper, 'an assimilated Kurd', is needed to overcome the language barrier, although the woman is often too embarrassed to translate the obscenities uttered by little Hejar. Most importantly, the judge (representing Kemalist doctrines as revealed by the *Cumhuriyet* newspaper he reads, and the official state ideology, which he belligerently orates) forbids Kurdish to be spoken in the house. He does not believe that Hejar, a citizen of Turkey, does not speak Turkish. The transformation of the judge comes when he is ready to utter the Kurdish word *Negri!* (Don't cry) to little Hejar, who misses her dead mother. In a climatic moment, the housekeeper reveals that her name is not Sakine but Rojbin.

*Hejar* was funded by the Council of Europe Fund (EURIMAGE) and by the Turkish Ministry of Culture. The latter tried to stop its screening after it was nominated as Turkey's entry for the Oscars,[26] and won prestigious awards in the national film festival in Antalya. The film was denounced for highlighting Kurdish nationalism and portraying Turkish police in a derogatory manner, particularly in the raid scene of

cold-blooded slaughter. The police asked for the revocation of the film's licence on the grounds that it promoted a 'chauvinistic' approach towards Kurdish identity and created the impression that the police carried out extra-judicial killings. They also held that the scene when the little girl pushes away a policeman was harmful to their image. Although *Hejar* was released in October 2001, it was withdrawn from the cinemas on 2 March 2002 by the Supervisory Council of Cinema, Video and Music Productions at the Ministry of Culture for violating the principle of the indivisible integrity of the state. İpekçi was brought to trial for 'insulting the police', but the charge was eventually dropped because 'no element of crime' was found and the ban on the film was lifted in June 2002.[27]

Despite its melodramatic mood, politically correct stand and mainstream attractions (such as the shopping spree of the reconciled duo at Benetton), *Hejar* is important as the first feature film to deal with the restrictions of the Kurdish language in a daring manner. The parallel theme of the deficiencies of the nationalist model of socio-cultural Westernization and the ignorance of the Kemalist elite to the realities of the less advantaged is equally important. The judge is deeply disturbed when he visits the shanty towns and sees Eastern Anatolia, with all its

Handan İpekçi's *Büyük Adam, Küçük Aşk*, aka. *Hejar / Big Man, Small Love*, aka *Hejar* (2001).

poverty, ignorance, feudalism and patriarchy, transplanted to the out-skirts of the modern city.

Just like *Let There be Light*, *Hejar* is a film with good intentions, which drew attention at a number of international film festivals, but was received with scepticism and even accusations from the Kurds and the Turks alike. In addition to the tribulations with the authorities, crit-icism from some of the Kurdish press was not favourable. 'To be liked by the Turks, does one have to be cute like Hejar or assimilated like Sakine?', one journalist asked. The amount of self-censorship exercised by filmmakers is an important factor for the reticence of films to take a concrete political stance. While Ustaoğlu succeeded in rising above such restrictions by creating a universal story, İpekçi and Çelik were trapped by the limitations they set for themselves, although *Let There Be Light* and *Hejar* are to be praised for appearing ahead of their time.

In the first decade of the new millennium, it is premature to speak of a Kurdish cinema. Even the term 'Kurdish cinema' is open to dis-cussion. What constitutes Kurdish cinema? The language, the subject, the approach, the ethnic origin of the director/producer or all of these factors? *Hejar* is adopted by Kurdish film festivals in the West as a Kurdish film because it is about the Kurds and Kurdish is partially spoken (with subtitles in Turkish). *Journey to the Sun*, a film in Turkish and by a Turkish director with two Kurdish actors in the lead, has also been embraced by many Kurdish film festivals. International film festivals generally identify films by Kurdish filmmakers according to the country of production. For instance, Bahman Ghobadi's films are classified as Iranian.

According to Kazım Öz, the concept of national cinema is very complicated. The Kurds are spread over several cultures. Instead of a Kurdish cinema one can speak of a cinema that reflects the lives of Kurds. In that sense any film about Kurds can be considered as Kurdish cinema. Yılmaz Güney is also part of Kurdish cinema. In his films the language is Turkish, but the characters, locations and stories are Kurdish. Due to political repression at that time, Kurdish is not spoken. 'But this is not about appropriation of films as Turkish or Kurdish', Öz points out,

> which is outside the problems of cinema. There are Kurdish film-makers who do not speak Kurdish. We can't blame them. One can discuss the possibility of a national cinema, but what is important is the national oppression. The Turkish national television does

not broadcast Kurdish programmes. Kurdish people have been oppressed in terms of using their language, owning an independent television station or broadcasting in Kurdish. All of these have reflected on the cinema. If there is a Kurdish cinema, even as a concept and even if it is a subject for debate, from the point of view of each identity to express itself, this can be viewed as an improvement.[28]

In the 1990s several films were made about the Kurds, some of which were by Kurdish filmmakers, although these were individual efforts, made by filmmakers, from the diaspora, or completed with aid from abroad. *Mem û Zin /Mem and Zin* (1991) by Ümit Elçi was produced in Turkey in Turkish but later dubbed into Kurdish. A Romeo and Juliet story adapted from the Kurdish bard Ahmede Xani, who lived 300 years ago, the film tells the story of two lovers who meet during *Newroz* (the Kurdish New Year) celebrations, exchange rings but are separated. One may also read the film as an allegory for the tragic fate of the Kurds, separated and dispersed. Elçi is probably not Kurdish, but the film was a 'Turkish film that was actually a Kurdish film, the first full-scale Kurdish film to be focused on the Kurdish way of life', according to Özgüç.[29] *Siabend u Xece / Siyabend and Xece* by Şahin Gök (1992) is also an adaptation of an old Kurdish legend about a tragic love between a precocious orphan named Siabend and his beloved Xece, but Gök inserted pictures of everyday Kurdish life in a attempt to comment on the history and struggle of the Kurdish people. The story was originally published in German because it was banned in Turkey and the film was shot in difficult conditions in the south-east.

Building on the tradition of Yılmaz Güney, Kurdish filmmaker Nizamettin Ariç made his directorial debut with a film in the Kurdish language, produced in exile and banned in Turkey. *Stranek Ji Bo Beko / Beko'nun Türküsü / Ein Lied Für Beko / A Song for Beko* (1992) is about the struggles of the Kurdish people against the Turkish state. In this film the protagonist Beko begins his long pilgrimage in search of his brother in the Kurdish areas of Turkey, where he escapes arrest. Fleeing into Syria, he makes his way to the beautiful highlands of the Kurdish areas of Iraq where he finds a homeland and identity in a nomadic community taking care of refugee children.

With the identity issue gaining more prominence in the world and with the relaxation of the political climate in Turkey several young

Kurdish filmmakers have emerged in the new millennium. Most of these newcomers start with powerful short films or try to find a voice in the documentary genre (thanks to the availability of the digital form) to expose the plight of the Kurdish people. Mesopotamian Cinema Collective, part of the Mesopotamian Cultural Centre in Istanbul, the only institution in Turkey actively engaged in the promotion of Kurdish culture, is usually behind such projects. According to Kazım Öz,

> the positive results of the liberation of the Kurdish language have reflected on the language of cinema. But the Kurds paid a high price to be able to speak their language when they stepped outside their home, which is impossible to explain to Westerners. Imagine you go to the army and the walls are covered with signs to remind you to speak Turkish. It is normal that these experiences would affect the arts, the cinema and the economy. You cannot think of a cinema that is independent of the conditions of life.[30]

Kazım Öz worked with Ustaoğlu in *Journey to the Sun* as the script supervisor assistant. His short film *Ax / Toprak / The Land* (1999) was about absence and loss, the most troublesome wound in the Kurdish psyche. The film begins as an old Kurdish man named Zelo places the shroud over the coffin of his wife. Then he closes the grave, which is on barren land save for one tree. Memories of his two sons, who are dead or gone, his departed wife, a raid by soldiers (only their boots are shown) who kill his dog and set fire to his bed haunt him, but he refuses to leave his village, evacuated by the Turkish army, and chooses to stay behind with his memories. The resettlement of the village appears as a distant memory for the old man as he ties the red scarf of his wife on her tombstone. There is not much dialogue, although the way the old man looks at the bust of Atatürk in front of the school building, emptied of its students, the Turkish flag still hanging nonchalantly on its post, is worth hundreds of words. The film was very successful at film festivals, national and international, although charges were brought against Öz for 'inciting people to hatred and enmity'. He was acquitted because the court concluded that 'the crime did not materialize in the movie',[31] although the film remained banned.

Öz made his first feature *Fotoğraf / The Photograph* (2001) with the support of the Mesopotamian Cinema Collective. The film can rightfully be considered as the first Kurdish production from Turkey. Work on the script began in 1995, but when the shooting started in 2000 there

was almost no money for production. The shooting was completed with contributions the film crew solicited from students, tradesmen, workers, engineers and businessmen and concerts they organized to raise further funds. They also worked on the film without monetary compensation. Just like the production, the distribution also had to be by alternative means, particularly due to the sensitive subject matter. An alternative distribution network was set up and the film was shown in Istanbul, Ankara, İzmir, Mersin, Diyarbakır, Van, Adıyaman, Elazığ and other cities, reaching a total of 25,000 people. It also participated in many film festivals and received awards nationally and internationally.

The narrative of *The Photograph* is rather schematic. On a bus journey from Istanbul to eastern Turkey, Ali and Faruk, two young men about the same age, sit next to each other. During the long journey they become friends, sharing cigarettes and the boredom of travel without revealing the true purpose of their journeys. As they approach their destination checkpoints become more frequent, heightening the atmosphere of oppression. In Diyarbakır they separate; one will go to the army to do his military service and the other will continue to Van to join the clandestine guerrilla operations; perhaps one day one will kill the other.[32]

Kurdish filmmaker Kazım Öz's *Fotoğraf / The Photograph* (2001) had to be made 'imaginatively' to avoid revealing its true subject.

The film had to be made 'imaginatively' to avoid revealing its true subject. Rather than dialogue, the narrative relies on gaze and silence. Öz gets his message across in small details, as when the minibus driver abruptly changes a cassette of Kurdish music to Turkish as they approach a checkpoint, or when the two passengers watch TV news footage of a bloody conflict between the Turkish army and the Kurdish guerrillas and make no comment, or the graffiti in the toilet, which reads: 'The soldier will come back in a coffin.'

Leading critic Atilla Dorsay praised the film, but he found some of the scenes that display the nationalism and militarism of the period imbalanced, especially the 'going to the army' festivities, the exaggerated images of Atatürk and victory statues, the constant presence of uniforms, a military exercise that 'reminds one of Stanley Kubrick's *Full Metal Jacket*', children who are called 'War' and a street named 'Turkish Power'. He admits that these are all part of the Turkish reality, but to ignore the events that create such nationalistic paranoia serves neither objectivity nor peace, he claims.[33]

Regarding the production of a Kurdish film in Turkey, Öz explains that there are no concrete restrictions, but the conditions are not favourable. For instance, you cannot shoot a film in Dersim.[34] There are obstacles. Distribution is another problem. The cinemas do not want to take a risk. One cannot pinpoint a concrete obstacle, but there are obstacles. He had therefore to exercise self-censorship and several issues that he planned in the script were not included in the film.[35]

Nazmi Kırık and Mizgin Kapazan, Berzan and Arzu of *Journey to the Sun*, also appear in *The Photograph*, which is largely in the Kurdish language. Turkish dialogue is dubbed into Kurdish, an achievement for Kurdish cinema within Turkey.

With *Dur / Uzak / Far Away* (2005), a documentary on migration and its aftermath, Öz returned to the theme of absence and loss that he had studied with *The Land*. The project began in 1997, when he visited his home village in eastern Turkey after a long absence and noticed an unbearable silence – no voice of children playing and no sign of life except a handful of silent old people. He decided to explore the stories of such villages that were emptied of two generations, mainly through migration. The film traces his journey from Istanbul to his village and then to Cologne in Germany, where many of the younger villagers immigrated. While the older generation left in the village suffers from loneliness and absence, the younger generation in Germany endures alienation. The old live with the memories of those who may never return, feeling the pain of severed communication ties, particularly with grandchildren born abroad who will probably never speak the language of their grandparents. The young daily experience the pain of homelessness, belonging neither here nor there: they are foreigners in Germany and *Alamancı* in their native village. Öz distributes pictures among those who are separated to renew the ties that have been broken and takes his village video to homes in Germany. An old woman cries as she watches images of her village on the TV screen: 'My neighbour comes to shoot my loneliness.'

The film does not dwell on the political reasons for migration but on the effects of migration. The underdevelopment and poverty of the east come out as the primary reasons for leaving home. Through stylistic narrative devices such as the staged return gaze and the non-matching voice-over, Öz tries to reveal the pain of loss and absence and at the same time attempts to bridge the spatio-temporal, generational and cultural gap experienced by the Kurdish people who do not have a homeland. Far from the omnipresent director who tells a subjective story, he withdraws to the edge of the frame and lets the characters reveal their stories while being part of the diegesis as characters address him by his first name.

Öz explains that, starting in the 1940s and '50s, Turkey experienced dense migration from the country to the city and then to Western countries, particularly Germany. But the rupture was felt more intensely in the Kurdish communities, where the villages were emptied rapidly. The numbers are much higher than official records show.

> The migration from the village in the film was not forced but there was no other choice. Unemployment, low standards of life . . . a large area experienced these problems. The villagers, who had never gone to the nearby town, found themselves in the middle of Europe in a situation they had not anticipated. Those who were left behind experienced the emptiness but those who left were not able to understand what was happening. One man in Germany thinks that he died and now he is in heaven. This is an extreme situation but if the exile did not happen, such depressive situations would not arise. Immigration resulted in drastic changes in societal relations, lifestyles and especially man–woman relations.[36]

The fact that several young Kurds have begun to choose the medium of cinema within the last few years is a positive step in terms of negotiating Kurdish identity. As in the old Iron Curtain countries, innovative filmmakers find creative ways to convey their message. There is no better model than Yılmaz Güney, who perfected the art of codified filmmaking, who knew how to deliver his political message to the audience by a simple gaze, or even by leaving words out of a dialogue.

Like the Kurds and other ethnic minorities, non-Muslims have also been invisible in Turkish cinema. Several ethnic minority personalities made their mark in the industry, but often their identity had to be masked. In the beginning, when Muslim women could not be actors, non-Muslim minorities assumed the female roles and the contributions of Armenians Eliza Binemeciyan and Bayzar Fasulyeciyan are significant in this respect. Özgüç states that 'without the contribution of the non-Muslim women who assumed the female roles, there would not have been a Turkish cinema today'.[37] Nubar Terziyan (Alyanak) remains an important character actor in Turkish cinema with his lovable 'uncle' image in over 400 films. Although he never hid his Armenian identity, very few people knew that Kenan Pars, who played the bad man in more than 500 films was actually born Kirkor Cezveciyan. Sami Hazinses, who devoted 45 years to Turkish cinema, had to hide his Armenian identity (Samuel Uluç) all his life for fear of reprisals; his secret was discovered only at his funeral when the procession had to be transferred from the mosque to the church.[38] Several Armenians have also served Turkish cinema as directors (Arşavir Alyanak, Aram Gülyüz), the most contemporary being Artun Yeres, whose daughter Natali Yeres is an art director. Hayk Kirakosyan is one of the most distinguished cinematographers of Turkish cinema and the Greek Kriton Ilyadis was one of the best cinematographers of the black and white period. Lazar Yazıcıoğlu was another noteworthy Greek cinematographer. Nişan Hançer was a Greek director.[39]

The depiction of non-Muslim minorities on the screen, however, has been one-dimensional. In the tradition of Yeşilçam, mature Armenian women were given the role of educating Turkish girls in the ways of the West. They represented the European culture through modern dress, classical music and table etiquette. They were rarely given a name, but usually called 'Madame', as in *My Dark-eyed One*. Greek characters were either old men (often fishermen) whom the family would adopt as 'uncle', or spinsters. Jewish characters would be connected with small commerce. This very stereotypical stand was not completely fabricated. In real life many Armenian women of limited means were hired as governesses; many families did have an old Greek/Armenian neighbour whom their children called 'uncle' (such as Agor Amca in *Bir Kırık Bir Bebek*, Nisan Akman, 1987); and many Jewish men (with Turkified names) were shopkeepers. The only non-Muslims that the Muslim population in general had some contact with were these 'assimilated' ones. Many non-Muslims were affluent and led lives that were beyond the dreams of the majority of the population. They lived in the European part of Istanbul with their churches and schools and owned summerhouses on the fashionable Prince Islands. They socialized with their own kind in their own language (in whispers, and behind closed doors, after the 'Citizen Speak Turkish' signs began to be mounted in public spaces during the Cyprus crises). Some had professional jobs like doctors or dentists, or owned factories. They were not in the service of the Muslim Turks; in fact, they hired Muslim Turks to work in their enterprises. Cinema showed no interest (perhaps intentionally) in showing these real lives. The non-Muslims existed only when they were like 'us'.

In the 1990s 'liberal' attempts were made to tell stories involving the now practically extinct *Rum* (Greeks from Turkey) population, but almost all these films were artificial and contrived, just like the accents of the Turkish actors who tried to imitate the accent of the Greek minority. A television series, *Yabancı Damat / Love Without Borders* (2004–5), by Durul and Yağmur Taylan, about the marriage of a Turkish girl from a traditional family in Gaziantep to a Greek, broke the taboo by showing a Muslim woman marrying a non-Muslim man. (The reverse could more easily be tolerated since the woman could be converted to Islam.) Produced by Türker İnanoğlu who used to import the popular Aliki Vuyuklaki films from Greece in the 1950s and '60s, *Love Without Borders* was very popular in Turkey and in Greece. The public opinion was that such films were ambassadors of peace. As soap operas they were too far removed from reality to disturb anyone. Turco-Greek relationships have not been approached in a serious and objective manner.

*Salkım Hanımın Taneleri / Mrs Salkım's Diamonds* (1999) by Tomris Giritlioğlu, a woman filmmaker who works for the state television, foregrounded the infamous property tax of 1942 levied on non-Muslims, which destroyed many families. Although Etyen Mahçupyan's and Tamer Baran's script tried to draw a picture of Turkey during the Second World War when government policies were detrimental to those with a different cultural and religious identity, the film's focus was three love stories that revolved around a necklace.[40] The handling of the property tax issue was as tame as one would expect from any work sanctified and supported officially, although it was produced privately. Even then, the film was still controversial, although it got 357,487 admissions on its release.

Yeşim Ustaoğlu's *Bulutları Beklerken / Waiting for the Clouds* (2004), about a Greek woman who lived under the identity of a Muslim Turk for fifty years, is the only noteworthy work so far that tells the unwritten history of the 'other'. Ustaoğlu's script, which had won the 2003 Sundance/NHK Filmmaker Award, is borrowed in part from the novella *Tamama* by Yorgios Andreadis, which is based on the true story of a woman like Ayşe/Eleni, the protagonist of the film, and on extensive research in the Ottoman archives in Sofia, interviews with people with similar experiences and accounts of Turkish and Pontus Greek historians.

Ustaoğlu was the first to approach another sensitive issue, a long-forgotten tragedy of Turkish history, the forced deportation of the Pontus Greeks after the First World War, and again after the founding of the Turkish Republic. The Pontus Greeks had lived in the Black Sea region for thousands of years and had thriving communities with schools, theatre groups and newspapers, but were forced into exile during the harsh winter of 1916 when the Ottoman army evacuated the villages west of Russian-occupied Trabzon and deported the Greek residents. It is estimated that 350,000 to 500,000 Pontus Greeks died from cold, hunger and sickness.

The one-nation policy of the Turkish Republic established in 1923 made life difficult for all minorities. Many converted to Islam for survival and kept their identity secret all their lives. In 1924 the rulers of Greece and Turkey agreed to repatriate the ethnic Greeks and Turks and another massive deportation took place (as in Kayaköy mentioned in chapter Two). In 1994 the Greek parliament adopted 19 May as the day to commemorate the Turkish genocide against the Pontus Greeks, claiming that between 1916 and 1924 the Greek Orthodox population of Turkey's eastern Black Sea region became victim of a systematic policy of extermination by the Turkish authorities. The Turkish government has been very sensitive about the unofficial part of the Turkish history that is not included in schoolbooks. As shown in the film, Turkey's first census to include all minorities was not until 1975.

The protagonist Ayşe was born as Eleni in the Turkish fishing village of Trebolu on the Black Sea coast about 90 km west of Trabzon.

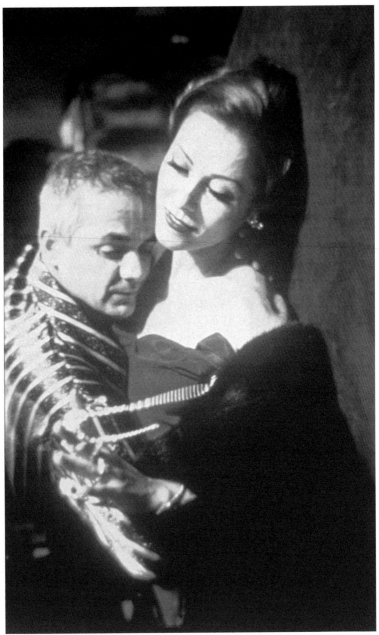

*Salkım Hanımın Taneleri / Mrs Salkım's Diamond*s (1999), dir. Tomris Giritlioğlu, foregrounds the infamous property tax of 1942 levied on non-Muslims.

The first part of the film takes place in this location, where the *Laz* ethnic minority (with Georgian roots from the Caucasus) live a harsh life under incessant rains and fog. The second part of the film takes place in the Kalamaria region of Thessaloniki, where most of the exiled Pontus Greeks settled when they arrived in Greece. Eleni was about ten when she was forced to flee with her parents and younger brother Niko. Their father was branded a 'rebel' and shot, and their mother died of starvation and exposure like hundreds of others. Eleni and Niko were saved by a Turkish family. Striving for security, Eleni chose to remain with them while Niko joined other orphans who were sent to Greece. Eleni became part of the Turkish family, assuming the name Ayşe and forming a strong bond with her adoptive sister, Selma. She hid her identity for fifty years, but the feeling of guilt for abandoning her brother and choosing to live like a Turk never left her.

Following the documentary footage of the deportation (which Ustaoğlu acquired from the Greek archives), the narrative unfolds with two men arriving for the census. Ayşe is evasive when giving information about her identity. Ironically, her sick sister Selma goes into a coma before she can tell the man her 'vital statistics'. After Selma's death the memories of her hidden past begin to haunt the ageing Ayşe. She begins to utter garbled words. As she slowly reclaims her mother tongue she assumes her real identity, which forces her to isolation; she fears repercussions

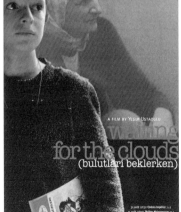

'What is a homeland? Who is a foreigner?'

Yeşim Ustaoğlu's *Bulutları Beklerken / Waiting for the Clouds* (2004).

denied identities | 113

from the closed society of the village where outsiders are still treated with suspicion. The period was marked by social and political upheavals and strong nationalism when paranoia in regard to the 'other' was rampant, although the Soviet Union and its ideology, which found its strength in the universities and unions, was the immediate target. While anarchists stick posters on the walls at night, during the day the children are indoctrinated in the school with the usual motto of Atatürk: 'How happy is the one who can say I am a Turk'! As they repeat 'The Turk cannot be quelled!' eight-year-old Mehmet wets his pants.

In fact, Mehmet is the alter ego of Ustaoğlu, who was about the same age when she lived in the area with her family. He observes Ayşe and notices the change in her. When a white-haired stranger arrives, Mehmet thinks that his accent resembles the nonsensical words Ayşe has been uttering. He introduces the two and helps Ayşe to deliver herself from her assumed identity. The stranger is Thanasis, who was transported to Greece with other orphans. During the war he joined the partisans (largely Pontus Greeks) and was then forced into exile in the Soviet Union. 'Russia became my home in exile,' he says, 'The Greeks said, "you can return home". Which home? The home from which I was expelled 50 years ago? I have no home!' Thanasis is a catharsis who brings Ayşe/Eleni to confront her past. For the first time in fifty years she gives an external voice to her feelings of guilt: 'we walked all the way to Mersin burying our dead one by one on the way. They gathered all the orphans . . . I never wanted to get on a boat again, or to walk . . . Niko stayed with the orphans . . . Süleyman Baba bought the house I was born in, he said my conscience will be eased, but it did not happen.'

Thanasis locates Niko. When Eleni arrives in Greece, she meets an old woman, a deportee, who is the other half of Eleni according to Ustaoğlu, who lives among Greeks but still maintains her Pontus Greek accent, misses her home and dreams of dying under her favourite tree one day. The scene when Ayşe meets her brother Niko is charged with emotion. Memory is selective and Niko had made a decision to erase his sister from his past. He shows her the pictures of his family, his wife and his children, and tells her she is not there. He has no sister. Eleni takes out the faded photo she has kept all these years.

'What is homeland? Who is a foreigner? The film tries to find answers to the thorny questions of identity and nationalism', Ustaoğlu explains. 'Identity and sense of belonging are felt deeply as death approaches. You may add to this the guilt feeling as we carry the burden of what has been taught to us for so many years.'[41]

The issue of identity is central to *Waiting For the Clouds* just as much as to *Journey to the Sun*. In *Journey*, Mehmet, after being subjected to prejudice and discrimination, tries to change the colour of his hair, but through his experiences realizes the futility of such action. To the soldier he meets on the train (who incidentally is from Tire, Mehmet's native town), he says he is from Zorduç (Berzan's Kurdish village) and he adds that he *had* a friend from Tire, who was called Mehmet Kara, in an action of 'releasing oneself from being a Turk (a post-colonial and counter-national film). It poses the question that a national community (and cinema) can never pose: the question of change and the conditions of possibility for change.'[42] By confronting the 'other' Mehmet steps outside himself and assumes a new relation to identity. In *Waiting*, to survive among Turks Eleni hides her Greek identity. The Greek and Turkish identities of one woman lacerate her life, while a young Turk can find his equilibrium only by acknowledging the identity of the 'other'.

# 4  Yılmaz Güney

I wish I could write conflict on a leaf
for the fall to come and the leaf to fall
I wish I could write anger on a cloud
for the rain to pour and the cloud to disappear
I wish I could write hate on the snow
for the sun to shine and the snow to melt
And friendship and love, I wish I could write
in the hearts of all new-born babies
to grow with them and engulf the universe.[1]

'I am a man of struggle and my cinema is the cinema of the liberation struggle of my people.'[2] This is how Yılmaz Güney, the most renowned filmmaker of Turkey, defined himself. From westerns and gangster movies to socially and politically engaged films the cinema of Güney systematically stood on the side of the common man trying to survive in an unjust world. The character Güney created (often inspired by his own life and played by himself on the screen) was the oppressed provincial whose main concern was to earn his bread. He did not want to get involved in events but was forced by circumstances. At one point he exploded and resorted to violence, but always lost, mainly because he tried to find individual solutions to his problems.

In his short life (1937–1984), a large part of which was spent behind bars, Güney's name appeared on more than one hundred films, as an actor, scriptwriter, producer and director. Many of these films disappeared into the vaults of censorship boards or were left to disintegrate except for about twelve that he successfully sent abroad before his escape from prison, having served seven years and one month of a long sentence for murder. Güney reappeared in France to receive the Palme d'Or at the Cannes Film Festival of 1982 for *Yol / The Way,* which shared this prestigious prize with *Missing* by Costa Gavras. The following year his citizenship was revoked, his films were recalled and his name was erased from the history of Turkish cinema. In 1984 he died in Paris from stomach cancer, a condition exacerbated by the long prison years. Audiences in Turkey were first able to see *Yol* on 12 February 1999, seventeen years after its Cannes success.

Yılmaz Güney (family name Pütün) was born in a village near Adana to a Kurdish mother from Muş and a Zaza Kurd father from Siverek. His mother's family migrated from the east when the Russians occupied the Eastern Territories during the First World War and his father's family because of a blood feud. Güney grew up under the state Turkification policies and spoke only Turkish during his childhood. He became aware of his origins when he visited his father's village for the first time as a sixteen-year-old, which made him understand the suffering of an uprooted family, although this experience did not turn him into a nationalist; he had already discovered socialism. He stood for the unity of all people and not one particular nation. However, he admitted that being a Kurd shaped his character. The Kurds were landless and poor. They were scattered around the country due to forced resettlements and exiles of post-First World War policies, as well as forced economic migration. Like migrant workers in Europe, the Kurds had the toughest jobs, Güney explained during an interview, and were considered as belonging to the lowest scale of society. 'In Turkish there are many mean words and expressions that are related to the Kurds. To say Kurd is almost an insult.' Many Kurds held prominent positions in society and reached the highest ranks of the state apparatus, but this was because they never said, 'I am a Kurd'. 'The Kurdish deputies in the parliament are elected as Turks living in a country that denies the existence of the Kurdish population.'[3]

Güney was introduced to cinema in Adana when he was thirteen. He began to frequent the theatres in the poor neighbourhoods, where action films were shown. During his high-school years he carried film reels from one open-air cinema to the other on his bicycle (and let the younger kids in through the back door, one of whom, Ali Özgentürk, would become another notable filmmaker). Slowly he established contacts with local representatives of major film companies and started to work for them. He also published short stories in literary journals. After high school he started at the Law School of Ankara University but switched to the Faculty of Economics in Istanbul to be closer to the world of cinema.

He entered Yeşilçam as a worker and did odd jobs on the set, occasionally as an extra, but soon drew attention as a scriptwriter and actor. He had his first real chance in 1958, when he was 21, in a film by Atıf Yılmaz, *Bu Vatanın Çocukları / The Children of This Nation* (a film inspired by the cinema of John Ford), as actor, scriptwriter and assistant director. Following several films in which he collaborated in a similar fashion, he was jailed in 1961 for communist propaganda, which aborted his university education. The sentence was over by 1962, but he was exiled to Konya for six months. On his return to cinema in 1963, he started working with small production companies as the main actor and often as the scriptwriter. In 1966 he made his first film, *At, Avrat, Silah / Horse, Woman, Gun*, a male bravura yarn, as the title indicates.

The cinema of Güney before *Umut / The Hope* (1970) was scorned as 'commercial trash' by bourgeois intellectuals, although, even within that mould, his films carried humanist elements that appealed to the masses and particularly Anatolian male migrants, whose identity was in conflict with the sophisticated urban middle-class identity exalted in Yeşilçam melodramas. With his dark skin, large nose and thin silhouette Güney broke the prevailing good-looking hero image, personified by blond, blue-eyed Göksel Arsoy, and created his own myth. The audience crowned him the *çirkin kıral* (the ugly king) of Yeşilçam, although he was the king of the periphery and not the centre. Nonetheless, he became a myth.

The reward of becoming a myth was that it would help Güney to move in a more serious direction without losing his audience. In Akad's *Hudutların Kanunu / The Law of the Borders* (1966), which Güney co-wrote with Akad, his natural and spontaneous acting displayed a clear departure from the exaggerated performances that had defined Yeşilçam. Güney could show the nuances of the human character through the role of a toughened lone smuggler, who could harbour deep paternal love, respect for women and reverence for education. (He would develop this character further in *Ağıt / Elegy*, 1971.)

In the earlier period of his career Güney had been conditioned by the audience and its expectations. Gradually, he began to condition the audience with realistic films depicting real characters experiencing real problems. The gangster scuffles gave way to social issues of oppression, poverty and inequality, and, most importantly, the narrative acquired political consciousness. Landless peasants who became smugglers at the borders, or flocked to the cities as migrant workers to feed their families; the 'lumpenized' people pushed to the margins by a society rapidly changing from feudalism to capitalism entered Turkish cinema.

The epic of *Seyyit Han* aka *Toprağın Gelini / Seyyit Han* aka *The Bride of the Earth* (1968) drew attention to the self-destructive mentality of the feudal system and the fate of the rural woman, often the victim of so-called family honour; *Aç Kurtlar / Hungry Wolves* (1969), which Güney shot during his military service in the east, was defined as an 'epic of banditry', while *Bir Çirkin Adam / An Ugly Man* (1969) was an experiment in *film noir*.[4]

The social realist movement of the 1960s had produced remarkable films such as *Gecelerin Ötesi / Beyond the Nights* (1960), *Yılanların Öcü / The Revenge of the Serpents* (1961) and *Susuz Yaz / A Dry Summer* (1963) by Metin Erksan; *Şehirdeki Yabancı / A Stranger in Town* (1962), *Gurbet Kuşları / The Birds of Nostalgia* (1964) and *Haremde Dört Kadın / Four Women in the Harem* (1965) by Halit Refiğ; *Otobüs Yolcuları / The Bus Passengers* (1961) and *Karanlıkta Uyananlar / Those Awakening in the Dark* (1964) by Ertem Göreç; and *Bitmeyen Yol / The Never Ending Road* by Duygu Sağıroğlu (some of which are discussed in chapters One and Two). Although these films were not sufficient to transform the established infrastructure of commercial cinema, the movement prepared the ground for the committed films of Güney by introducing the concept that cinema was not only a vehicle for entertainment but also an art that could transmit individual or societal messages.

*The Hope* is considered a landmark in the history of Turkish cinema. An authentic portrayal of Turkey (the epic of *verité*, as Güney would define the film) in a period of transition to market economy, it is regarded as the first 'truly realist' film of the country and the best Turkish film up to the year it was made. With *The Hope* Güney defied the established nomenclature of the dominant Yeşilçam by abrogating the gilded studio sets, the star system and the formulaic narratives and cliché constructions that had one aim: box-office success. To tell the story of an anti-hero leading an unheroic life he chose natural decor and non-professional actors. Using the phaeton driver Cabbar (played by himself) as a metaphor, he was able to promulgate the tragedy surrounding daily lives and the apathy and ignorance of others caught in the same vicious circle. While systematically referring to destiny in his films, Güney did not think that the reason behind poverty and desperation was destiny.

Cabbar is a quiet family man, burdened with the responsibility of earning a living for his wife, his ageing mother and his five children with two worn-out horses that pull a rundown phaeton. The opening shots showing the phaeton drivers and food vendors at Adana train station are significant in establishing the fundamental issues of the film. As the phaeton drivers wait for the arrival of the passengers, the camera pans along the billboards and we see impoverished Cabbar relieving himself under the billboard for a bank; Coca-Cola logos decorate the kiosk where he buys his newspaper and the advertisement for *Güney Sanayi* (the Industry of the South) comes into view: the new economy that promises prosperity while Cabbar is left without a customer.

The focus shifts to Cabbar's home and his financial problems. He refuses his wife's suggestion that he should return to the cotton fields. However, he has no other solutions to the economic impasse except buying lottery tickets. Solidarity with his class in organizing resistance against exploitation and inequality does not occur to him; he only wants to save himself.[5]

The second part commences with the consultation of the *hodja*, reputed to have supernatural powers. Cabbar has once more chosen a fruitless alternative, and his effort is again individual and for individual gain. The treasure hunt does not give the expected results. All hope gone, Cabbar turns around with his eyes folded in an exceptional moment of 'the abstraction of hopelessness'.[6]

The theme of the futility of seeking solutions to poverty and oppression in sources outside one's control is foreshadowed in the open-

*Umut / The Hope* (1970) by Yılmaz Güney, 'a milestone for Turkish cinema'.

ing scene when Cabbar is the only driver left without a customer. The theme of alienation and degeneration fed by poverty in the urban environment is underlined when the small merchants and artisans in the marketplace (who will all be affected by the arrival of the taxi system) refuse to deal with Cabbar because he owes money to all of them. At home his children fight over a slice of watermelon they find in the rubbish. The mother beats the children and the husband beats his wife. A private car hits and kills Cabbar's horse, but the owner blames Cabbar for leaving the animal unattended. At the police station the accused magnanimously 'forgives' the victim, and Cabbar is thrown out. His desperation culminates when he is obliged to sell his gun, symbol of manhood and tool for the oppressed man to claim justice, as in his 'ugly king' films.

The first part of the film has certain similarities to Vittorio De Sica's *Ladri di biciclette / Bicycle Thieves* (1948), whereas the second has been compared to John Huston's *The Treasure of the Sierra Madre* (1948). The loss of the object that is the livelihood of the protagonist is at the centre of the narrative in both *Bicycle Thieves* and *The Hope* (the bicycle for Antonio and the horse for Cabbar); both protagonists seek supernatural deliverance by consulting someone reputed to have psychic powers; both are disillusioned by condescending policemen, who are not at the service of the poor; both try 'to do to others what is done to them' (Cabbar tries to rob a man and Antonio tries to steal a bicycle) and both fail miserably.[7] Furthermore, both are driven by motives of self-interest for personal and familial benefit and oblivious to the needs of others. Unlike De Sica, whose approach to his character is rather sentimental, Güney is critical of Cabbar, evidenced in the scenes that show him humiliated (his old bosses refuse a loan; a pick-pocket tries to steal the money he receives from selling his gun; and he receives a beating from the black American soldier that he tries to rob). For Güney the film represented the corrupt order; the man whose feet are firmly on the ground does not build his hope on false dreams.

Despite similarities to other films, *The Hope* does not share the trend of its period when imitation was the norm rather than the exception among filmmakers of both artistic and commercial concerns, according to historian Nijat Özön. '*The Hope* is authentically local from its subject, characters and environment to the inter-personal relationships that it displays . . . The closest it would come to is perhaps, the works of the author Orhan Kemal, who also narrates the stories of downtrodden characters of Adana, from where he originates.'[8] Cabbar's house in the film is the house where Güney spent his childhood. He remembers his father digging in the yard for treasure. The *mise-en-scène* is constructed from actual memories of growing up among the impoverished cotton workers of Adana. Through the images of the familiar landscape Güney exposes the contradictions of the society with precision. A fantastic level is moulded into these realistic elements, which one could define as magic realism.[9] As Stephen Slemon argues, magic realist texts are often preoccupied with images of borders and centres, and they work towards destabilizing their fixity.[10] In *The Hope* Güney attempts to achieve this by working within the borders of the cinematic screen, where he perceptively examines the effect of the subtle fantasy at play within the perceptions of reality, formed both by Hollywood, which shaped his cinematic tastes as a young boy in Adana, and by the Yeşilçam film industry of which he was a part.

Despite its revolutionary message *The Hope* does not conform to the revolutionary cinema of the West, or the Third Cinema movement in South America, although comparisons have been made, particularly to the work of Brazilian Glauber Rocha and the 'cinema of agitation'. Güney, who was often identified as a 'Third World filmmaker' or a filmmaker practising 'Third Cinema', was disconcerted by the compartmentalizing of films and filmmakers. 'I am a man of cinema. This identifies me', he said. 'A filmmaker should be approached within the context of the concrete circumstances of that country's class struggles . . . We are the filmmakers of a country in search of its language. And just like our country, our cinema is trying to find its way', he asserted.

> But what is the first world, or the second world, and why this is so, have to be discussed. I believe there are two cinemas: cinema that serves the oppressor and the cinema that serves the oppressed. There is no third cinema. In the US, Britain and other capitalist and imperialist countries, there is also young, new and revolutionary cinema. This cinema and the revolutionary cinema in the colonialized or semi-colonialized countries complement each other. At the same time, in the colonialized or semi-colonialized countries, there is reactionary cinema that is on the side of the oppressor . . . The distinction has to be made from the point of class and not geography.[11]

While hailed as 'a milestone for Turkish cinema' and 'the harbinger of Italian neo-realism' (albeit twenty-five years after Italy) by the *New Cinema* group that advocated authorship, *The Hope* was not a welcome departure for some circles. The fact that Güney lets himself be beaten by a black American shocked some of his audience and irritated his producers, who preferred 'the ugly king' of roughneck melodramas and revolver romanticism. Novelist Kemal Tahir had praised *The Bride of the Earth* as a film that possessed all the elements of the people's cinema and Güney as an artist of the people who could effectively demonstrate the difference between the reality of cinema and the reality of life (particularly in the scene when he receives so many bullets but does not flinch) but dismissed *The Hope*, saying: 'How could one create drama with a phaeton driver!'[12]

*The Hope* was chosen as the Best Film at the Altın Koza (Golden Cocoon) Film Festival in Adana, but was subsequently banned for propagating class differences in a country where officially there are no classes (drawing attention to poverty by showing the torn clothes of the phaeton driver; giving the impression that the rich car owner would not be punished for hitting the horse of the poor; exposing discrimination when Cabbar hunts for a job); for alluding to American imperialism (presenting a soldier from the military base in Adana); for degrading religion (the morning prayer scene is shown while the sun is rising); and for provoking workers to resist authority. As a reaction, a local journal would protest, under the heading 'The Enemy of the Beautiful, Good and Honest', that the censorship board was trusted with the responsibility of preventing every opinion and every attempt that the dominant class would find against their interest. They would give free reign to pornographic films, films that debased Turkey and its citizens and films that would serve as opium for the audience, but consider it their duty to prevent attempts at exposing the problems of Turkey and its citizens that aim to seek a solution.[13] *The Hope* was later smuggled out of the country to be screened at the Cannes Film Festival. (Ten years later *Yol / The Way*, scripted by Güney while in prison and directed by Şerif Gören would have a similar fate.) The veil of censorship was lifted from *The Hope* only in 1990.

In the 1970s, when political murders, economic crisis and censorship tore society apart, few films comparable in quality to *The Hope* were made, except perhaps the Anatolian trilogy of Lütfü Ö. Akad (discussed in chapter Two) and Güney's trilogy *Ağıt / Elegy, Acı / Pain* and

*Acı / Pain* (1971) by Güney with Güney himself in the lead

*Umutsuzlar / The Hopeless Ones* and also *Baba / The Father*, all made in 1971. (During this period Güney also made a few films in his previous 'ugly king' style.) *Elegy* is a poetic epic about a gang of smugglers who fight against the system; *Pain* a spaghetti western *à la turca* about the custom of revenge in the harsh realities of Anatolia and *The Hopeless Ones* a melodrama about sacrifice to love in the underground world.

*Elegy*, the most accomplished film of the trilogy, foregrounds the problem of smuggling in the south-east, where few choices are available to landless peasants. The character Güney had built in *The Bride of the Earth*, the humane bandit who searches for the truth despite perpetual persecution and long prison sentences, is extended to *Elegy* through the smuggler, a man used by so-called upright citizens to do their dirty jobs yet disdained by society for trying to earn his bread. The legendary Çobanoğlu (Güney), an outlaw the villagers compete with each other to inform on to the gendarme for the reward money, is a man with feelings just like Hıdır, the smuggler in *The Law of the Borders*. The drama of Çobanoğlu unfolds through the striking images of the rocks falling incessantly over the ruins, petty villagers selling their soul for a piece of bread, barefoot kids playing with scraps they find in the rubbish and women in rags queueing in front of the doctor's house to have their screaming children inoculated. The smuggler observes but says very little as if he has lost hope in communicating with other human beings. In one instance only he uses language to concretize his misery: 'our villages were destroyed by the rocks and the blood feuds. If they considered us as human beings, would we hide in the mountains'?

Güney had already tried his hand with epic realism with *The Bride of the Earth*; with this film he shows remarkable mastery in the way he weaves the two genres using close-ups for the concrete details of village life and extreme long shots for Çobanoğlu, the legend many have heard of but few have seen. The verticality of the natural decor of Göreme, with the pitiless landslides that claim villages, contrasts sharply with the horizontality of the arid landscape where the silhouette of the lone hero with his white pants and white umbrella often becomes a dot on the horizon, more legend than real. The relative long shots that in Italian neo-realist films highlight the characters' interrelationship with their physical environment, accentuating their vulnerability and aloneness, are used effectively to build a universal dimension to the drama of the poor peasants. The camerawork of Gani Turanlı gives the narrative a supernatural aura, particularly during the cave scenes that he shot without artificial light but like a *camera obscura* used a hole in the rock as a lens and focused the light rays with a mirror on the opposite wall. The resulting play of light and shadow invokes the traditional art of *Karagöz*, the shadow play that Güney also employed in *The Hope* during the treasure hunt scenes.

Like *The Bride of the Earth*, where Güney's performance is reminiscent of Clint Eastwood, *Elegy* also toys with the Western genre that heroicizes the outlaw. Çobanoğlu is a rugged and dogged individual who has made the mountains his home, although a new village is established after the destruction of his village by falling rocks. There is a woman, the village doctor, who inspires the community (she is seen teaching other women to boil water, to inoculate their children, etc.). She operates on the outlaw to remove a bullet from the gendarme's rifle; she brings him back to life, but she cannot bring him back to the community. Like the lone cowboy of the Wild West he is a restless individual, although one with deep feelings. He takes a chance on his life to go down to the village to thank the doctor for saving his life and he visits the grave of his beloved when he knows the end is near. However, death is the unchangeable destiny of the smuggler; censorship would not have it otherwise.

The 'bandit' films such *The Hungry Wolves* and *Elegy* are significant as Roy Armes points out, in the sense that they are both exciting adventure stories and also works that comment on Turkish society through their omissions; the lack of a concerned government bringing help or even defense to the villagers, the non-existence of religion as a positive force, the inability of women to achieve a real participation in life, and the failure of the bandits to offer a way forward beyond instinctive revolt (they remain bound by the retrogressive codes of honor, revenge, and vendetta).[14]

*Baba / The Father* is noteworthy as a film that merges the two filmic personae of Güney, the political, committed artist and the populist man of cinema. The protagonist is a poor man named Cemal (Güney) who receives a prison sentence of 24 years when he assumes the crime of a wealthy man's son, with a promise that his family will be well provided while he is inside. When he is released he learns that the man he protected seduced his wife; his son became a hit man for the mob and his daughter a prostitute. He vows to take revenge but he is shot by his own son.

The opening scenes are similar to *The Hope*, showing the desperation of a family man who is unable to provide for his family. Cemal does minor jobs for a gangster/businessman. He ties his hope to finding work in Germany as many others around him do, but fails the physical examination. The prison transforms him into a bitter and vengeful man, respected by the other prisoners. The rest of the film resembles Güney's 'ugly king' films. Although the prison scenes, the socio-economic analysis of prostitution and the scenes of confrontation between the victim and the villain carry the signature of Güney as an *engagé* artist, the focus is a personal story. The film does not invite the spectators to delve into the causes behind the ordeals of the protagonist; instead it draws the audience inside the narrative emotionally as in his populist films.

Several other Güney films are about prison. Considering he spent twelve years of his life incarcerated, in fifteen different prisons, this is not extraordinary. Prison is generally a trope for entrapment in his films. Ironically, in *Zavallılar / The Poor Ones* (1974) the prison is a shelter for the poor, the unemployed and the desperate and a place where one can feed oneself. The protagonists, Abuzer (Güney), Arap and Hacı, are homeless men excluded by society. Release from prison would mean a return to the streets where there is neither shelter nor food. They beg to stay at least until the spring. The film draws on several elements from

In Güney's *Zavallılar / The Poor Ones* (1974), the prison is a shelter for the destitute.

the Yeşilçam melodramas – child crime, love for a fallen woman, prison relations – without resorting to melodrama. Instead, a subtle criticism of the anomalies of a society that pushes men behind bars comes to the fore. Arap's situation is an indictment of the exploitation of labour when workers have no social security; he was imprisoned because he reacted against the injustice shown by his employer, who used him as a guard without pay during the construction of a building, with a false promise that he would be given a place to open a tea-house once it is completed. Hacı's drama is a strong critique of the capitalist order that contributes to social disorders such as prostitution; he was imprisoned because the prostitute he wanted to share his life double-crossed him. Abuzer's story shows the fate of an innocent child when society is indifferent to the less advantaged; as a child he witnesses his mother killing the man to whom her husband had sold her and he is pushed to crime when left on his own. The film exposes the inequalities and injustices in society, but like Güney's other socially and politically motivated films does not offer a solution; it prepares the ground for the audience to find their own, which Güney claimed was his understanding of revolutionary cinema. Soon after he started *The Poor Ones* in 1972 Güney was imprisoned for hiding anarchist students and the film was completed three years later with the same actors by Atıf Yılmaz, who had been instrumental in introducing Güney to Yeşilçam.

*Arkadaş / The Friend* (1974), the last film Güney was able to direct in Turkey, was a second turning point in his career after *The Hope*, and in some ways complements it. *The Friend* is not only a settling of accounts for Güney with his 'ugly king' image, but also with the audience who crowned him as the 'ugly king'. In this film he plays Azem, an educated public worker with a certain charm for urban women, who visits his childhood friend, Cemil, in his villa in an affluent summer resort. Azem is disturbed to see his friend distancing himself from his humble roots in an atmosphere of decadence and emptiness. His critical eye is not welcomed by Cemil's *petit bourgeois* wife Necibe, although the young niece Melike is very impressionable.

*The Friend* is a strong indictment of revolutionary youth who turn into apathetic *bourgeois* as middle age approaches. The film does not have a dramatic structure in the classic sense. The narrative depends on observations. Güney deliberately puts distance between the images and the audience to avoid any identification that may reduce the impact of the message. Azem also observes from a distance and in a sense becomes the eye of the audience. He can see the futility of such a meaningless existence, unlike the people in the holiday village who are not able to see its superficiality.

*The Friend* is the least-appreciated film of Güney in the West, although its impact was very strong in Turkey. Many Turkish critics considered it an apposite documentation of the 'culture shock' the urban educated middle class encounters when faced with the other, the poor, abandoned to their destiny in their invisible villages. The weakness of the film lies in the way Güney exhibits the idle lives of the *bourgeoisie*, where he resorts to the clichés of Yeşilçam – parties, bikinis, whisky, casual and empty sex – to illustrate its decadence. His didacticism creates caricaturized cardboard characters. He is more in his element when he shows the lives of the disadvantaged in the second half of the film as Azem and Cemil visit their home village. In fact, the shock of the misery Cemil witnesses is so strong that it leads to his suicide; he is unable to bear the contradiction between the life of materialism he leads and the values of the people he has scorned.

Güney filmed *The Friend* following his release from prison during a general amnesty after having served 26 months. Three months later, while shooting *Endişe / The Anxiety* (1974), he was arrested on a charge of having killed judge Sefa Mutlu during an argument.[15] Şerif Gören, one of his assistants, finished the film, which was scripted by Güney during a previous jail sentence. The next time he was behind the camera was in 1983 in Paris when he shot *Duvar / Le Mur / The Wall*.

The reputation of Yılmaz Güney in the West is built around two very important films which he did not direct in the literal sense, but which he scripted while in prison and instructed his assistants to direct. The first of these is *The Herd* by Zeki Ökten (with whom Güney also collaborated in *Düşman / The Enemy*, 1979) and the second is *Yol / The Way* (1981) directed by Şerif Gören. Both filmmakers were influenced by Güney's cinema and ready for change, despite several productive years they had spent within the confines of Yeşilçam.

*The Herd* problematizes the disintegration of a nomadic Kurdish tribe and its patriarchal structure with changes in the economic structure of the country. The film is a realistic portrayal of a Turkey rapidly embracing capitalism. Berivan from the Halilan tribe is given in marriage to Şivan, the eldest son of the Veysikan tribe, to stop the animosities that had already claimed several lives. Although the couple love each other, happiness and peace are denied to them by Hamo, the patriarch of the Veysikan tribe. When Berivan loses one child after another Hamo blames her for purposefully draining their heritage. Şivan tries to defend his wife, reminding his father that Berivan represents the 'honour' of their family, but Hamo is convinced that love for a woman makes a man weak. After the loss of her third child Berivan becomes mute. Şivan's hopes to find a better life in the city and a cure for Berivan's illness collapse when many of the sheep they were supposed to sell in Ankara suffocate on the train journey from inhaling the fumes of DDT sprayed on the wagons. Berivan dies alone in the corner of a construction site for luxurious apartments.

The film is spatially divided into three parts, all of which have the characteristics of temporality, in-between-ness and the uncanny: the encampment, the train to the capital Ankara and the capital itself. In the encampment the nomadic tribe is in the open air, which is like home for them. They have the security of being together, although a feeling of the uncanny has already permeated this temporary shelter. The nomadic life is documented meticulously, almost ethnographically. The camera moves from one silent face to the other as eyes deliver the message of suffering. The women and children occupy themselves with daily chores while the patriarch Hamo sits and watches. The ritual of the women preparing their men for the long journey to Ankara has a lyrical quality, although it also magnifies the alienation of the nomads when faced with the routine of modern life encountered in the capital.

We do not hear the women utter a word when they are outside; inside their tent, they are scolded and humiliated. Hamo's aged wife is not allowed to leave the table before he grants her permission; one of the sons almost chokes his wife for contradicting Hamo and saying Berivan is sick; another brutally rejects his older wife's advances in bed while he fantasizes about a prostitute. Hamo beats Şivan for disobeying him; in return, Şivan beats Berivan for refusing to talk when she is asked. Moments of conflict are indoors, in claustrophobic spaces, inside the tents or close to them where one can easily be cornered and trapped.

*Sürü / The Herd*
(1978), dir. Zeki
Ökten.

Berivan's image on the train, sitting with her face down beside her father-in-law in a packed compartment of sad faces, transmits her feeling of oppression and her wish for invisibility. The asphyxiation of the sheep metaphorizes this sentiment of suffocation. From time to time the camera turns to the arid landscape; the faces of the people waiting at stations show similar expressions of pain and suffering as those in the encampment. A handcuffed bard with his *saz* (traditional string instrument) gets on the train with two gendarmes. He sings a traditional ballad from the War of Independence: 'The bandit cannot rule the world'. Someone asks what his crime was. 'To sing songs', he responds. (The song is sung by Zülfü Livaneli, musician, author, filmmaker and political activist who in 1974 escaped to Switzerland as a political refugee.) As the train moves, we see graffiti on the walls of the ruins outside: 'Down with the Landowners!'

During the long march with the flock through the boulevards of Ankara the camera pans from the desperate tribe to the conspicuously

visible Turkish flags, the towering statues of Atatürk on horseback, the giant Yeşilçam movie posters, the modern architecture of the mausoleum of Atatürk, the high-rises, the slums and passers-by in modern clothes staring in amazement at the men in black *shalvar* trying to move the flock through the dense traffic and Şivan carrying his sick wife on his back. When the two Turkeys come face to face, there is confusion and chaos on both sides. The reforms intended to bring the country to the standards of civilization of the West did not benefit all citizens.

A countryman shelters Şivan and Berivan inside a construction site. The unfinished room, open to the elements, is a false shelter, just like the capital. The young son of the man has already acquired political consciousness. He reminds his father who believes that the rich in the city are not like the landlords back home: 'You have no home and no money, neither to educate me nor to pay the doctor. Just like Uncle Şivan. Millions of workers have nothing. Three–four people have millions. Where does it go, the work of the millions? The rich of here is the same as the landowners over there.' However, the father is hopeful that he will be the superintendent when the building is completed. He shows Şivan and Berivan how big the kitchen is; how you can eliminate cooking smells by just pressing a button. Bedroom for yourself, for your children, for your guests and for the maids . . . The son interposes: 'you are dreaming again, father. They won't let you live like that. Who lives in those places? In this society, there is the working class and the class who makes them work. How do they accumulate their capital? By exploiting you, him . . .'. After this conversation the father proposes to go to the music hall to listen to the arabesque music, the 'opium that keeps the masses pacified', according to Güney.

Berivan dies in the construction site, a space that promises comfort and security. The views of Ankara, the towering mosque, the city with all its sacred and secular elements are accentuated to show the alienation of Şivan, who is arrested for attacking a callous man who does not consider the death of a woman significant. Berivan's unclaimed corpse is dragged from the construction site by the friend who is bewildered by the thought of losing his job. One could not find a more appropriate display of the degeneration of an otherwise kind-hearted, generous and simple peasant in the urban environment.

Woman as metaphor for the oppressed land and its peoples is a common trope that has had precedents in world as well as Turkish cinema. Placed in liminal spaces, women are at a double disadvantage to men, although *The Herd* shows that feudal oppression destroys men and women alike. When the loss of identity is not a conscious one (as in the case of ethnic minorities in Turkey) its power is more destructive. Berivan stops speaking after she loses her third baby. Her silence is a metonymy for the oppressed people without a voice (the poor, the women), but particularly for the Kurds who are silenced, not even able to speak their own language. However, this message is very subtle in the film to thwart state censorship.

*Yol / The Way* (1981) written by Yılmaz Güney while in prison, shot by Şerif Gören according to Güney's instructions and later edited in Paris, recounts the stories of five prisoners on leave, although the overriding theme is the half-open prison outside the prison walls and oppression, be it the oppression of the military regime of the time, the oppression of the state or the embedded feudal oppression, remnants of which still rule the lives of ordinary citizens. At the same time the film is about the sufferings of the Kurdish people.

*Yol* begins with a group of men receiving their mail inside the half-open prison on the island of İmralı. Permissions for temporary leave have been frozen after the military coup of 1980 but there has been some hope recently. When the list of those who will be allowed to visit their families is posted, it creates a different kind of anxiety for the chosen ones. The film follows the parallel journeys of five such prisoners. Güney describes his characters:

> Yusuf and Mevlüt are both from Antep. Yusuf is a naïve young man who enters the prison as a married adolescent, but stays away from the bad habits of prison life . . . Before they leave, Mevlüt receives the news of the death of Yusuf's wife, but it is very difficult to tell this to Yusuf . . . because it is difficult to give bad news in prison. Therefore, Yusuf goes on leave with longing for his wife and takes his canary along to give to her as a present.
>
> Mevlüt comes from a feudal family; he is soft and friendly. He is engaged. During the leave, he'll see his fiancée and his homeland.
>
> Ömer is a young Kurd from Urfa. He lives in a smugglers' village near the Syrian border. Landless peasants, his family earn their living as smugglers. That is why he is in jail. His heart is filled with love for his horse and for nature. He is silent and introverted. He thinks he will not return to prison; that is why he is on leave. He is a bachelor.

Memed Salih who earns his living as a driver was involved in an aborted armed robbery and convicted. He feels the pain of coming to terms with the event because his brother-in-law was killed by the police when he left him and ran away. The family of his wife know about this and are very angry. In her last letter, his wife was asking if he really left Aziz behind. Is this why Aziz was killed? During the journey, Memed tries to find the answer to give to his wife . . .

And Seyit Ali Fırat. A young Kurd who hides his bruised feelings that are shaped by the feudal life and thinking. He is married and has a son . . . But his wife has become a fallen woman . . . He is crushed. His honour is wounded. There is only one thing to do now: he must hurry to Siirt and then to the town of Sancak where his wife is and punish her himself. He wants to kill her . . . A new voyage begins for him, a voyage of hate and pain and the rebellion of broken honour.[16]

Yusuf never makes it to his village and therefore never learns about the death of his wife. At a checkpoint he is unable to produce his permission document and is sent back to prison. Mevlut goes to Antep. In his father's house, he eats with the family while his fiancée Meral waits outside. When the couple take a tour in town, they are chaperoned by two female relatives hidden inside black *chadors*. To vent his anger Mevlut gets drunk and visits a prostitute. Ömer finds his village surrounded by gendarmes. His arrival creates anxiety in his family; they fear that his brother Abuzer, who is an outlaw, would try to return to see him. Abuzer *does* return and is killed. Ömer is obliged to marry his sister-in-law and father her children as custom dictates. The dreams of a young girl whom he saw on the way, his beloved horse and the possibility of escape are all shattered. Memed Salih (Halil Ergün) reaches Diyarbakır but cannot go near his wife. When he confesses his cowardice her family throw him out. Later, he convinces his wife to go with him, but the couple are killed on the train by the youngest brother-in-law. As for Seyit Ali (Tarık Akan), from a conversation he has on the train with Memed Salih we understand that he loves his wife Zine (Serif Sezer) dearly and his heart is filled with the dilemma of love and pity and hatred and revenge. Through impenetrable snow, he reaches the village where she is chained for eight months in the basement of her parents' house. He does not kill her. He devises a cruel plan to revenge himself:

*Yol / The Way* (1981), written by Yılmaz Güney while in prison, shot by Şerif Gören.

to leave her to the elements of nature, where another woman had recently been frozen to death. Although his conscience overrides him at the end, it is too late. With her thin clothes and the weak body that had not seen the light for eight months, she is already frozen in the blizzard.

*Yol* thematizes state oppression, particularly during the military dictatorship, with episodes of checkpoints, inspections, body searches of civilians, curfews, inserted dialogues and silently observed signs. In the opening scenes the prisoners are told by a loudspeaker that after the intervention of 'our glorious army' all permissions for leave are frozen. A prisoner comments under his breath: 'Instead of ranting, why don't they learn about human rights?' Stories of beatings and torture are whispered among the prisoners. Such conversation is repeated when the army stops the travellers from continuing their journey because of the curfew. Seyit is advised not to protest when the gendarme keeps the passengers overnight, as 'they broke the heads of two men only few days ago'. A friend of Memed was shot by the 'fascists' and left in a bad shape. On the streets of Gaziantep a poster of Kenan Evren, the general responsible for the coup (who has been compared to Pinochet, but has not yet been brought to justice), is seen side by side with that of Kemal Atatürk.

The poverty, which increases as you go further east, is documented unsparingly in the slums of Diyarbakır, essentially a Kurdish city. Children sell *simit* (doughnuts) on the street, fight with each other to have a turn on the rental bike (a reference to *The Hope*), and six seven-year-olds in rags puff cigarettes. In Adana little Gypsy boys mount the bus to sing a few songs to earn a piece of bread. Obviously, none of them goes to school. The poverty in the countryside is tenfold. 'Smuggling is over now', says the father of Ömer, who does not know how else to earn a living. 'And if you are a Kurd, you are finished.' When the gendarme brings the dead body of their son, the family cannot claim it in fear of reprisal.

Despite the grim picture it drew of a society chained to oppressive traditions and more oppressive government policies, *Yol* is a film of hope, according to Güney. He stated that the remorse Seyit Ali feels after his wife's death should be perceived as the melting of the ice; Ömer's decision to change his life by choosing to combat oppression is already an advancement and the courage displayed by Memed Salih at the end to tell the truth despite losses is significant. The film does not have schematic progressive elements in the classic sense, but there is a forward change that is the result of the changes within the characters: 'what makes a society evolve is its inner conflict and what makes a human being evolve as an individual is his/her individual inner conflict, the conflict between the old and the new, the positive and the negative.'[17]

Discussion continues as to the real director of *Yol*, especially abroad, where some critics have been creating a myth that Güney made *Yol* by 'remote control' from prison, although Güney was very clear on this issue: 'Instead of defining me as a director who makes films from prison, it would be more accurate to say, someone who prepares from prison the conditions for a film to be created . . . it's wrong to present the success of the film as the success of Yılmaz Güney because the essence of cinema is collective.'[18] However, as leading critic Atilla Dorsay would point out, viewing *The Herd*, *Enemy* or *Yol* one cannot help asking if these are truly films by Zeki Ökten / Şerif Gören. Not only the dialogue and the script but the atmosphere in these films carries the signature of Güney. The fact that neither Ökten nor Gören have made any other films as powerful illustrates the very important influence of Güney on these works.[19]

*Duvar / Le Mur / The Wall* (1983) was the last film Güney directed, made in France and funded partly by the French Ministry of Culture. It did not receive the acclaim accorded to his work accomplished in Turkey. Shot outside Paris in an old abbey, the narrative was spatially placed entirely inside a prison, which was divided into men's, women's, boys' and anarchists' cells. The subject of prison is the principal issue in most of Güney's films. He had spent the best years of his life behind bars, and prison was the determining element in many scripts he wrote, films he directed or roles he played. As in *Yol* the trope of prison often had a triple function in his films: to represent the concrete one he knew well, the imprisonment of society en masse and the prison of our minds. Now an exile in Paris he chose the prison motif to expose the political situation in Turkey, where 40 death sentences were carried out following the 1980 military intervention.

He claimed that *The Wall* represented the outsider's point of view, and he tried to tell the story of the hopes of the prisoners and the 'dead end' of these hopes, the concrete example of which was the riot of the boys demanding transfer to a better jail. The children do not think of freedom or liberation; they just dream of a better jail. They pray: 'My God, send me to a better jail'.

People could change their life not by escaping from their reality with empty dreams, but within their realities, Güney reiterated. There was no such thing as a 'good prison'. In oppressive regimes all citizens were held prisoners; the apparatus of the state, the police, the army and the gendarme were entrusted with the job of protecting such a world, a world of filth, both inside and outside. '[W]hat is narrated in this film is the re-collating of events that were lived. They looked for the light and the water in the blood, fire and tears, in the darkness of the walls . . . I dedicate this film to them, to my little friends who grope in the dark searching for the light and the water.' It is a harsh and vengeful film carrying the bitterness of an exceptionally talented artist condemned to spend the best years of his life behind bars and to die in exile.

Hailed worldwide as a humanist artist, Güney's stance on women has been problematic for some viewers. His early image as the 'ugly king' of Yeşilçam and rumours about outbursts of physical violence in his personal relationships with women have distanced some from his cinema, who consider his point of view masculinist with violent tendencies against women. Roy Armes points out that in Güney's cinema the role of the woman is subservient to the man. 'Throughout his work, women are stolen and abused, seduced and abandoned, sold, killed, or driven to suicide. To have a woman – as wife or daughter – is to be vulnerable: she will be killed or will betray you, and in either case the called-for response will be violent revenge – the vendetta that runs as an undercurrent through society in all Güney's work.'[20] Atıf Yılmaz, who supported Güney throughout his career, believed that Turkish cinema in general was a cinema that answered the demands of a macho society and that 'Güney made films degrading women.'[21] Ali Özgentürk, who knew Güney both personally and professionally, did not agree, arguing that the violence in Güney's cinema was 'the violence inherent in society, in man–woman relations', although he supported the view that Turkish cinema was a 'macho' cinema that endorsed the status quo.[22]

For Güney, men–women relations were not a question of gender but class. If men oppressed women, this was a manifestation of their being oppressed. In *The Hope* the woman exists only within the borders of the house. She does not have a name. She is referred to only through her attributes: wife and mother. The children are afraid of their mother but she does not have the same authority as the father. She curses them ('I hope you all die!) when her helplessness against poverty turns to cruelty. However,

> within the shanty that the family calls home, wife and children stand as the would-be voice of common sense. Güney clearly shows that they do not participate in Cabbar's delusions, that they literally do not see what he sees (the promise of treasure). Yet, wife and children seem cowed, bullied into accepting the adult male delusion as their lot – their luck – in life. Within this traditional yet disintegrating family, there is no place for effective opposition to masculine will. Güney pointedly marks the place where sanity could reverse the progress of illusion but marks also the *if only* of the tragedy – if only the woman (and the children) were not placed *a priori* outside the realm of possible truth; if only they could intervene to convert the monologue of male delusion into dialogue; if only . . . At this point in *UMUT*, Güney pauses to imply the alternatives, the potentialities, just as he earlier presented Cabbar, lost in his own preoccupations, blindly trudging past a workers' demonstration.[23]

In several of his films, Güney exposes the plight of women within traditional patriarchal societies. In *The Bride of the Earth* Keje's fate is decided by her brother and her husband; she cannot disobey because, as she is reminded, she represents the honour of the family. In *The Anxiety* the feudal system of *başlık parası*, the money the father receives from the groom in return for the daughter, is underscored through the story of the cotton-worker Cevher who decides to give young Beyaz to the head farmer, a middle-aged married man, but she elopes with the man she loves.

Güney draws a picture of a thoroughly independent woman in *Elegy*. The village doctor is a woman with a profession, and she is free to make her moral decisions to treat a wounded outlaw without informing the police, but not to protect him when he is cured (even though she has now developed a soft spot for him).

Prostitution is systematically denounced as a social evil that, according to Güney, is fed by the capitalist order that considers the woman as a commodity. *The Father* and *The Poor Ones* as well as *Düşman / Enemy* (1979), written by Güney and directed by Ökten, are examples. In *The Enemy* a parallel is drawn between the workers who line up to attract employers and the prostitutes who exhibit their wares. The workers are shown devoid of any humanity in the struggle for survival. Hungry and hopeless, they push each other to get on the truck first to grab the scarce jobs; they do not bother to look back when a man falls and is mortally injured. The only time the corpse in the middle of the town square draws attention is when someone notices the half-naked pictures of women on the pages of the newspaper covering him. Man's cruelty to man is displayed in another powerful scene, when a desperate prostitute tries to jump off the balcony of the brothel. The sex-starved men of all ages pay more attention to her naked body than to her misery. In *The Herd* a lame prostitute services the men in the toilet of the train. Hamo's youngest son, so ignorant as to sell the ancient tablets he finds in a cave to a middleman for a few pennies, loses all his money to have pathetic sex among the sheep in the wagon.

Social and cultural oppression at the macro level contributes to the oppression at the micro level, where the family unit and women are at the worse end. Just like Hamo, the patriarch in *The Herd*, who vents his anger on his children who then unleash their frustration on their wives, in *Yol* the feudal patriarchy is instrumental in the tragedy of the women. The 'crime' of Seyit Ali's wife, Zine, is not very clear in the film, although there is no dispute about her punishment. She grew up with Seyit Ali and still remembers him playing his flute. Why would she deceive him if not oppressed by the same mechanism that oppresses him? The macho delivery of Mevlüt to his fiancée about the rules of their planned married life ('when we get married, my word will be the law in the house . . . I'll decide what you'll do, or I'll get very mad') is almost a premonition for the fate of the young woman, who listens admiringly.

The underlying theme of *Yol* is women and honour, although for Güney the question was not a struggle between men and women. Each character is in a quandary with women but also with the homeland. We do not know the circumstances of the death of Yusuf's young wife, but Mevlüt is trapped inside the customs and traditions that squeeze him in a corner, like his prison cell. Ömer's home is surrounded by the gendarmes. Memed Salih's return will be his end and Seyit Ali is more broken on his return journey than when he started. Güney believed that the liberation of women was possible through the liberation of men. 'A society where women are not free cannot be free', he stated. 'A nation that oppresses another nation is a slave itself. To show symbolically that the whole Turkey is imprisoned and oppressed, *Yol* focalizes the subject of women and the Kurdish nation.'[24]

The cinema of Güney serves as a role model for generations that follow with its authentic film language and realistic approach in terms of acting, directing and scriptwriting. Most of the characters and the stories Güney narrates are inspired by his experiences. Cabbar of *The Hope* is modelled after his father. The blood feuds (as in *The Anxiety*) carry memories of a childhood trauma when his father was shot in front of his eyes, although he did not die. The story of the Veysikan tribe in *The Herd* is based on his mother's tribe, Cibiran. When a character in *Pain* says, 'We saw so many handcuffs in our life . . . So many handcuffs got rusty on our wrists', the reference is to Güney himself and his life behind bars.[25]

Güney may be best described in the words of intellectual/author Murat Belge:

> a brilliant filmmaker and artist; a 'politician', who always remains an amateur, an 'us' who wants to share everything he owns with the masses and a 'me', individualistic enough to name the journal he publishes, 'Güney'; a disposition befitting the populist rebel heroes of the world before socialism and a brain that gives vital importance to comprehend the theoretical fine points of historical

materialism; a fearless warrior of the world of guns, action and bravery and a dervish that calls people to peace, serenity, education and love. As a result of all of these, inevitably a very lonely man.[26]

# 5 Gender, Sexuality and Morals in Transition

The provincial girl: Who said I'll marry you?
Her boyfriend: But we slept together.
The provincial girl: Just because I slept with you once,
do I have to sleep with you for the rest of my life?[1]

Women have been the focus of Turkish cinema since its beginnings, although their visibility has not always been beneficial to their identity. Cinema arrived in Turkey as an entertainment for men by men and remained so for many years. At the beginning of the twentieth century armed fundamentalists were occupying theatres threatening to knife any woman who dared to enter. Women had to wait even longer to become actors. All female roles were played by non-Muslims until the foundation of the secular Turkish Republic in 1923.

As early as 1917 the 'fallen woman' motif was established with *Pençe / The Clutch*, by Sedat Simavi, which featured two 'promiscuous' women, one with an insatiable appetite for men and the other an adulteress. This was followed by Ahmet Fehim's sex vaudeville *Mürebbiye / The Governess* (1919), presenting Angélique, an amoral French beauty, who seduced all the men in a rich household. Filmmakers habitually exploited the female body through the medium of comedy, the camera objectifying the female and turning her into a spectacle, confirming Laura Mulvey's contention that the spectatorial look in mainstream cinema is implicitly male; the image represents the ideological meaning that 'woman' has for men: the male as active and powerful and the female as passive and powerless as a subject, on which power is exercised, either as a victim or as an object that needs to be protected, and the spectator identifies with the male look.[2]

Yeşilçam portrayed love as the first condition of marriage in a period when marriages were still arranged; love involved individual choice and paved the path for the emancipation of women. Ironically, for the majority of society love was not considered as necessary for marriage and in fact was a threat to morals. Although films showed love that ended in marriage as a victory for the woman, the same love would limit the woman's freedom and reinforce the man's dominance. The woman who fought familial and societal pressures to marry the man she loved was expected to adhere to the patriarchal laws of society or she would pay for her misdemeanour.[3]

'Women's films' dominated the industry in the 1950s and '60s when the female audience was a gold mine for the producers. The star system born in the 1960s typecast four top stars according to audience expectations: Türkan Şoray, the oppressed sexual woman; Hülya Koçyiğit, the oppressed asexual woman; Filiz Akın, the well-educated asexual bourgeois woman; and Fatma Girik (who became the mayor of an uptown municipality in the 1990s), the honest 'manly' asexual woman, known as *erkek fatma* (male Fatma, which did not mean masculine, but rather honest and straightforward like a man). According to Atıf Yılmaz, these stars represented masks similar to those worn in traditional Eastern arts, such as the Kabuki theatre of Japan. When communications advanced with television, the Internet, etc., and the borders with the rest of the world blurred, the stereotypes began to turn into self-reflexive characters who would question their identity and their role in society.[4]

Yeşilçam endorsed the conservative values of society and the sacrosanctity of marriage. Sexuality was reserved for 'bad women'. The vamps and the prostitutes could kiss, undress and make love, but innocent 'family' girls never took off their clothes and never went to bed, and 'fallen' women, although honourable, never found happiness. As social evils they had to be eliminated. Producers ensured that family

*Çinliler Geliyor /
Chinese are Coming*
(2006), dir. Zeki
Ökten.

values were not offended, particularly in the provinces and rural areas, where Islam played a fundamental role in patriarchal lifestyles. To protect their careers stars had to refuse roles that would compromise their reputation.

In *Meryem ve Oğulları / Meryem and her Sons* (1977) Fatma Girik sacrifices her singing career for an honourable marriage, but has to go to the mosque and ask for Allah's forgiveness first. When a good man comes along and tries to make an 'honest woman' out of a prostitute, the first manifestation of the change is the veiling. In Lütfi Ö. Akad's classic, *Vesikalı Yarım / Licensed to Love* (1968), Şoray, a *konsumatrist* (bar girl), dons the scarf to be worthy of her honest man, a grocery owner from Anatolia (although the length of her coat remains short enough to show her beautiful legs to the audience).

Şoray entered Yeşilçam as an adolescent and instantly charmed the new urban audience, the migrant workers from Anatolia. Unlike blonde Cahide Sonku of earlier years, who fascinated the urban elite with her mysterious sensuality but failed to reach the Anatolian audience, Şoray was claimed as the typical Turkish woman. Film magazines claimed that 'Şoray was more beautiful than the stars of Italian and French films because of her big brown eyes, her expressive face, and her plumpness, wet lips and misty eyes. The audience was captivated by her, the extra weight did not bother them because they loved the soft curves of the Eastern woman.'[5]

Initially Şoray accepted roles the stars would not, showing bare legs and kissing without inhibition. Once her popularity was established she switched images and created the myth of the 'woman to be worshipped'. Close-ups of her face, her wet lips and dreamy eyes were accentuated to arouse not only the male characters on the screen but also the spectators. (Remarkably, Şoray has evolved into an intelligent and independent woman on screen and in private life and directed a number of noteworthy films of her own in the 1970s and '80s.)

The figure of the *lumpen woman* whose trademarks were macho muscle power, vulgar jests, foul language and dress code of black leather jacket and *casquette* (peaked cap) of the male sub-culture was very popular, a phenomenon that seems rather odd for the conservative masculinist Muslim society of 1960s Turkey. The audience accepted cross-dressers and gender-benders on screen against the social, cultural and religious structure as long as the *lumpen woman* was not a manifestation of transvestism or trans-sexuality (they were expected to be wives and mothers at home) and the genre turned into a fetish.[6] In a society where male prowess is glorified and in a film industry dominated by men, women could become heroes only by assuming male characteristics.[7]

The *lumpen woman* vogue was started with *Şöför Nebahat / Nebahat, the Taxi-Driver* (1959–60) by Metin Erksan, centring on a young woman who takes over her father's job after his death. Although the film is about Nebahat's struggles in the world of men and her revolt against the established structures of society, the implication is that in her subconscious she harbours a secret desire to be male. Erksan's *İntikam Meleği* aka *Kadın Hamlet / The Angel of Vengeance* aka *Woman Hamlet* (1976), with Fatma Girik in the lead, is also about distorted female identity,[8] a theme explored in an earlier film, *Fosforlu Cevriye* (Aydın Arakon, 1959), which depicts a married woman with split sexual identity who is brought back to 'normality' by the aid of her second husband, a psychiatrist. Within a social structure that did not consider woman equal to man, such films distorted issues of women and their layered identities by showing them as reckless and aggressive in their envy of the male persona.[9]

Women's entry into the workforce in large numbers during the free market policies of the 1980s and the widening of education possibilities transformed the traditional identity of the woman as an obedient daughter/wife whose honour was to be preserved behind closed doors, and consequently her fictional identity gained a more humanist dimension. Talented filmmakers such as Şerif Gören, Zeki Ökten and Ömer Kavur joined Atıf Yılmaz, pioneer of films about women and their issues, in narrating stories of the new woman, 'neither a virgin, nor a prostitute' but a human being with sexual desires. Foreign soap operas were instrumental in bringing topics considered private in Muslim societies – divorce, abortion, marital abuse, infidelity – to public view and paved the way for cinema to break some taboos. Müjde Ar, a totally 'liberated' young woman, was the initiator and star of a new image of an independent modern woman with intellect, but also sexuality. With Ömer Kavur's *Oh Beautiful Istanbul* and Atıf Yılmaz's *Delikan* (1982) to lead the way, the emancipated woman motif became one of the most common topics of the 1980s. These two films launched Müjde Ar as the prototype of *hayat kadını* (literally 'life woman', a euphemism for a prostitute), but Ar's character was far from Yeşilçam's image of the 'fallen woman' with a bad destiny and, rather than an exploited sex

star, Ar moulded herself into a sex symbol that exploited cinema clev-
erly. *Mine*, made the following year by Yılmaz, starring Türkan Şoray
as an unfulfilled woman whose sexuality obsesses the village men and
exposes their hypocrisies, broke box-office records with an unprecedented number of female spectators. Yılmaz reminisces: 'When *Mine*
was shown in the city of Samsun, a cinema had a 200-seat capacity and
190 women arrived. They did not let the men in! *Mine* coincided with
the arrival of the feminist movement in Turkey and it is more or less the
beginning of the theme of women's search for identity.'[10] These were the
same spectators who flocked to see a sex film in 1980, *L'anti-vierge* by
Francis Giacobetti, the second of the *Emanuelle* series, that played in
downtown Beyoğlu for fourteen weeks in a woman's matinee. One single
screening was attended by more than 200 women. They seemed to be
starved to see a part of their lives on screen.

For rural women and the women from migrant families who settled
in the peripheries of the big cities, it took longer to achieve financial and
social independence. Meryem of *The Bride*, discussed in chapter Two,
was perhaps the first woman on the screen to rebel against the patriarchy and find a job in a factory. Unfortunately, more than three decades

*Gündelikçi /
Housekeeper
(2005), dir.
Emel Çelebi.*

later, many Anatolian women from the shanty towns still earn a living cleaning the houses of the rich and hand over their meagre earnings to their husbands or brothers, not to offend their 'manhood', thus facing double exploitation. Emel Çelebi's insightful documentary *Gündelikçi / Housekeeper* (2005) is a realistic rendition of the sufferings of these women, who are still victims of the customs and traditions prevalent even in urban settlements.

The sexual liberation of women from the shanty towns appeared on the screen with Aygül in Atıf Yılmaz's love comedy *Bir Yudum Sevgi / A Taste of Love* (1984). Dissatisfied with her lazy loser husband who cannot provide for her and their four children, let alone satisfy her sexual needs, Aygül takes destiny in her own hands and first finds herself a new man and then a job in the factory. The film shows Aygül as a bold woman ready to take initiatives. She succeeds in seducing Cemal, who pleases her eye (especially when he is on the soccer field), and she arranges for an empty apartment to make love (she visits the local 'expert', an ex-prostitute, beforehand to learn a trick or two). She is a living woman, all flesh and blood, far removed from the one-dimensional 'Kabuki masks' of a generation earlier.

The films of Yılmaz best display the evolution of Turkish cinema regarding women's issues. In the 1960s and '70s the general contention was that solutions to social or economic problems would automatically solve women's problems. *Ah Güzel Istanbul / Oh, Beautiful Istanbul*

(1966), *Kuma / The Second Wife* (1974) and *Selvi Boylum Al Yazmalım* (1977) present this point of view. *Mine* (1983), *A Taste of Love* (1984), *Dul Bir Kadın / A Widow* (1985), *Asiye Nasıl Kurtulur? / How Can Asiye Be Saved?* (1986) and *Adı Vasfiye / Her Name Is Vasfiye* (1986) consider women's issues as possessing an intrinsic importance independent of other elements. Beginning with the 1990s when women, particularly in the urban milieu, attempted to free themselves from the clutches of tradition and dogmatic religion, sexual choice became of great concern. *Düş Gezginleri / Walking After Midnight* (1992), on lesbianism, and *Gece, Melek ve Bizim Çocuklar / The Night, The Angel and Our Gang* (1994), about transvestites and male prostitutes, are the best examples of this period.[11] Yılmaz's last film, *Eğreti Gelin / The Borrowed Bride* (2005), was a period film that celebrated free love.

*Eğreti Gelin / The Borrowed Bride* (2005), Yılmaz's last film, revives the old custom of hiring 'experienced' women to give young men sexual education.

*Gece, Melek ve Bizim Çocuklar / The Night, The Angel and Our Gang* (1994), dir. Atıf Yılmaz. The focus is the world of transvestites and male prostitutes.

*Her Name Is Vasfiye* is particularly noteworthy in exhibiting the slippery nature of moral values in transitional periods. The fate of the woman without male protection is a common trope of Yeşilçam cinema, but in this collaboration of Atıf Yılmaz with Müjde Ar it gains a new dimension. Four western Anatolian men, each one a realistic typification of Turkish machismo, recount their version of the story of one provincial woman, whose search for an identity is at the core of the film. All four men are the same men, played by the same actor; but their gender privileges them to change their identity at will, or to express layers of identity. However, each time Vasfiye wants to put one foot forward she is hampered by men.

Yılmaz underscores the masculinist mentality of men who consider women as objects to be owned, and draws attention to the relativity of morality in Turkish society. So long as men determine what is considered moral or immoral, whether the woman has good intentions or not is inconsequential, which shows the immorality of men, according to Yılmaz.

What makes *Her Name Is Vasfiye* different from other films of Turkish cinema that systematically deny women visibility is that while following the status quo, a critical point of view is also presented. The film's focus is a woman who does not exist, which illustrates that in patriarchal cultures, women's visibility is possible only through her absence. Paradoxically, in the process of the criticism of gender politics, the woman is erased from the screen altogether. As a result, not only the young writer who pursues Vasfiye's story in the narrative, but also the filmmaker propagate patriarchal representation.[12]

The film industry in Turkey is monopolized by men, as are most film industries in the world, and this reinforces the male point of view. Until the late 1990s the career woman was depicted as an anomaly that had to be resolved by domestication before the end of the film. Films that ostensibly focused on working women were often not about emancipation, but a process of regaining the femininity lost by the desire for emancipation. In the portrayal of sexuality and the consequences of sexual freedom double standards have prevailed: while men are allowed extramarital sex, 'good' women enjoy sex only within monogamous relationships. Özgüç comments:

*Adı Vasfiye / Her Name Is Vasfiye,* dir. Atıf Yılmaz (1986).

the *macho* tradition in our society, fed by male hegemony, considers man's infidelity as normal, but adultery committed by a woman is contrary to the moral fibre and contrary to the censorship, therefore filmmakers are reticent to take a chance. Atıf Yılmaz, who justified the infidelity of the woman by delving into the motives behind the adultery with *A Taste of Love* and several other films, was the pioneer. He exposed the hypocrisy on moral issues and eased the way for other and younger filmmakers, such as Seçkin Yaşar, whose *Sarı Tebessüm / Yellow Smile* (1992) is the most daring film until now.[13]

Women are regularly used as a metaphor for the nation in different cultures and periods, particularly when the nation is exposed to danger. One of the earliest examples in Turkish cinema is *Vurun Kahpeye / Strike the Whore* (1949) by Lütfi Ö. Akad, based on a 1926 novel about the War of Independence by a woman writer, Halide Edip Adıvar. *Strike the Whore* shows the local *imam* as a religious fanatic who incites the villagers to lynch the progressive schoolteacher, Aliye, whom he labels a shameless prostitute. Aliye's character is important, as she reconciles opposing elements. After the founding of the Republic, the image of the veiled housewife, brought up in the Islam-Ottoman tradition, was considered a symbol of backwardness by intellectuals, whereas the Westernized modern woman was regarded suspiciously as someone severed from her roots and confused about her values. Adıvar's women, like Aliye, were Westernized, but faithful to the national values; educated and free but with a sound sense of morals and honour. They could play sports like men, even ride a horse if necessary, but still succeed in preserving their femininity.[14] They were ready to die for their men and their country. In short, they represented the ideal woman Atatürk envisioned for Turkey.

The film was adapted for screen three times by different filmmakers and each version reflects the concerns of its period and convictions of its director. The Akad version takes the lynching in the final scene outside the village; the individual blows by the villagers are not shown since Akad is more concerned by the act as a social phenomenon than its violent dimension. The dead body of Aliye is immediately covered with the Turkish flag. In Orhan Aksoy's version (1964) the locale is indeterminate; after the death of Aliye the medallion her fiancé gave her is found in her hand. As the film was made after the 1960 military intervention and during the threat of reactionarism, nationalist sentiments are in the foreground. Halit Refiğ's version (1973) begins with the images of a mosque. Aliye is killed in the village square. In her hand, a small Qur'an is found. Refiğ adds dialogue to the original script such as 'when the infidels invade an Islamic country, the Muslims must take up arms' and 'the first duty of Islam is *jihad* [holy war], isn't it?' With the prevailing Cyprus conflict, the 'enemy' of the main theme becomes the Greeks, although the film foregrounds religion rather than nationalism.[15]

During a period of political unrest when Yeşilçam turned to soft porn for survival, cinema with a religious agenda (*Milli* cinema as discussed in chapter One) used the woman as a symbol for a nation that had to be rescued from bad elements: secularism and Westernization. Yücel Çakmaklı's *Kızım Ayşe / My Daughter, Ayşe* (1974), a very popular film of its period, uses the clichés of Yeşilçam liberally, particularly the binaries of the good (rural folk) and the bad (urban people). The urban lifestyle (modernism *à la franca*) is equated with parties, drugs, whisky, motorcycle rides, Western music, mini-skirts and *nouveau riche* furnishings. In the opening scene a widow wearing a headscarf laments at her late husband's grave: 'It was not for us to educate a girl in Istanbul.' With this statement, the 'us' and 'them' motif is established. Ayşe, an intelligent village girl, goes to Istanbul with her mother, Huriye Bacı, to study medicine and takes off her scarf to enter the university as required by law. When poverty settles in, an old village acquaintance that made it rich in the West takes the mother and daughter under his protection, and Ayşe is lured by the carefree lifestyle of his daughter, Melahat. Melahat's decadent boyfriend tries to seduce Ayşe, but Melahat intervenes with a gun, only to be savagely beaten by the boyfriend (a lesson to all girls who deviate from the true path). Huriye Bacı arrives to save the girls. She beats the man, who shows no resistance (even the evil respect the elders). He dies rolling down the stairs (the fall of the sinner). Ayşe is reunited with her village boyfriend and they leave hand in hand with the view of the Blue Mosque in the background. The conflict is resolved when the 'bad elements' are eliminated and the 'good values' reinstated.

Political scientist Alev Çınar points out that the body is one of the most important sites where modernizing interventions and negotiations take place. Just as the newly founded Republic of Kemal Atatürk 'liberated' the body from the oppressive restrictions of Islam by 'unveiling' it and giving it a modern Western appearance, the Islamist interventions have 'reveiled' the body using the headscarf as 'the symbol of their political struggle toward rescuing the nation from the ill effects of the secular state and reinstituting its true culture and identity founded upon the notion of an Ottoman-Islamic civilization'.[16] In *My Daughter, Ayşe*, Çakmaklı uses the body of the woman and her veiling or unveiling as a conduit for the film's message. When Ayşe takes off her scarf (unveils) and dresses like Melahat, she is pulled towards a precipice. Several years later, with the revival of religious cinema under the banner of 'white cinema', Mesut Uçakan resorted to exploiting the woman and her veiling and unveiling for the Islamist message. *Yalnız Değilsiniz / You Are Not Alone* (1990) shows Serpil in mini-skirts and riding a bicycle before she embraces Islam and covers her hair, while her 'feminist' cousin's clothes and short hair suggest androgyny (a common contention in Turkey, which equates feminism with lesbianism). The film was very successful since the issue of banning the *türban* (which covers the hair entirely as opposed to the headscarf, which is not firmly fixed) in universities appealed to young women experiencing a crisis of identity, but the sequels to the film did not get the same interest. The *türban* remains a burning issue, but the subject has not been approached by conscientious filmmakers with cinematographic originality.

Secular cinema also employs the woman as a metaphor for the nation and 'parallel to the worsening of the conditions, the presentation of the woman as an independent-subject becomes difficult' according to Eyuboğlu. In films from the late 1990s such as *Eşkıya / The Bandit* (Yavuz Turgul), *Güneşe Yolculuk / Journey to the Sun* and *Propaganda* (Sinan Çetin), which carry the common theme of a 'Turkish Apocalypse', the deplorable condition of the country – flooded villages and forced migration in the first two films and a country divided by a barbed wire as an allegory for ethnic strife and self-serving bureaucracy in the third – is conveyed through the woman as a metaphor, although in most of these films the relation of the woman to the nation is more of a metonym. When women represent the nation, they represent only one aspect or appear as an extension of the nation. Eyuboğlu points to two films by Ali Özgentürk, *Su da Yanar / Water Also Burns* (1987) and *Mektup / The Letter* (1997), where foreign women (French in *Water* and American in *The Letter*) identified as 'frigid' are abandoned by the male protagonist. While the foreign women represent his alienation to his country and its problems, the Turkish women who replace the foreign women represent the 'brighter face' of the nation. However, in a period when the struggle for independence and Westernization is in danger, political films such as Güney's *Arkadaş / The Friend* (1974) show the woman as representing the evolution of independence. The character of Melike, a young, beautiful and naïve woman who is indecisive about her choices, stands for Turkey, and her attraction to the Güney character suggests that she (or rather Turkey) needs men like Güney who represent change and revolution.[17]

Several women are active in the film industry in Turkey although they have not been mobilized by diverse cinematic forms of intervention to locate themselves inside a universe of shared self-definition with other women filmmakers of the world. Neither have they taken responsibility as outspoken and leading advocates for women's problems to use cinematic art purposefully to document a new feminist social realism. More than a decade after her death Bilge Olgaç (1940–1994) is still considered the only fully fledged 'woman filmmaker' of Turkey. She made several 'male macho films', including some with 'ugly king' Yılmaz Güney, before she had the chance to explore her real interest, the plight of women in a macho society. Unfortunately, her committed films gained little distribution and she did not receive the attention she deserved.

Olgaç's first film was a gangster yarn, *Üçünüzü de Mıhlarım / I'll Nail the Three of You* (1965), with Güney killing everyone to restore the family honour. Disillusioned by the splatter films and the sex fare Yeşilçam was churning out during the politically repressive 1970s, she withdrew, only to return in 1984 with *Kaşık Düşmanı / Spoon Enemy* aka *A Wedding Room*, a black comedy about the plight of women in the rural milieu, where they work in the fields all day but are still considered a *spoon enemy*, a term generally attributed to women and children in the local vernacular, meaning a consumer who does not contribute to the family income. The film satirizes the helplessness of men when all women of a village, except a half-wit, die in a gas explosion. *Gülüşan* (1986) exposes the suppressed sexual world of a man whose yearning for a son reaches fanatic proportions. The film shows how in masculinist societies oppressed women express their anger through intrigues and devious means and show no pity for other oppressed women. When the first two wives cannot revolt against the husband who brings a younger third wife and obliges them to serve her, they abuse her handicap (she is blind) and build traps to kill her. Lack of solidarity among oppressed women has been pointed out in *Yol*, when the sister-in-law refuses Zine's gold bracelet because it was bought with 'stained' money; she has already judged Zine according to the opinion of her husband. In *Mutluluk / Bliss* (discussed below), the stepmother offers Meryem a rope to hang herself because Meryem is 'soiled', and again this is based on the opinion of men.

Olgaç said that she did not want to look at the woman as a woman and she did not propose a solution to women's predicaments.[18] Although her films, starting with *Spoon Enemy*, focus on the plight of women, her social and political stance is systematically in the foreground. She questions the feudal structure and the patriarchal system. In her films marriages between young girls and older men result in the madness or death of the woman. She condemns violence against women, harassment, rape and beating, and shows how honour, an important value, turns into a power tool in the hands of men. She also points to the fact that women's ignorance and lack of awareness plays a role in the continuation of the system of male hegemony. But above all she calls for an end to economic inequality, social exploitation and the oppression of revolutionary movements. At the end of her films the uninitiated poor lose. In the feudal system women are sexual objects for rich and poor men alike; they are doubly exploited. The only solution is to teach men and women political consciousness and to change the system to end exploitation.[19]

Parallel to the movement of 'women's films' by male filmmakers (Atıf Yılmaz) that gained popularity in the 1980s, a number of women filmmakers also entered the industry with stories that spotlighted women. However, their contributions in general do not represent a true picture of the life of the real woman; while trying to depict the modern woman, they reinforce the standards of morality established by men. In some of these films women in powerful positions delegate their power without much resistance to the man they love, or a career woman's achievements are measured not through her professional advancements but through her dealings with the opposite sex.

Mahinur Ergun presents the modern woman as an anomaly in her fourth film, *Ay Vakti / Moon Time* (1993). The film places the binaries of good woman / bad woman, housewife / free woman in their traditional context. The 'modern woman' is the young, urban and 'liberated' mistress of an older man. She is irresponsible (a bad mother) and ill mannered: she insults people, gets drunk, abuses those less powerful than her and simply runs in circles. The image the woman filmmaker draws of a free modern woman is that of a lost kitten. On the other hand, the provincial wife is

focused and in complete control. She is devious; while pretending to be under the authority of her man, she uses her housewifely skills (preparing her husband's favourite dishes, appearing calm and commiserating) to get him back. She may not succeed. But her character is better developed and is certain to arouse audience sympathy.

Women who oppose the classification of 'woman filmmaker' and prefer to deal with universal socio-political issues that touch men and women alike are more successful in creating films of artistic quality, although their female characters are in general designated secondary roles. Ustaoğlu's *Journey to the Sun* presents a world of men, where women play traditional roles, but within that context the character of Arzu, the girlfriend, is well drawn. In her conservative world she manages to find outlets. She is not afraid to search for Mehmet at the police station, or to bribe the authority at the morgue with her gold bracelets for the release papers for Berzan's coffin. However, it is Mehmet who goes through an evolution. Arzu supports him with her feminine instincts but this is not her journey. She works in a lauderette, the modernized version of a traditional job for women. Mothers, wives or girlfriends (the passive females) go to the police station to enquire about their

gender, sexuality and morals in transition | 155

'disappeared' men (the active males). Women take small risks: Arzu defies social customs by drinking beer in public, but she would not dream of carrying the coffin of a police victim and a Kurd all the way to the south-east. (In *Waiting for the Clouds*, discussed above, Ustaoğlu created a woman protagonist, but her alter ego in the film is not Eleni/Ayşe but the little boy Mehmet, who in a sense is the childhood of Mehmet in *Journey to the Sun*.)

Turkish cinema has traditionally followed the one-nation, one-language, one-religion official policy of the state, and its position on issues of gender and sexuality has not been different. One sexuality, heterosexuality, has been endorsed, designating the family as the ideal medium to practise this sexuality. 'Man–man and woman–woman sexual relations have been shown under a shroud, the intended meaning shifting according to audience sense of perception', Özgüç claims.[20] Such reticence is not peculiar to countries like Turkey, where Muslim tradition has conditioned society to conformism and has encouraged hypocrisy and double standards that have alienated individuals from their own selves. Alternative sexual identities have been gradually becoming more visible in Turkish life with repercussions in cinema, although filmmakers still exercise self-censorship and evade issues that would create controversy and endanger wide distribution.

Özgüç cites *Ver Elini Istanbul / Istanbul Give Me Your Hand* (1962) by Aydın Arakon, written by celebrated poet, author and columnist Atilla İlhan, as the first attempt at depicting lesbian relations. 'Two women tried to kiss each other with trepidation, but the rationale behind the kiss was obscure and the scene was cut by the censors.'[21] Atıf Yılmaz, with one eye on artistic concerns and the other on the box office, was the pioneer with *İki Gemi Yanyana / Two Ships Side by Side* (1963), showing two women kissing each other on the lips. Halit Refiğ's *Haremde Dört Kadın / Four Women in the Harem* (1965), a period film, drew attention to the oppressive atmosphere of the harem with several scenes of closet lesbianism and was criticized severely. From 1974 to 1980, however, the subject of lesbianism was exploited in what was called 'sex comedies' to evade censorship.[22] The year 1974 was the heyday of pornography. Censorship was very severe on political issues but closed its eyes to debasing women on the screen. Police began to raid porn movie houses only in the 1980s.[23]

Atıf Yılmaz's *Dul Bir Kadın / A Widow* (1985) was the most discussed film of 1985 with a new approach to sexuality. The erotic fantasies of two women and the comfort they found in each other – a tongue-in-cheek lesbianism – aroused an awkward curiosity in the audience, but also disturbed some. The premise of the film was two women's descent into hell while looking for an identity in a degenerate society. The settling of accounts with the opposite sex was also integral to the narrative: Ergun sleeps with two women using his masculinity as a weapon but at the end his masculinity is rejected by both. The film was denounced for smearing the image of men, particularly in the sentence 'men take their egoism all the way to bed'.

*A Widow*'s focus is an upper-class woman, widow of a diplomat, who tries to determine her place in a conservative society that expects the widow to resign from womanhood and live like a hermit. Where customs dictate that unmarried girls stay virgins, widows are most desirable and most vulnerable. Although moral values are flexible in the upper echelons of society, guilt feelings prevail, which prevent many women from coming out of the shell of widowhood. The uncustomary nature of this story is foreshadowed in the first few minutes of the film when the protagonist (the inimitable Müjde Ar) is shown with her eyes closed and her lips half open with desire while a flock of birds flies over her face, her naked shoulders, her arms and her breasts. Feminist overtones of the film in its approach to women are visible and commensurate with the feminist movements that gained ground in Turkey in the 1980s. (The fact that Yılmaz's wife was the feminist activist Deniz Türkali also contributed to this point of view, as Yılmaz admitted during our interview.)

Atıf Yılmaz's *Dul Bir Kadın / A Widow* (1985) aroused an awkward curiosity in the audience with its tongue-in-cheek lesbianism.

Following the official abolition of the censorship laws (1989), a large number of films experimented more openly with previously taboo sexual subjects. For a Turkish cinema that had perfected the art of 'wet lips' and 'eye-eroticism', this was no small revolution. *Denize Hançer Düştü / Balcony* (1992) by Mustafa Altıoklar, about two women attracted to each other while acting in Jean Genet's *The Balcony*; a young widow from a conservative immigrant family seeking auto-satisfaction in *Berlin in Berlin* (1993) by Sinan Çetin (Hülya Avşar masturbates while her brother-in-law watches through the keyhole); *Yellow Smile* (mentioned above), about a respectably married career woman yearning for a second partner for sexual pleasure; *Dönersen Islık Çal / Whistle If You Return* (1993) by Orhan Oğuz, the story of an unusual friendship between a dwarf barman and a transvestite prostitute, are examples.

*Düş Gezginleri / Walking After Midnight* (1992) by Atıf Yılmaz was the first film to show openly two women making love on the screen, although Yılmaz insisted that his aim was not to break taboos; lesbian relations existed in the Ottoman harem as well. His focus was not homosexuality but rather the distribution of power in society. 'The economically and culturally more privileged exercises power over the less privileged.'[24] And the film was criticized, notably in feminist circles, particularly for this aspect, for reducing the woman-to-woman relationships to an exercise of power.

Two childhood friends meet years later in a small town. One has become a doctor with a bourgeois lifestyle while the other is a prostitute. The doctor is presented as superficial and imbalanced while the prostitute is a 'working woman' with honour. The relationship, which the flashbacks confirm is more than platonic, is broken due to class difference. Eyuboğlu reads the prostitute as a metaphor for the working class and the nation trying to keep its head above water and the doctor as a metonym for the country. The latter's true face is revealed through her relationship with the prostitute, he points out, and the message is similar to that of the Bertolucci masterpiece, *Novecento* aka *1900* (1976) that inspired the film: there is nothing the *bourgeoisie* would not sell, not even their best friend, to safeguard their preferred status.[25]

*İki Kadın / Two Women* (1992) by Yavuz Özkan, released the same year, was also about a woman-to-woman relationship. A member of parliament rapes a sophisticated call girl who calls him impotent. The story is told from the point of view of the call girl and the narrative develops along her efforts to seek compensation. When she meets

*Düş Gezginleri / Walking After Midnight* (1992), dir. Atıf Yılmaz, the first film openly to show two women making love on the screen.

GEZGİNLERİ
MERAL OĞUZ-LÂLE MANSUR
yönetmen
ATIF YILMAZ

the MP's wife, the two women form an unusual friendship. Eyuboğlu claims that the film uses sexual impotence as a metaphor for politicians. The women of different socio-cultural and educational backgrounds have one common ground: they are both victims and in that sense they represent the nation 'raped' by impotent politicians. Like *Walking After Midnight*, Eyuboğlu asserts, *Two Women* does not try to approach the issues of women, but rather confirms Jacques Lacan's statement that the woman is 'absent'.[26] The woman is identified through relationships and associations with men.[27]

Lesbian stories possess intrinsic commercial value appealing to the fantasies of frustrated men, but homosexuality is taboo in societies that exalt manhood. Homosexual tendencies are usually kept under leash, and occasional escapades are dismissed as part of manhood as long as it is clear who plays the male role. According to Asuman Suner in Turkish cinema the homosexual man is typecast as a marginal character, whose parodying of feminine traits is intended for laughs. He often comes from the bourgeois class and works as a hairdresser, fashion designer or make-up artist. In general, homosexuality is used as an expression of decadence in society and the loss of moral values.[28]

Kutluğ Ataman, a multi-disciplinary artist and activist for gay rights, is the only filmmaker who takes the issue of identity, particularly sexual identity in a modern society, seriously and effectively throughout his work. He explores the fragility of personal identity through characters who have become dislocated from conventional categories and are compelled to reinvent themselves, be they a transvestite Turkish belly-dancer at the heart of Berlin (*Lola und Bilidikid / Lola and Bilidikid*, 1997) or an androgynous young rebel from the outskirts of Istanbul (*İki Genç Kız / Two Girls*, 2005). Ataman continually crosses the border between the past and the present and reality and fiction. He favours characters outside the norms, as in his Carnegie Prize-winning video installation *Kuba* (2004), a 40-channel video installation exposing a neighbourhood in Istanbul, home to criminals, drug addicts, teenage delinquents, religious radicals and the very poor, or *semiha b. unplugged* (1997) about the first opera singer of Turkey, an eccentric woman in her eighties, who dialogues with the camera for 465 minutes, recounting and at times reinventing her remarkable life without inhibitions (including a love affair with exiled poet Nazım Hikmet) in her baroque boudoir.

Tortured by the police during the 1980 military coup for filming political events with his Super-8 camera, Ataman left Turkey for the US and remained in exile for several years. After his first feature, *Karanlık Sular / The Serpent's Tale* (1994), an experimental mystery thriller, he turned his attention to video installations, exploring the boundaries between reality and fiction through the medium of documentary. His focus of interest has been the way that individuals construct their identities through telling stories about themselves and their experiences. For Kutluğ Ataman, who maintains that the subject of identity is taboo in Turkey, 'there are as many centres as there are individuals'.[29]

*Peruk Takan Kadınlar / Women Who Wear Wigs* (1999) is composed of four simultaneously run videos placed in a row. Ataman interviews four Turkish 'women' who wear wigs, each for a very different reason. Melek, a legendary figure in the political struggles of the 1970s, recounts how she escaped arrest during the military dictatorship by wearing a blonde wig and disguising herself as a stewardess. We never see her face – instead we are presented with the back of her head; the camera gets closer as she handles her wig while narrating her story to a dressing-table mirror. Nevval, a television personality, tells of her battle with breast cancer, the chemotherapy and its consequences on her self-image as a woman. She chose to wear a wig to maintain her feeling of femininity and to continue her career in television. An anonymous young Muslim student gives an account of her religious reasons for wearing a wig. She protests that her university does not allow Islamic women to cover their

*Karanlık Sular /*
*The Serpent's Tale*
(1994), dir.
Kutluğ Ataman.

hair. As she feels uncomfortable revealing herself, Ataman chooses to present a blank screen to the audience instead of her image, which may also be interpreted as a metaphor for the secular wish to render these women invisible. Demet Demir, a well-known transsexual activist who became a woman through surgery, uses the wig to maintain her income when the police cut her hair for prostitution or when it falls out due to stress. The work is a dialogue between the characters and their 'female identity', of which hair is the most important aspect. Beautiful long hair, desired by most men (endorsed by commercial cinema, television ads, etc.), connotes femininity. Devout Muslim women must forego femininity in public and hide their hair as a protection against the male gaze. Ataman considers *Women Who Wear Wigs* 'an aggressive political work, which is not about the wig but about women; the four women who seem different are in the same predicament'.[30]

*Never My Soul!* (2001) is a video work that takes its title from a clichéd phrase in Yeşilçam cinema: when the virginal female character is forced to have sex, she first struggles and then relents, exclaiming to her violator: 'You can have my body, but never my soul!' The focus of this work is Ceyhan Firart, a transsexual dialysis patient living in Switzerland. She is asked to assume the role of a Turkish star and, at the same time, play herself. In six different locations we are exposed to six different chapters of her life, a life of abuse, persecution and violence. Ataman first filmed Ceyhan narrating her story, which he then transcribed for Ceyhan to learn as a script before filming a second version. The result, which is deliberately incoherent as a single narrative, is what Ataman calls a 'parallax view' – a formal expression of Ceyhan's parallel situation as a transvestite.

Ataman's second feature film, *Lola und Bilidikid / Lola and Bilidikid* (1997), focuses on Turkish transvestites within the 'guest worker' community of Berlin, who are subject to social prejudices by their own people in an environment where discrimination is already a threat. 'The Turkish community refutes the prejudicial behaviour of the Germans but displays the same discriminatory attitude towards their homosexuals and their women', Ataman explains. 'The film is not only about homosexuals, it is also the reflection of all ethnic identities in Turkey. I tried to tell the conflict between the minority culture and the dominant culture.'[31]

*Never My Soul!* (2001), dir. Kutluğ Ataman.

*Lola and Bilidikid* develops parallel themes of homophobia, the search for visibility in a foreign environment and the yearning for a sense of belonging. Osman, Lola and Murat, sons of a guest worker family, live in Kreutzberg, the Turkish ghetto in Berlin. Osman, the eldest, becomes the head of the family after the death of his father and begins to rule with an iron fist following patriarchal tradition. Within the confines of his imposed identity he represses his natural instincts, except when he is in a position to exercise power on the meeker. (We learn at the end of the film that he raped his brother, later called Lola, several times before throwing him out for 'not being a man'.) Lola is the star of a transvestite show called *Die Gastarbeiterinnen / The Female Guestworkers* and in love with Bilidikid, who loves him (her) but cannot forego his machismo. Sixteen-year-old Murat is curious about gay life. He is not aware that he has a brother called Lola, but in Lola he finds the brotherly love denied at home. Violence erupts when family secrets come out of the closet.

Ataman underscores the alienation of the individual to his being in the industrialized and cold atmosphere of Berlin. The night scenes in desolate parks that shelter men who try to forget their loneliness in the comfort of another warm body reflect the stark reality facing outcasts anywhere and these images resemble the night scenes in *The Bus*, when the Turks react to the land of the unknown with trepidation but also curiosity. Ataman's handling of the question of sexual identity, however, is very precise. Lola's lover Bilidikid thinks he is a man because he is the one who penetrates. He wants Lola to have an operation so that they can move to Turkey and live as man and wife, like normal people do. Notwithstanding his *macho* appearance, Bilidikid yearns for an uncomplicated identity that would help him belong to a society without facing discrimination. He wants to be invisible while being visible. On the other hand, Lola fears that a 'normal life' will destroy his relationship with Bilidikid, who likes him for his 'otherness'.

Murat is introduced to the dark side of Berlin against the background of the statue of an angel, the redemption and hope in the film.[32] He explores his own sexual inclinations with a German school friend. Then he discovers that Lola is his brother. After the neo-Nazis beat him, he questions his mother about Lola but all she can do is warn him to stay away from Lola, who was disowned by the family. Murat wants to help Bilidikid to avenge Lola's death. Wearing Lola's red wig he lures the neo-Nazis into a deserted building, where

the two radical characters of both cultures, Bilidikid, who embodies the machismo of the Turkish male, and the Hitler-inspired neo-Nazi leader, attack and kill each other. After the self-destruction of the extreme elements of both cultures, director Ataman places Murat and one of the neo-Nazi youth at a corner in the building, abandoned both physically and metaphorically. There, in a state of panic, beaten and bloodied, the two are stripped of their cultural differences, they become human, and they become the same.³³

Lola is actually killed by his brother Osman. This revelation releases the mother from the role of the passive female veiled inside the house; she walks out into the public space leaving her scarf on the pavement. Unlike Turna of Başer's *40m² of Germany,* the mother here is capable of 'unveiling' herself from the traditions that had imprisoned her under the pretext of false security. Murat, representing the second generation, also rejects the patriarchy that has oppressed his identity. Powerless Osman is left behind in the Turkish ghetto.

Women are no longer depicted as victims, asexual nonentities or sexual toys. The dialogue from a 2007 movie quoted at the beginning of the chapter would have been unheard of in a Yeşilçam movie. Times have changed and so have the moral values of a once tightly closed society. However, serious studies of women and their predicaments are new to contemporary Turkish cinema. In the films of some accomplished film-makers women still appear as less-developed secondary characters, in their traditional roles and within the confines of Muslim traditional ethics.

The films of Nuri Bilge Ceylan focus on men. In *Distant* women are represented as wife, mistress, sister and mother, the traditional roles that Turkish cinema has attributed to women; they do not have names and exist only in the presence of the protagonist, Mahmut. For the audi-

gender, sexuality and morals in transition | 165

ence to hear their voices, Mahmut must press the button of the answering machine. Except for two scenes, when the mistress cries silently in the toilet and when she walks out of the building and into her car under the scrutiny of the Anatolian building superintendent (another male gaze), the women need Mahmut's gaze. His mother is hardly visible in the low light of her hospital room and when he takes her along a dimly lit corridor (to the memories of his childhood, perhaps), she is only seen from behind.

Mahmut's sister walks in and out of doors in a clearly reproachful manner (reminding the protagonist of his past negligence of his family). In her apartment, furnished in a clearly different style from his (leaning more to the bourgeois tastes of the modern middle class rather than the middle-class intellectual artist), his ex-wife's picture is still on the mantelpiece. Who are these women? What do they do in life? Why can't Mahmut openly recognize his mistress in public? The narrative is indifferent to aspects that do not directly involve Mahmut. Regarding his ex-wife, we are privy to one event in their past life together: her abortion. Even on this subject she says the words he would like to hear: 'I am not blaming you.'

In *İklimler / Climates* (2006), also by Ceylan, the female protagonist has a name and a profession apart from her identity as girlfriend/partner. (She is played by Ceylan's real-life wife, Ebru.) Bahar is the artistic director of a minor TV series; an insignificant position compared to her partner's, the university lecturer writing a thesis on Roman ruins. In the opening scene Isa, the scholar, is immersed in his work onanistically (even on holiday, at the expense of neglecting Bahar), taking pictures of ruins. For him Bahar's job is so insignificant that towards the end he crosses the country to tell her to leave it and come back with him. Isa is a macho Mediterranean male with difficulty relating to women, especially if they are gentle like Bahar. He cheats on her with a woman who will give him violent sex and who can beat him at his own game. The fact that this woman is his friend's mistress adds to the sense of victory. The conversations with his equally macho colleague (with an equally fragile ego), taking place in the office, tennis court or sauna, and in the absence of women, are revealing about male–female issues in Turkey, which seem not to be much different in the urban milieu among the educated elite than in the countryside. Although the thrust of the film is the disintegration of a relationship, the structure of the narrative sides with the male character. The point of view of the female partner,

In *İklimler / Climates* (2006) by Nuri Bilge Ceylan the female partner's feelings and dilemmas are conveyed through her silence – the traditional attribute of women in society and in cinema.

her feelings and her dilemmas, are felt through her silences (the traditional attribute of women in society and in cinema).

The protagonist of Tayfun Pirselimoğlu's first feature, *Hiçbiryerde / Innowhereland* (2002), which has had national and international success, is a woman who undertakes a journey across the country in search of her missing son. In the last two decades more than 3,000 people have disappeared in Turkey; some while in police custody, others just vanishing without a trace or being found dead in a morgue, like Berzan in *Journey*

*to the Sun* (incidentally based on a story by Pirselimoğlu). For a time the mothers (most of them Kurdish) protested peacefully every Saturday in front of the Galatasaray University in Beyoğlu (The Saturday Mothers), but gave up due to intimidations, arrests and beatings.

Pirselimoğlu presents Şükran, who works at the ticket counter of the central train station, as a passive woman who feels inferior to men and is treated accordingly. When she enters the office of her boss the camera shows her as a diminutive figure in front of the heavily built man. Her behaviour has a timid and submissive aura; her head is bent to the side, almost like a beggar asking for something she has no right to ask, or she looks down like a schoolchild reprimanded in the office of the principal. Consequently, her boss treats her like a lost kitten and says he will help her only for the sake of her dead husband, who was enough of a trouble-maker. In her refusal to accept the political involvement of either her husband or her son she uses official channels – the police, the governor's office – for news, the least likely places for that kind of information, according to Pirselimoğlu. They all tell her: 'Go home, lady!'

The first part of the film reinforces the dominance of men and the notion of their superiority. Men act (Şükran's husband was an activist; her son Veysel is probably an activist) and women wait. They wait for destiny, or God. Şule, Veysel's girlfriend, vents her anger on the more vulnerable, raging like a bull, but only running in circles. She is present-ed as an unattractive tomboyish woman, wearing fatigues, the usual cliché for the woman activist, whereas passive Şükran is feminine even in her misery. (The rationale for creating such a passive woman charac-ter is rather obscure and her passivity is not very believable considering she is a working woman surviving on her own in a metropolis.)[34]

The dramatic effect is heightened when Şükran, who is 'invisible' as a woman in a modern city like Istanbul, embarks on a long journey to a part of the world where women are irrefutably invisible – not a single woman on the streets of Mardin. Pirselimoğlu uses the conventions of the *road movie*, which had been male-oriented until recently, to plunge her without defence into the world of men. On the train journey small signs of the transformation of Şükran's character are visible. Offering grapes to the two gendarmes and their prisoner shows her motherly instincts, but letting the prisoner escape while the guards sleep is an indication of active involvement. Although in Mardin she tears down the walls of her submissive world and yells at men to find her son, the final scene when she returns home to her empty apartment and caresses her son's jacket hanging in the doorway is ambivalent. Has she evolved through her experience? The poster of the film shows Şükran covering her face with her hands except for a slight opening of the fingers on one side.

In depicting the modern woman in a society where morals are in transition, the films of Zeki Demirkubuz (discussed in chapter Six) are more insightful. In *Masumiyet / Innocence* (1997) Demirkubuz exposes the double standards of a society where a man kills his sister's lover to preserve the family honour, but willingly pimps for a prostitute. A woman who is judged as 'fallen' by society can be someone with individuality, who merits respect (like Uğur who Yusuf loves madly), while another woman can be punished with violence for 'innocent' love (the sister Yusuf shoots for trying to elope with her lover). Yusuf is the personification of the double standards of men. The irony in the title is a reminder to the audience to re-examine their convictions before passing judgement on others. Demirkubuz shows that both Yusuf's sister and Uğur live in a world dominated by men. The sister is a typical 'family woman' from the poor class whose honour needs to be protected; Uğur is from a world that considers women as merchandise. The difference is that Uğur's 'fall' is her liberation, whereas the sister's 'honour' is a curse. Uğur chooses the life she lives, but Yusuf's sister does not have this chance.[35]

In the second half of the 2000s several courageous works have appeared exposing sexual taboos, particularly regarding violence against women, drawing attention to the reality that social maladies will not disappear through denial of their existence. Semih Kaplanoğlu's *Meleğin Düşüşü / Angel's Fall* (2004) is about incest. The film opens with Zeynep walking slowly up a hill wearing layers of baggy clothes and heavy boots. She holds a spool of yellow thread in her hand, which she ties to a wooden post and pulls, but the string snaps. The distraught Zeynep goes down, re-wraps the thread and begins to climb, but the thread breaks again. She starts to cry as she clomps down the hill, back to the post. She loops the thread around the post a few times and proceeds up the hill again. As she walks off the frame the screen turns black and the title appears in a bold yellow font.

In the next scene Zeynep stands on the edge of a precipice, the landscape beneath her feet like a pretty picture on a wall, timeless and elusive. In the last scene of the film Zeynep stands naked (and light like a feather)

*Masumiyet / Innocence* (1997), dir. Zeki Demirkubuz, exposes the double standards of a society where morals are in transition.

in front of a high balcony. Over her shoulder we see the city with the overpowering Galata tower in the distance and the waters of the Golden Horn almost beneath her feet; the city looks very much alive, a flock of birds in the sky suggesting hope. Between these two elevated places, darkness prevails. The long corridors of the hotel where she works are dark; her father's workplace is dark and the streets are dark. The homes are also very dark. Everything important happens in darkness.

Zeynep works in a hotel, a transitory and impersonal space, but home is not a shelter either; on the contrary, home is foreboding and uncanny. Zeynep's body is violated each night by her father. In another part of town Selçuk's wife, Funda, walks out of her home that harbours lies and deceit, only to return to witness her husband having sex with a neighbour and to slash her wrists.

For the characters of Kaplanoğlu there is no home; it is a nightmare. In that sense, what the young man from the hotel who is in love with Zeynep suggests at the end is significant: 'Let's go to my home town,' he says, 'we would live happily there', which implies the possibility of a third space, but Zeynep knows that for the dis/misplaced, there is no return. Before Zeynep appears naked in front of the balcony, she drinks several glasses of water. Water is life. Will the 'angel' fall (to the earth) as the title suggests? Or fly high?

Kaplanoğlu asserts that home is also connected to identity. Zeynep wears someone else's clothes and wishes to be another woman, perhaps like the woman she observes in the hotel corridor. While she is watching a television programme dressed in a red negligee and wearing high heels, clothes that had belonged to Selçuk's dead wife, her father arrives. Their eyes meet for a second. Zeynep, like a typical young Turkish woman, is very embarrassed to be seen by her father in seductive clothes despite what goes on between them in the darkness of the night. In her guilt she rushes to change into her usual oversized clothes and prepares the dinner hurriedly, her body language revealing her wish to be invisible. Her father waits until she serves his meal, then slaps her before proceeding with his dinner. Sexuality is sin when it is visible. Later, when we see her dragging her father's body, we think of an earlier scene when she had to drag her badly beaten and drunk father from the street as he muttered: 'let's go *home.*' But this time it is different. The bathroom is splattered with blood. When divine justice does not arrive Zeynep takes justice in her own hands.

Sexuality is sin when it is visible. Semih Kaplanoğlu's *Meleğin Düşüşü / Angel's Fall* (2005).

Weight – arising from the feeling of guilt, helplessness and loneliness – is a strong leitmotif in the film.

The thread Zeynep unspools in the opening scene is an allusion to a Turkish tradition: before the religious holidays, women tie a piece of thread to wooden posts and begin to walk up a long winding hill. The thread represents a wish. If they reach the top without breaking the thread, then their wish will be granted. On numerous occasions Zeynep plays with the spool, unwinding the thread and muttering prayers, an indication of her obsession with the eventual fulfilment of her wish.

Weight, arising from the feeling of guilt, helplessness and loneliness, is a strong leitmotiv in the film. Just as she pulls her estranged body up the slope in the opening scene, Zeynep pulls luggage full of a dead woman's clothes up another slope, the luggage that promises her a new identity and with a twist of fate will be instrumental in her releasing herself from the heaviest burden of all, her incestuous father.

*Angel's Fall* is a charged but silent film. Until six minutes and eighteen seconds into it, there is no dialogue, then one single word. The first dialogue is heard seven minutes and eighteen seconds after the film begins. For Kaplanoğlu,

> the silence in this film is a metaphor for the sufferings of the women who are victims of incest. They are so ashamed of themselves that they remain silent, confiding in no one except God. Words are replaced with the language of the body. Zeynep is a stranger to her body, the only home she could claim ownership. Most incest victims are in a state of denial. They continue their lives in normalcy as seen in the scene when the father and the daughter sit down and have tea together discussing mundane matters.[36]

During the national film festival, Golden Orange in Antalya, in 2007, three films specifically dealt with honour killings. The subject is not new to Turkish cinema. Yeşilçam favoured the exploitative nature of the topic, but committed filmmakers such as Yılmaz Güney boldly exposed violence in the name of customs and traditions. Şerif Gören's *Yol* is built around the theme of honour killing. A lesser-known work, nonetheless a classic of Turkish cinema, is *Berdana* (1974) by Süreyya Duru, a strong indictment of the customs and rigid morals of Anatolian society.

*Mutluluk / Bliss* (2007), dir. Abdullah Oğuz.

More than thirty years after *Berdana* honour killings are conspicuously on the agenda. Abdullah Oğuz, director of *Mutluluk / Bliss* (2007), was motivated by a news item in a magazine: in one year 64 girls between the ages of 13 and 16 were killed and all deaths were staged as suicide.[37] The film is based on an eponymous novel by Zülfü Livanelli. In the southern part of Anatolia, Meryem, a young girl, is found unconscious lying in the mud in a compromising manner and her family declares her to be 'soiled'. She is locked in an ominously dark storage room just like Zine in *Yol*, waiting for a man to do the honourable deed: to kill her. Meryem is offered a rope by her stepmother, but she is too young and full of life to hang herself as other girls have been doing when faced with the same situation. A solution is found by appointing a killer, Cemal, a cousin about to finish his military service. He will take her to Istanbul on false pretences and kill her there and no one will know about it. Cemal was a commando in the army and he is proud to have done his duty by killing terrorists (i.e., Kurds). 'Her Türk asker doğar' (every Turk is born a soldier) is his favourite motto. Just as he has done his duty to his country by eliminating 'subversive elements' without blinking an eye, now he will prove himself worthy of his family by cleansing their tarnished honour by killing Meryem. It is of little importance that Meryem was a childhood friend and perhaps she is innocent. A soldier's duty is to follow orders. However, through the mediation of a third element, a disillusioned intellectual, the young couple fall in love, and forgive and forget when the real culprit is finally exposed.

Beautifully shot from the east to the west of the country like a road movie, with remarkable performances by the talented young duo and without resorting to melodrama, the film has a powerful impact on the audience. A less subtle aspect is that in order to heighten the dramatic impact of the innocence of Meryem, other women in the film are shown in their stereotypical 'bad' roles: a heinous stepmother, a spoiled student who appears in a bikini (a Yeşilçam cliché) and a rich wife too proud to accept desertion. However, *Bliss* is remarkable as the first attempt in emphasizing not only the issue of honour killings but also

the vulnerability of women, particularly in rural areas, who are often abused by members of their families and pay a high price when the culprits go free.

Despite its tragic premise, *Bliss* is a hopeful film, showing how the old customs of the East gradually fade and younger generations acquire a different set of values when they move to the cities. The older brother, who is settled in Istanbul, thinks it is insane to kill a young girl to save the family honour. Freed from the pressures of his claustrophobic village where relatives decide one's destiny before one is born and men prove their manhood by exercising brute force over women, Cemal is able to listen to his conscience and see the absurdity of equating family honour with the so-called purity of women. The happy ending, although fashioned after Hollywood, is significant in pointing out the possibility of a 'third space' for Meryem and Cemal. In that sense, the killing of the uncle by the girl's father is symbolic: the one who orders the *fatwa* for Meryem's execution is the one responsible for the ugly deed and freedom from oppression is possible only by destroying it.

For Handan İpekçi (*Hejar*), however, there is no reprieve for women so long as they do not revolt against archaic customs. The feudal mentality does not change with the move to the West or the passage of time. In *Saklı Yüzler / Hidden Faces* (2007), about a young woman killed for having a sexual relationship out of wedlock, the obsession to cleanse the 'tarnished' honour of the family is carried to new environments, Istanbul and Germany, for over five years. İpekçi is also interested in how men who kill their mothers, daughters, aunts or sisters deal with their consciences. Zühre's father kills himself rather than killing his daughter and the brother is deeply scarred by the monstrosity of killing Zühre's new-born baby, an act he commits under threat. However, studies show that most perpetrators of honour killings do not show remorse, and in prison they are treated like heroes. İpekçi points out the dichotomy in Turkish society. On the one hand, women become judges (as in the film), journalists and filmmakers; on the other, they are slaughtered. Mothers do not fight against the murder of their daughters or their sons becoming murderers. Instead, they endorse honour killings. 'The only solution lies in the women taking destiny in their own hands, to stop the mentality that considers women as men's property and to fight against the notion that virginity is a commodity.'[38] Although the protagonist cannot be saved and her mother is helpless, at the end of the film an aunt who has already established authority over the men of the clan metaphorically takes over the video camera of the documentarian who has been recording the honour killings.

*Janjan* (2007) by Aydın Sayman, which focuses on the malaise of 'bought brides', also draws attention to an important social problem involving unemployed youth in the closed societies of small towns, whose anger as well as sexual repression is ready to explode. An important aspect of modernity, the Internet, is added to the narrative, pointing to the dangers of cyber-cafés as hang-outs for misguided youth, with easily available porn sites that endorse violence against women. The film is very timely, as a new term has been coined in the Turkish media, 'neighbourhood Islam' meaning 'neighbourhood pressure', which can have fascist dimensions that may lead to lynching when the question is honour, not unlike the fate of school teacher Aliye in Lütfi Ö. Akad's *Strike the Whore*, made almost six decades ago.

Despite the bleak picture these films paint, there has been significant openness in recent years regarding sexuality and alternative sexual choices. Sexual freedom for women is still relative and honour killings *do* exist, but at least in the urban milieu the younger women have better opportunities than previous generations to take charge of their bodies, their careers, their emotions and their intellect.

In Istanbul, the young are out until late hours, walking freely around Beyoğlu, the SoHo of Istanbul that some decades ago was a trap for country lads and deceived and deserted maidens, as Yeşilçam showed us. They have a drink with their friends at the cafés, shop for books until midnight, go to the movies or the disco. No one seems to be concerned about sexual preferences. However, this part of Istanbul is like 'liberated territory', metaphorized as a local hang-out in Serdar Akar's *Barda / In the Bar* (2006), where the 'grey Turks' of Nilüfer Göle (see Introduction) are outsiders. Violence explodes when the 'other' from the outskirts of town, from the traditional devout families with conservative values, trespasses.[39] For the 'intruders' the choices are not about free sex or abstinence, abortion or marriage, or the choice of a private university for postgraduate studies (discussions heard in the beginning of the film, among the 'beautiful' middle-class children with educated families who support them). The boys from the periphery, usually belonging to conservative migrant families, are conditioned to respect only women like their mothers or sisters: obedient, devout, faithful and virginal. Whether the bloodbath that ensues justifies the message is another issue, but the film draws attention to the widening

Serdar Akar's *Barda /
In the Bar* (2006)
draws attention to
the widening of the
gap between social
and economic classes
in Turkish society,
which disadvantages
women.

of the gap between classes in Turkish society, which greatly disadvantages women.

Crossing over the Golden Horn, the streets are deserted after 9 p.m. Secrets remain behind closed doors, like the porn magazines hidden under the bed of Behiye's upright brother in *Two Girls*, or Zeynep's incestuous father who arrives beside her bed in the dark in *Angel's Fall*. Those who search for an identity that clashes with their environment grab their bag and leave like Behiye, from the periphery, to be consumed by the city and rejected, or like Zeynep commit parricide to liberate their souls from the oppressive feelings of guilt. In a multilayered society that evolves constantly, where morals are in a constant transition, there are as many outlets as there are problems. Turkish filmmakers' interest, particularly in the new millennium, in the real issues of men and women alike, in a sincere, honest, analytical and non-judgemental way, is a feat for Turkish cinema and perhaps a liberation for Turkish society.

# 6 A Modern Identity or Identity in a Modern World

How do young artists approach the shifting values of a society in a constant move to secure its place in the modern world while preserving its identity? What do they think when they gaze at the breathtaking sunsets behind the polluted skyline of the Byzantine churches and the Ottoman mosques? Do they read about deaths, disappearances and unsolved crimes in the daily papers? Do they join the silent majority and live day by day without a vision for a better future? Or do they assume responsibility as artists to mirror their society and through creative awareness make it more respectful of its individuals, regardless of gender, religion, race or political allegiance?

The new Turkish cinema that emerged in the late 1990s is in search of new economic, aesthetic and thematic models in interpreting Turkish national and personal identity in the modern world. From art-house films to box-office hits, the main concerns of the films of the new generation are similar: unemployment, survival in the urban jungle, search for an identity in a changing society, the threat to physical and/or mental space/territory and the general atmosphere of fear and not belonging when faced with the question of identity: national, social, religious, political and sexual. 'This thematic fixation can be seen as a response to a growing anxiety in Turkish society around the questions of identity and belonging following the 1980 military coup', claims Asuman Suner, stressing the fact that the neo-liberal policies of the 1980s have led to technological reforms, particularly in the information and communication sectors, and eased the way for Turkey's integration into the capitalist system, but have also resulted in widening the gap in income levels. Coupled with the civil war that has been raging in the south-east against the Kurdish guerrillas, 'questions of belonging and identity in Turkish society have become sites of intense and conflicting emotions, manifest-ed in the growing popularity of nationalist discourses on the one hand, and increased cynicism about, and distrust of, community relations and collective identity on the other'.[1]

Film-school graduates or products of the traditional apprentice-master system, the filmmakers of this new vitality are familiar with the national cinematic tradition, but they have also had the opportunity to study the cinema of the West, not only the theory and the aesthetics, but also alternative modes of production and exhibition. Derviş Zaim, Nuri Bilge Ceylan and Zeki Demirkubuz, who have entered the industry with improvised films about the ordinary lives of ordinary people, are the pioneers of the independent low-budget film in Turkish cinema.

A significant point is that the New Turkish cinema (which is called the New New Turkish Cinema by some critics, not to confuse this development with the New Cinema started in 1970 with Güney's *The Hope* or the new trends in the cinema of the 1980s) is not a *nouvelle vague* in the French sense. There are evident similarities in terms of the dominance of the *auteur* and the *mise-en-scène*, the self-reflexive counter-cinema practices, a deliberate distanciation to avoid audience identification, the subversion of genres, the use of counterpoint and elliptic editing, the attention to camera work and the script (often written by the filmmaker) and the use of professional actors sparingly, but New Turkish Cinema is not a 'wave'. The conduit each filmmaker chooses is unique to them, despite thematic and artistic convergence points and parallels in modes of production.

Derviş Zaim calls his generation 'alluvionic filmmakers': they flow in the same direction, but the linkages take different forms; they work 'inde-pendently but also parallel to one another, similar to the sediments of alluvium that together form an alluvion. At times, they come together, and at times, spread apart, as do alluvia'. This analogy, he believes, is accurate in defining the dynamics and diversity of the group, which pursues differ-ent styles and different forms of production, financing and distribution.[2]

Zaim's debut feature *Tabutta Rövaşata / Somersault in a Coffin* (1996) can be considered a landmark in the emergence of this new period in Turkish cinema. The film was shot in 24 days, although the project had existed for eight years. The budget was negligible; the actors, except two, were non-professionals. The originality of *Somersault in a Coffin* lies in the manner it alternates neo-realism, science fiction and fantasy. The nar-rative, the dialogues, the decor and the acting are all very simple. The *Sufi* overtones of the background music are unobtrusive but effective in building the mood. Its unpretentious and minimalist approach is an antidote to the hyperbolic and theatrical tradition of Yeşilçam commercial cinema.

Trying to do a 'no budget' film was harder than trying to do a somersault in a coffin, according to Derviş Zaim, who got the idea for an underground project while taking a course in London. He wanted to tell the story of a down-and-out character he knew: a thief with a heart of gold who washed the cars he stole before returning them to the spot from where he had stolen them. Well-known theatre actor Ahmet Uğurlu volunteered for the lead; Tuncel Kurtiz of international fame (*The Herd*) accepted the supporting role as Reis; the fishermen's hangouts along the Bosporus served as decor and this is how Turkey's first *guerrilla style* film was born, a film that represents 'the aesthetics of lack' according to Zaim.[3]

The original title of the film uses a soccer term, *rövaşat*, meaning bicycle kick, replaced by 'somersault' in the English title. Both are impossible to perform inside the closed space of a coffin. From the manner it was produced to the dispositions of the characters towards life, the film is about pushing the borders. What makes Mahsun and the others around him dramatic characters is that they try to build an equilibrium in their lives – to have a home, a shelter, someone to love – under impossible conditions, but have the capacity to reject this equilibrium and anything else that seems normal or rational.[4]

Mahsun (which ironically means strong and firm in Ottoman Turkish)[5] lives on the street and steals cars to find a warm place to sleep and to satisfy his yearning for high technology. Mahsun has no home, no past and definitely no future. His life oscillates between the cars he steals (a transitional shelter from the cold nights of the Bosporus) and the police station (where he is beaten and tortured). Both are claustrophobic spaces, but the outside world does not offer any respite either. One day, as he watches a television crew shooting a film in front of the Rumelihisarı fortress built by Conqueror Sultan Mehmet II during the siege of Constantinople, he learns that the peacocks, which were considered a symbol of prosperity and abundance by the Ottomans, were brought from Iran to the fortress by Mehmet II before the siege, but after he died the birds slowly disappeared. The President of Turkey, Süleyman Demirel, receiving 50 peacocks as a gift from the Iranian president, decided to donate these to the fortress as part of the new policy to decorate the historical landmarks of the city to attract tourists. For

Mahsun the peacock becomes the symbol of love and beauty he can never attain. Real love and beauty arrive in the form of a young woman named Fulya, an outcast like himself who regularly shoots heroin in the washroom of the *çayhane* (the seashore tea-house where Mahsun hangs out with his fishermen friends).[6]

The cruise boats that ply the currents of the Bosporus with loud music that disrupts the night are unaware of the homeless on the shore. At the entrance to the fortress Japanese tourists take photos, but when Mahsun tries to pass through the gate he is stopped by the guard. Now he needs a ticket. As the city engages in the global race for tourism, people like Mahsun are rejected. He has to wait for the night to jump over the fence. In his exclusion the peacock becomes Mahsun's sole connection with the outside world; he can express himself only through the peacock. He confides in the bird, telling him all his troubles but when he is hungry he decides to eat it. The irony is clear. Flag-waving nationalism does not fill the stomach![7]

The story of Mahsun's 'transgression' reaches his pals at the tea-house through the television screen, which has penetrated the lives of the ordinary citizens, particularly in the 1990s with the spread of private channels, making private public and widening the distance between human dramas and human feelings with nonchalant and monotonous

Derviş Zaim's debut feature, *Tabutta Rövaşata / Somersault in a Coffin* (1996).

a modern identity or identity in a modern world | 183

repetition of crime and terror, global, national or individual. In this scene the television is heard but not seen by the audience. In a high-angle shot that emphasizes their vulnerability, the characters look at the spectators as they watch in amazement the absurd drama of someone familiar recounted in a matter-of-fact, distant, but also judgemental manner. The announcer repeats the declaration of Mahsun at the police station: 'I am unemployed, I am hungry, if they did not catch me, I would have eaten the peacock.' Then she adds: 'if you want to know the details of the story, stay with us. We'll be back after the commercials.'[8]

Istanbul, the minarets, the bridges, the hilltops and the shores of the Bosporus, are an integral part of almost every film, as mentioned in the Introduction. The Bosporus is a venue for the rich to indulge in expensive restaurants and bars. But in *Somersault* the Bosporus is not a decoration. The tea-house, a familiar hang-out for pre-1980s youth, as critic Sungu Çapan reminisces, is turned into a cement block;[9] the only regulars are a heroin addict, some fishermen and desperate Mahsun who has not paid for the 600 glasses of tea he drank in three months, a reminder of Turgut Özal's 'rags to riches' policy that widened the gap between the poor and rich. The camera often juxtaposes the shots of the suspension bridge that links the two continents, the symbol of modernity as many Turks would proudly declare, with the destitute men nibbling a piece of dry bread in the cold of the night, presented in foreboding grey tones. Mahsun tries to rebel against the societal impositions that compartmentalize individuals according to their class status; the lifestyle of Fulya is a reaction to the society that standardizes individuals. For those who do not belong, the cold and cruel Bosporus, on the shores of which a man can freeze to death (fisherman Sarı), is a bitter reminder of their exclusion.

The legendary charm of Istanbul that had been the inspiration of countless films and poems is replaced with an atmosphere of fear and terror in the films of the new generation. The element of terror under-lining the narrative of *Somersault* reflects a society that has experienced the terror of military regimes and civil war and has become dangerously immune to tragedy thanks to the aggressive mass media that have chosen ratings rivalry over professional ethics. The crimes of passion or honour, graphic images of daily traffic accidents or ethnic oppression and violence have now penetrated into the familiar private space (such as one's living room), contributing to collective indifference and creat-ing characters like Musa in *Yazgı / Fate* by Zeki Demirkubuz, who can no longer show a reaction. The violence next door (the neighbour beating his mistress) or outside the window (a blurred image of the poor scavenging in the dark while Musa's eyes are glued on the TV screen) is little different from the violence on television one can watch while sitting on a comfortable sofa. It is 'someone else's agony'.

Zaim's next three films, *Filler ve Çimen / Elephants and Grass* (2000), *Çamur / Mud* (2003) and *Cenneti Beklerken / Waiting for Heaven* (2006), show coming to terms with the past and the collective memory as a means of interpreting the present, although the question of identity and belonging is at the core of all his work. 'The preoccupations with history and memory, closely tied to issues of identity based on nationality, gender, race, and sexual orientation, is one of the major indications of a "fin de millennium" cultural and economic crisis that often comes disguised within the notion of "an end to history"', according to Marcia Landy, although 'as Derrida has cautioned, we may not be witnessing an end to history so much as an end to revered and traditional notions of historicity'.[10] *Elephants and Grass* and *Mud* approach two highly political issues of recent Turkish history, respectively the criminal organization within the state, identified as 'deep state', and the trauma of the partition of the island of Cyprus for its inhabitants. Both films begin with the Turkish army flexing its muscles: a military parade in *Elephants* and soldiers receiving the daily pep talk from the commander on the island of Cyprus in *Mud*. In the latter, ironically, a veteran of the '1974 Peace Operation' (the invasion of the island by the Turkish army) collapses before the sermon is over while the camera gives us a glimpse of the famous emblem of Atatürk, 'How happy is the one who says I am a Turk!', hanging on the door of the barracks.

*Elephants* is loosely based on the 'Susurluk' scandal of 1996, when a traffic accident near the town of that name exposed the involvement of the government and the police with the mafia and other illegal elements. The former deputy chief of the Istanbul police; the leader of the Grey Wolves (a violent nationalist youth organization), a convicted fugitive wanted for drug trafficking and murder; and a beauty queen turned mafia hit-woman died in the incident. A member of parliament who was also at the head of a large group of village guards in the southeast, where war was raging against the Kurdish guerrillas, was injured. Several handguns, silencers and narcotics were found in the car. The fact that they were travelling together exposed the connection between the security forces, politicians and organized crime, and resulted in the resignation of the Interior Minister and the suspension of the police chief of Istanbul. But the issue of what came to be known as 'deep state' has remained a burning issue, as revealed in other instances, including the assassination of the Armenian journalist Hrant Dink.

The title of the film refers to an old saying 'when the elephant stomps, the grass suffers'. Using fictional characters, the narrative is built around a woman athlete named Havva Adem (Eve Adam, symbolizing 'everyman'), who needs sponsorship for an upcoming marathon. If she wins she will use the prize money for an operation on her brother, confined to a wheelchair after stepping on a mine while fighting Kurdish guerrillas during his military service.

Havva works in an *ebru* (a Farsi word meaning cloud) atelier, practising the Ottoman art of marbling on paper. Havva's life, just like the drops in the marbling pot, is directed as if touched by a superior power. At the end, she tries to do the impossible. As it snows, she does *ebru* in the pool of the atelier, which is against the nature of the art. 'Perhaps *ebru* cannot be practised under the snow but for the sake of freedom, we must continue to try it.'[11]

The film is overcharged with a plot-sub-plot labyrinth that at times confuses the spectator (politics, mafia, PKK, suicide bombers, drug-trafficking Colombians, the secret intelligence service, Alevis), but it is an important manifestation of cinema's contribution to the preservation of collective memory,[12] to which end Zaim uses several symbols, including the eraser, which gives the capacity to obliterate mistakes, but also the incentive to repeat them.

The war in Cyprus and the partition of the island following the Turkish invasion of 1974 is an important issue that was not approached by Turkish filmmakers conscientiously and from the point of view of the Cypriots. As mentioned in chapter Two, at the time of the invasion Yeşilçam exploited the subject to churn out nationalist war melodramas exalting the feats of the army, but no attempt was made to tell the stories of the uprooted people. *Mud* by Zaim, a Turkish Cypriot, is the first fiction film to underscore the trauma of the displaced and victimized as pawns in a political match. Through the tropes of earth, mud and the confinement, *Mud* tries to tell the story of an island where ethnic identity, manipulated for political gains, resulted in mortal clashes. Zaim uses different modes of narrative in a manner commensurate with the character of the island, where reality is constantly changing. Destiny and free will, the central theme of *Elephants*, is fundamental in *Mud* as well. The film won the UNESCO prize at the Venice Film

*Çamur / Mud*
(2003) by Derviş
Zaim is the first
fiction film to
underscore the
trauma of the
partition of the
island of Cyprus.

Festival, but received mixed reviews in Turkey. According to local critic Elif Genco, just like *Elephants and Grass*, *Mud* displays Zaim's inability to be political, 'unless not being able to be political about a subject that has been presented as a historical impasse and used to feed animosities is also a metaphor'.[13]

Zaim's fourth feature, the historical costume drama, *Cenneti Beklerken / Waiting for Heaven* (2006), is a parable that uses the past to understand the present and the question of identity in a modern context by extrapolating the dichotomy of Eastern art versus Western. The themes of individual and collective memory, the emotional distance created by its loss and the search for identity when values are transitory are also prominent in this film.

Eflatun is a miniaturist living in seventeenth-century Istanbul, then capital of the Ottoman Empire. When his son dies, to preserve a realistic image, he draws the boy's face in the Western tradition, contrary to the tradition taught to him by his masters.[14] Instead of punishment for his transgression, he is sent by the vizier on a mission to draw a Western-style portrait of Danyal, the pretender to the throne, as proof of his decapitation. With a group of palace guards Eflatun sets out on an arduous journey to the heart of Anatolia, torn by mutinies and rebellions, while his apprentice Gazal is held hostage to ensure his return. Eflatun's dramatic encounter with a painting similar to *Las Meninas / The Maids of Honour* (1656), the *magnum opus* of Diego Velázquez,[15] is a turning point. He understands that cultural differences are not tools for conflict, but rather serve to enrich both cultures. Zaim uses the meeting point of Western art with the Eastern art of miniature painting as a trope for Turkey and its unique advantage, geopolitically and socially, to amalgamate two diverse and at times oppositional cultures.

The film incorporates the art of miniature aesthetically into the Western art of cinema. Miniature art is devoid of depth, light and shadow, Zaim explains. The miniaturist does not try to achieve a sense of perspective or the optical illusion of three dimensions. Figures or objects never overlap or conceal each other. Time and space are fluid. A place depicted in one miniature will be redrawn in the next, with both colour and form transformed. In a succeeding drawing of the same location, objects may be added or may disappear. Events that are known to have occurred at different times or in different places may be drawn together. These characteristics may appear contrary to the nature of

*Cenneti Beklerken / Waiting for Heaven* (2006) by Derviş Zaim uses the past to understand the present and the question of identity in a modern context.

cinema; but many features of the miniature art are invaluable in terms of their potential contribution to the cinematic language.[16]

In the film the Western art of the illusion of light, shadow and depth is incorporated to the Eastern. Until Eflatun begins the journey the colours of miniature art are dominant; during the journey the Western style of lighting is employed and at the end we return to the pure reds of the miniature. The shadow, the cave and the mirror are allusions to Plato and the name of the protagonist is the Turkish translation of the philosopher's name. Space and time are indeterminate. During the first voyage, as the convoy rides towards a rock, the camera descends and we notice the caves; a different space appears in each cave and a different narrative takes place. In a dream sequence the hut where Eflatun had spent his childhood enters the frame. When Eflatun gazes at the mirror, instead of his own image he sees the image of Prince Yakub, whom he met in the desert. On his return journey Istanbul first appears in the caravanserai frames, then it enters the actual frame. When Eflatun is face to face with the Western painting that resembles *Las Meninas*, he notices that the concepts of time and space are also indeterminate there. The painting also depicts a mirror and the time and space reflected in the mirror is different from that depicted in the painting itself. Encountering this feature of Western art leads Eflatun to re-evaluate his earlier beliefs about cultural differences and meeting points. Zaim stresses that the film does not oppose different cultures to show them as the 'other', but instead tries to show how different cultures mutually enrich each other. This is extended to the personal identity of the characters: Eflatun is a Croatian converted to Islam; the slave woman Leyla who becomes involved with Eflatun cuts her hair and assumes a male personality for reasons of security. Zaim maintains that the fundamental question of identity is not discussed in Turkey. The main reason for such reticence is the 'paranoia ethos that stems from the trauma Turkey had experienced from the nineteenth to the twentieth century during the transition from the empire to the nation-state. The difference between "us" and "them" has become very clear making dialogue extremely difficult.'[17] His sentiment is shared with other filmmakers (Ataman, Ustaoğlu, Öz, Çelik and archivist Özgüç), who have stated that 'the question of identity is a taboo in Turkey'.

To draw a distinction between films such as *Elephants and Grass* or *Mud*, which use direct political references, and the films of Nuri Bilge Ceylan and Zeki Demirkubuz, who insist on not being political, would

*Cenneti Beklerken / Waiting for Heaven* (2006).

be misleading since the films of both are highly political, particularly from the point of view of mirroring the search for a modern identity and a place to belong in a modern world where values are constantly shifting.

Nuri Bilge Ceylan has been chronicling his family since 1995 in very personal films. He made his directorial debut with the twenty-minute black and white *Koza / Cocoon*, followed by his first feature *Kasaba / The Small Town* (1997), again in black and white, then *Mayıs Sıkıntısı / Clouds of May* (1999) in colour, followed by *Uzak / Distant* (2002), also in colour, and *İklimler / Climates* (2006), shot digitally.

The first three feature films, like the preceding short film, were shot in the filmmaker's home village; they are variations on the same theme and all actors are Ceylan's relatives. *The Small Town* was made with a $15,000 budget with no aid from the government; the Ministry of Culture would not lend money to a project in black and white without bankable actors. For lack of funds the film was shot silent and dubbed in the studio. Ceylan regretted that he did not have enough film rolls for more editing; one can no longer buy black and white film stock in Turkey.[18]

*The Small Town*, based on a short story, *Corn Fields*, written by Ceylan's sister, Emine Ceylan, is inspired by their childhood in the 1970s. Although the narrative follows the seasons, the general structure is day followed by night. In the first part we watch a rural classroom in winter, where a young teacher dreams away while the children read from a patriotic textbook about the rules of social life and the family as the nucleus of society. A feather flies, the lightness juxtaposed with the heavy atmosphere inside. Distracted children observe the world outside. A poor boy arrives late drenched in wet snow. The water from the wet socks he hangs over the stove sizzles. Tears roll down a girl's cheeks when the teacher discovers the stale eggs in her bag. Images follow one after the other like pictures in a gallery. On a spring day, the long road home

Neither a town nor a village, *kasaba* signifies an in-between space where the inhabitants are neither villagers nor townspeople. *Kasaba / The Small Town* (1997), dir. Nuri Bilge Ceylan.

that the children tread daily is full of new discoveries for little Ali, but his sister has grown and learned to look at her surroundings from a distance.

The second part of the film evokes Ceylan's memories: his childhood and the warm summer nights during the harvesting of the corn when he spent the evenings in the fields listening to adult conversations. Sometimes the talking was loud; other times soft like a murmur and the repetition of the same old stories would be reassuring to the children, Ceylan reminisces. Such private moments would expose them to different stages of adulthood with all its complexities.[19] During the conversation, freely borrowed from Chekhov, the question of belonging to a homeland and the possibility of return, the central elements of Ceylan's work, are introduced through grandfather Emin's (the director's father, Mehmet Bilge Ceylan) stories of his adventures in foreign lands during the war and the nostalgia he felt for his home. Such stories carry autobiographical elements for Ceylan, who tried to live in London when he was younger. The seeds of the search for identity and belonging, essential questions in his films, were sown after his encounter with the West. Everything looked meaningless to him. 'It was a very exotic relationship. The West would not show its true face to us.' However, the feeling of 'meaninglessness' would haunt him even in the Himalayas just like grandfather Emin in *The Small Town*, who says: 'Wherever you look, the same tree, the same cloud . . .'. Sitting in a Buddhist temple one day, Ceylan realized how much he missed home.[20] *Clouds of May* echoes the same sentiment. Muzaffer advises Saffet to stay at home. 'In Istanbul, you cannot tell the seasons apart . . . only from a little toilet window. In Istanbul they are trying to escape, too . . . you have security here.' In *Distant* a disillusioned Mahmut tells Yusuf, who wants to work on ships to see the world, 'all places are alike'.

Local critics diverge on the merits of *The Small Town*. Akarsu claims that Ceylan combines the techniques he borrows from the neo-realists with his deep knowledge of provincial western Anatolia to build a new narrative language that displays local sensibilities. The fact that he uses clichés from Antonioni or Tarkovsky copiously does not disadvantage the film because, in addition to his narrative erudition, other elements are also at work: the artistic craft he has acquired while working as a photographer, the depth of his philosophical concerns, his courage as an artist and a very important asset that is rare, 'a perfect family that support him wholeheartedly'.[21] For Erdem, *The Small Town* uses the main characteristics of Italian neo-realism by employing non-professional actors, displaying long sequences that simulate real time, manipulating images unrelated to the narrative ('if there is a narrative', Erdem questions) and ending abruptly. However, there is a major difference between *The Small Town* and the masterpieces of neo-realism.

> The still images of Ceylan remind us of his photographic background, but when the camera moves, his amateurism stands naked with all its clumsiness. While neo-realism considered cinema a visual art and avoided dialogues and especially monologues, *The Small Town* includes a section that stretches endlessly with a series of monologues that are presented as dialogues. The superficial nature of these conversations is in conflict with the film's search for realism. One cannot say that *The Small Town* narrates a story; it could be considered a narrative photo album. With smart editing, it could have been a promising short film.[22]

In *Clouds of May* Muzaffer (Muzaffer Özdemir), an independent filmmaker, works on non-paying projects, much to the dismay of his simple provincial parents. He returns to his home village to make a film (*The Small Town*) and disturbs the tranquillity of the lives of his relatives, especially when he asks them to play in it. The father, Emin Bey (Mehmet Bilge Ceylan, who played the grandfather in *The Small Town*), is about to lose the land he nourished for years to prospectors for lack of foresight. Cousin Saffet (Mehmet Emin Toprak, also from *The Small Town*) still cannot pass the university entrance exams and is suffocating in the tranquil but claustrophobic atmosphere of his small town. Saffet's only hope is Muzaffer, who he thinks can find him a city job, but instead Muzaffer uses him for his own purposes by giving him false hopes during the shooting but drops him at the end with the unwelcome advice that he is better off staying where he is. (Saffet as Yusuf arrives at the door of Muzaffer/Mahmut in *Distant*.) Little Ali keeps dreaming of a musical clock, but now he has learned the survival skills of cheating. Mother Fatma (the director's mother) is still the foundation of the family, though father Emin is the more colourful character with his idiosyncrasies and intuitive insights.[23]

*The Small Town*'s Turkish title, *Kasaba*, means neither a town nor a village; it signifies an in-between space alluding to the questions of identity it raises among its inhabitants who are neither villagers nor townspeople. The literal translation of the original title of *Clouds of May* is 'Boredom of May'. Despite the beauty of the scenery, the normalcy,

An independent
filmmaker returns
to his native
village to make a
film and disturbs
its tranquillity.
*Mayıs Sıkıntısı /
Clouds of May*
(1999), dir. Nuri
Bilge Ceylan.

the conformist and family-centred complacency of the small town and its insularity evoke a sense of claustrophobia with its 'squabbling couples and marital dramas, of petit bourgeois shopkeepers, neighbourhoods, and afternoons in front of television' as Fredric Jameson would define it, 'the pain and sting of absence from the center',[24] felt most deeply by Saffet as established in the opening sequences when the camera focuses on him gazing through the window with boredom and anxiety. '"Hometown", in both films, appears as an engulfing space limiting the social horizon of its inhabitants . . . The only time that Saffet appreciates the beauty of his home town, he explains in *The Small Town*, is the morning that he left it to join the army . . . To see the beauty of "home", it seems, distance is required.'[25]

The character of Ali is reminiscent of Ahmad in Abbas Kiarostami's *Khaneh-ye Dust Kojast? / Where is the Friend's House?* (1987). He has the best intentions but adults are not sensitive to his needs. The scene with Muzaffer in the children's park brooding on a swing is significant. Ali appears in the next shot, but only his back is seen. Muzaffer thinks about his childhood and sees himself in Ali as he earlier mentioned to his mother. Nostalgia for what is lost is the dilemma of Muzaffer, who is cut off from his roots, who knows there is no going back 'home'.

The episode in the classroom resembles that of *The Small Town*. Again, a system of education that hardly teaches anything useful to the children (repeated in Yeşim Ustaoğlu's *Waiting For the Clouds*) is exposed with humour. When Muzaffer asks Ali what they teach him at school, he answers: nothing. Ceylan alludes to modernity infringing on the traditional way of life in a humorous manner through Ali's fascination with the lighter that plays *lambada* when you click. The destruction of nature as small towns advance towards modernity is dramatically staged in the episode when the father walks out of the set – like the little girl in Jafer Panahi's film within film, *Badkonak-e sefid / The White Balloon* (1995) – and rushes on his bicycle to the woods that the employees of the Ministry of Agriculture have marked for destruction.

The loss of innocence and what is lost forever in nature evoke the passage of time. The mother is distressed to see herself look old in the videos. She asks: 'Does this tool make one look older?' Muzaffer does not bother to be tactful: 'Not at all.' 'Time flies', she responds. 'We have grown old.' The passage of time is also integral to *The Small Town*, where Ceylan juxtaposes his 'cultured' point of view with 'nature' and reflects on the dichotomy.[26] In *Climates* the opening scenes take place among ruins, which, according to the Bengali master Mrinal Sen, who has made several films in ruins, facilitate a continuous dialogue between the past and the present.[27]

The US critic A. O. Scott underscores the influences of Kiarostami's cinema on the work of Ceylan in these terms:

> a painterly regard for rural landscape, an unsentimental interest in children and an unobtrusive curiosity about the ways movie reality parallels and intersects with ordinary life. Mr Ceylan's protagonist, an Istanbul filmmaker . . . who returns to his small provincial hometown to make a movie, is a bit like the displaced engineer in Mr. Kiarostami's film "The Wind Will Carry Us": an urban outsider whose inquisitive presence throws the rhythms of country life slightly off kilter.[28]

According to French critic Jean-Sébastien Chauvin, Ceylan, who knows how to manipulate the audience, indulges in self-criticism through Muzaffer, an unsympathetic character, who is making a film that does not satisfy anyone, and apart from images that bring 'wrinkles to the forefront', he has little to give anyone, though he does not hesitate to use them for his personal gain.[29]

Most French critics were very favourable to *Clouds of May*. *Le Monde* praised the film for its journey from the individual to the collective, from documentary to fiction and from lies to truth, which, it argued, is similar to the journey of cinema.[30] *L'Humanité* called Ceylan 'a Turkish Chekhov', commenting that the richness of *Clouds of May* does not stem only from its distance from the characters. The film also speaks about the village life that is disappearing, the longing for big cities and the dreams of toys that won't leave the kids alone. 'In short, it reflects the situation in today's Turkey, which is not much different than other places.'[31]

*Uzak / Distant* continues the central theme of home, identity and belonging explored in *The Small Town* and *Clouds of May*. Protagonist Mahmut (Muzaffer Özdemir) has made a niche for himself in the big metropolis; in a sense, he is both inside and outside. Mahmut is distant to the women in his life: his ex-wife, his mistress, his mother and his sister. He is distant to his cousin who reminds him of the roots he thought he had severed while trying to build a new identity in the urban environment. He is distant to his work, having chosen the shortcut of material gains rather than pursuing his artistic dreams. He is distant to commitment to a human being: he coerced his wife to have an abortion. He treats his cousin with disdain; his mistress with detachment; and is unable to express his true feelings to his ex-wife who seems to be important to him. He is also distant from his immediate environment. Although the apartment seems large, his bed is placed in the living room and he sleeps in a sleeping bag like a traveller passing through.

The film starts with an early morning country landscape covered in snow. A tiny figure slowly approaches the camera. A bus stops in the distance and the young man hops on. Cut to a blurred image of a woman taking off her stockings. A man in the foreground watches her, sighs and takes off his shoes. The woman is waiting and the man watching. He arrives in bed. The image is blurred, facilitating its obliteration from memory once the act is over and the feeling of shame settles in. Later he would be seen cleaning the dirty spot on the bed in an annoyed manner.

Cut to the building superintendent, an Anatolian man as customary, watching the woman come out and get into her car. His gaze clearly reveals his disapproval since 'women who come and go in the dark' are against his traditional family values. But there is something special about this gaze, which suggests the resilience of the rural migrant to adapt to new situations, or at least to keep silent. The clash of the two cultures is foregrounded in another scene, again involving the superintendent, when a middle-aged gay tenant walks out of the building with his young lover. Ironically, the superintendent is nicer to the man whose sexual behaviour is against his moral convictions, but distant and judgemental to the country cousin, who reminds him of a past he tries to forget. At their first meeting he literally closes the door on him.

The fact that the provincial 'other' is not welcome, even by other provincials, is evident throughout the film. Yusuf acts the part to confirm prejudices: he follows women; harasses them on the bus (with his eyes or his leg); does not flush the toilet; smokes cheap cigarettes; leaves his smelly shoes around; prefers pop singer Sezer Aksu to Bach, whom he has never heard of, and sit-coms to Tarkovsky, who puts him to sleep. Earning money is his only aim in life and, worst of all, he does not know how to put a distance between himself and other people. He brings the claustrophobic proximity of small-town living with him (like the turtle in the two previous films that carries its home on its back) to the isolating but at the same time liberating anonymity of urban life that city cousin Mahmut has chosen to live.

While Mahmut is 'distant', Yusuf is 'distanced'. The provincial is permitted to exist in the metropolis as long as s/he is invisible. Mahmut divides the apartment, pushing Yusuf to the back room at the end of a long corridor. Yusuf keeps leaving the lights on and Mahmut keeps switching them off, like the doors that he keeps closing as if to protect his home territory and the identity he chose for himself. The 'other' must be left outside. But by locking the other out, one also locks oneself in. In this respect the trope of the mouse trapped in the kitchen is applicable to both characters, although the method of each for eliminating the animal is quite different.

*Uzak / Distant* (2002) continues the central theme of home, identity and belonging explored in *The Small Town* and *Clouds of May*.

The relationship between Mahmut and Yusuf reflects the tension between the urban and the rural milieu in Turkey and the transformation of the intellectuals who have chosen to serve the system. In the process they have distanced themselves from their ideals. Mahmut, once an ambitious photographer, now makes commercials for a ceramics firm. (Just like several 'engaged' filmmakers of yesterday who work on TV commercials and banal television series.)

Algan points out that the character of Yusuf as the unemployed provincial, abandoned and aggrieved, is presented with empathy, whereas Mahmut's character is selfish and opportunistic. Severed from his traditional and societal ties, Mahmut is in tune with the existing economic system. The tension between the two cousins, which is experienced deeply inside an apartment at the centre of the city, is a powerful trope

for Turkish society. A new type of urban intellectual was created in the 1980s with the social and economic changes and the hegemony of the neo-liberalist world view. The 'new' intellectuals – journalists, propagandists, advertisers, company executives, public relations experts are some of the typical professions – felt autonomous from the society, and in practical life gave all their creativity to the service of capitalism. Mahmut is one of these 'new intellectuals'. The lifestyle of Mahmut has been approved and exalted, whereas the 'other', represented by Yusuf has been humiliated. The cinema of that period endorsed this point of view, advocating neo-liberal lifestyles,[32] and *Distant* is the first film to look at this period critically.[33]

During an interview with a national newspaper Ceylan was asked if the identity crisis of the Turkish intellectual stemmed from being caught between East and West and whether being at the crossroads could be a source of intellectual richness. He responded that more than being caught between East and West, the crisis stemmed from the Third World status of Turkey; he did not think that intellectuals in Argentina or Mexico felt differently.

> The underdeveloped countries emulate the West that has been imposing its culture through various means. Imperialism has succeeded in making the underdeveloped countries feel slightly ashamed of their culture and traditions. This influence is more obtrusive on the third world intellectuals who have better possibilities to communicate with the West. Those who assimilate the point of view of the other see their own customs and traditions as extremities created by ignorance.

Ceylan also pointed out that he believed a Turkish person carried Eastern characteristics, but the idea that 'to be caught between East and West could be a source of richness' always gave him the feeling of a consolation prize.[34]

If the focus of Ceylan's first three films is homecoming and escape from home, *Climates* is about an escape from a sense of establishing roots and belonging to someone. The turtle motif, which is used both in *The Small Town* and *Clouds of May*, is significant in this context. In Turkey the turtle is compared to a nomad travelling with his home. One may also think that the turtle is a prisoner of its home, 'the turtle actually *is* its house . . . the turtle as a symbol perfectly embodies the comforting as well as the uncanny side of belonging. What protects and comforts also captures and imprisons.'[35] The same can be applied to relationships. Both Mahmut of *Distant* and Isa of *Climates* are better off when they have sex without attachments. Although Mahmut feels the emptiness that comes after the impersonal act, Isa is not even privy to such feelings.

Dishonesty and cheating are parts of the narrative in all films of Ceylan and perhaps serve as a metaphor for the art of cinema. Even the little boy Ali learns at an early age that survival means cheating. He is asked to carry an egg in his pocket for 40 days without breaking it and if he can accomplish this feat he can have the musical watch he wants. When Muzaffer suggests that he can boil it and that way it won't break, he answers adamantly that it is cheating. But when he actually breaks it, he steals another egg and replaces it. In *Distant* Mahmut puts on the Tarkovsky tape to get rid of his country cousin, but once Yusuf is out he starts to watch porn. Meanwhile, Yusuf is phoning his mother without asking Mahmut's permission. When his mother asks why he is whispering, he says because Mahmut Abi (older brother) is sleeping. Later on, Mahmut accuses Yusuf of stealing an old watch and even after he finds it in the drawer, does not tell Yusuf. Isa of *Climates* is equally hypocritical (as discussed in chapter Five).

Zeki Demirkubuz also makes independent low-budget films, but his style is different from the cerebral aesthetics of Zaim or the visual self-reflexivity of Ceylan. He draws his inspiration from the traditional Yeşilçam cinema that he had experienced at first hand during his years as assistant to established filmmakers including Zeki Ökten. Within this tradition, with crafty neologism, he narrates personal stories that are also very political. 'His films uncode, decode and deconstruct the customary clichés of Yeşilçam and deliver a fatal blow to the status quo, its trademark.'[36]

Demirkubuz was jailed for three years by the junta for his Marxist and Maoist beliefs when he was only seventeen. His first film, *C Blok / Block C* (1994), which he calls 'an atmosphere film about modern architecture', was about the malaise felt by the inhabitants of big apartment blocks.[37] At the Istanbul International Film Festival that year, he refused the award given to him, stating that he did not want to be part of an industry that could easily forget the pains of the past – the atrocities of the military intervention of 1980 – an industry run by 'dinosaurs'.

(Until the arrival of the New Cinema with its alternative modes of production, it was very difficult for filmmakers outside the established circle to receive financial support. It took Demirkubuz about eight years to shoot *Block C*.)

Demirkubuz's second film, *Masumiyet / Innocence* (1997), is a road movie but also a hotel movie. (The latter genre has its precedents in Turkish cinema, particularly in the films of the middle generation, notably Ömer Kavur's *Anayurt Oteli / Motherland Hotel*, 1987, and *Gizli Yüz / The Secret Face*, 1991.) Scripted by Demirkubuz and shot in nineteen days with a $90,000 budget, the film is a minimalist story about a loner named Yusuf who lost all his family, except his sister and brother-in-law, during an earthquake. His sister hates him because he aborted her elopement, killing her lover; he is imprisoned as a result. After his release Yusuf heads for the city looking for a job, and destiny brings him face to face with an odd couple: a prostitute named Uğur and her pimp Bekir, who keep moving from one town to the next dragging Uğur's mute daughter Çilem with them. Without better prospects, Yusuf becomes part of the lives of the trio and falls hopelessly in love with the cynical Uğur, becoming her pimp after the suicide of Bekir. (Demirkubuz's 2006 feature *Kader / Destiny* goes back to the youth of the characters and fills in some of the blanks.)

The plot of *Innocence* is not very different from that of Yeşilçam melodramas watched on TV in decrepit hotels: crimes of passion, desperate men who pimp the women they would like to marry, deaf and dumb little girls, unbelievable coincidences and suicides for love. ('They tell lies to make you cry,' comments Yusuf. 'It can't all be lies,' retorts another hotel guest.) When adopting the familiar themes of the once-popular Yeşilçam melodramas, but stripping them of their exploitative nature and exaggerated sensationalism, Demirkubuz seems to be saying perhaps it is not the story but how it is told that counts. His settling of accounts with Yeşilçam does not end there. His own film, *C Block*, also appears on the TV screen and the filmmaker himself is among those watching.[38] In fact, people watch television incessantly in the films of Demirkubuz. As Fredric Jameson points out, in a society changing from a peasant economy to a capitalist industrial one, along with the struggles with loneliness in modern urban life, the pervasiveness of the media has become a pressing issue for New Turkish Cinema.[39]

Demirkubuz continues his Yeşilçam-style melodramas with *Üçüncü Sayfa / The Third Page* (2000), a love, sex and murder story that would normally appear on the third page of a tabloid. The characters are again marginals oppressed by society. Isa is beaten as the suspect for the disappearance of $50 from a small mafia operation. Unable to cope with the blows of life, he contemplates killing himself, but instead kills his landlord, who comes to collect the overdue rent. Hence begins a chain of events in the life of this Raskolnikov character. (Demirkubuz cites Dostoevsky as the only influence on his career.) Meryem, a young village woman who has had her share of the blows of life, helps him when he is accosted by the mafia thugs and it looks as though love will develop between the two. However, Demirkubuz favours twists in the script. Meryem was the mistress of the landlord with the sanction of her husband. But she is happy he is dead. Now she wants Isa to kill her husband. When the husband is accidentally killed, Meryem disappears, to resurface in the apartment of the landlord's son, who was her lover all along.[40]

The film is a realistic rendition of life in Turkey including the shaky social structure and the fragile economy. In the opening scene the mafia thug is sitting under the portrait of Tansu Çiller, the woman prime minister of the period, whose dubious dealings in the acquisition of her fortune are yet to be investigated. The bullies who come to collect from Isa ask for dollars, not Turkish lira. Everyone walks around with a calculator and a mobile phone and everyone knows the exchange rate of the day. Everyone is pushed in a corner and of course will hit back, argues Meryem.

The role of the media in Turkish daily life, where unlimited private television channels broadcast a wide range of programmes from Italian variety shows and Brazilian soap operas to local *arabesque*, is again underscored in this film. Isa earns his living playing minor roles in TV series; the walls of his bachelor pad are adorned with film posters of his heroes (such as Cüneyt Arkın in *Dört Yanım Cehennem / The Mummy*, Çetin İnanç, 1982). As for Meryem, she is a woman caught between tradition and modernity. 'Extricated from her roots, she is confined to a basement flat where her only connection to the outside world is the TV screen. In her liminal state, the soap operas she watches day and night shape all her actions and reactions. Often it is not evident whether she is able to see the difference between real life and make believe.'[41]

The economical style of Demirkubuz places all key events outside the frame almost like a Greek tragedy. *Innocence* is more about what the characters have already lived than what they are living now. In *The Third Page* it is as if the narrative has two faces: the seen and the unseen. A fight is heard in the next room. A woman screams. The hero grabs a knife and listens. The fight is not shown. The director takes a deliberate distance. Interviews with ordinary citizens on the street who represent three different age groups interrupt the narrative as if to link the surface melodrama with something more tangible.[42]

*Yazgı /Fate* and *Itiraf / Confession* were both made in 2001 as part of a trilogy that Demirkubuz calls *Karanlık Üstüne Öyküler / Tales about Darkness. Fate*, a loose adaptation of Albert Camus' *L'Etranger / The Stranger*, while it explores the essence of the feeling of guilt, turns the traditional values of society upside down, and *Confession* is a highly charged drama about a man whose wife cheats on him. Both films 'denormalize' bourgeois myths about marriage and the family.[43] Musa (Serdar Orçin), the protagonist of *Fate*, is an ordinary man who works in a custom's office: he gets up in the morning, has his breakfast, takes the bus to work, has lunch with colleagues and comes home in the evening. What makes him different from the others is his inability to show the reactions society expects. He is unable to display any emotion when his mother dies unexpectedly; he is even relieved and he does not hide this sentiment because he believes he should be truthful. He marries the mistress of his boss when she asks him and keeps silent about her infidelity. When he is arrested for a crime he did not commit, he does not bother to defend himself. He knows it would make no difference. He is even indifferent to his release.

Demirkubuz claims that the interior world of Musa is no different from many others in society. No one wants to suffer; no one wants to be sad at the death of their mother; no one wants to be hurt by the infidelity of a partner. The burden of images that do not belong to us forces us to act according to expectations. The difference of Musa is that he rejects an existence made up of assumed status and identity. 'Pain arises out of expectations, from the image and identity we cut out for ourselves.'[44]

The predominant issues of Demirkubuz's films are homelessness, physical and material, distance (from one's roots or inner being) and the lack of a sense of belonging. His characters are either thrown from one city to the other, as in *Innocence* and *Destiny*, from one socio-economic class to the other, as in *Block C*, *The Third Page* and *Confession*, or in and out of jail, as in *Innocence*, *Fate* and *Destiny* (2006). Dismal interiors, impersonal hotel rooms, dark corridors, dingy basement apartments intensify the feeling of claustrophobia and entrapment. The prison of metaphor is in every film beginning with *Block C*.[45] The door, also a symbol Ceylan favours, appears as an object that exists in connection to

The characters of Demirkubuz are in a flux, but they go around in vicious circles.

*Üçüncü Sayfa / The Third Page* (2000).

*Yazgı /Fate* (2001).

*Itiraf / Confession* (2001).

what is behind it. It may forbid the street, or it may forbid the room in a system of traditions and prohibitions. In the last episode of *Fate*, when Musa is obliged to sit through an unofficial interrogation by the prison governor, the door refuses to close, no matter how many times the governor tries. Does the governor have a secret wish to keep behind bars those who do not fit into the mould, who are unlike the normal citizens who believe in God (or keep it a secret if they don't), who are sad at funerals and happy when they are exonerated of the crimes they did not commit?

a modern identity or identity in a modern world | 205

Thresholds are places where many interactions take place, most of them violent. When the thugs harass Isa in *The Third Page* Meryem comes to his aid on the threshold and pays the money. In *Fate* Musa and his neighbour get to know each other between the two doors when the latter is wounded and bleeding; the violence the neighbour exercises on his ex-mistress and the arrival of the police to arrest him also take place on the threshold. Musa observes the adultery of his wife without really entering the apartment, catching a glimpse of her naked back in the bed and seeing an unfamiliar pair of men's sneakers beside the door (later, he notices the boss wearing the same sneakers). When he returns home after his release from prison he witnesses the domestic life of his neighbour across the corridor when the ex-mistress/prostitute rings the doorbell to ask for some eggs.

The characters of Demirkubuz are in a flux, but they go around in vicious circles. Bekir, who appears as a young man in *Destiny*, tries to cut his ties with Uğur and marries a woman of his parents' choice (someone who wears the headscarf), although he keeps returning to Uğur, who does not want him. Distant from their pre-proscribed identities, these characters are at home nowhere. One city looks like the other. In fact, except for *Destiny*, cities are rarely identifiable in Demirkubuz's films. Movement does not bring change. Meryem's ascent from the claustrophobic basement to the large apartment on a well-lit upper floor leads her to a false paradise, where she looks like a character from the soap operas she has been watching. Yusuf of *Innocence* is unwilling to leave the prison where he had spent ten years because he has nothing to do and nowhere to go; he is a character similar to Fassbinder's Franz Biberkopf, whose head spins when the prison doors close behind him in *Berlin Alexanderplatz* (1980). (Susan Sontag would call Biberkopf one of Fassbinder's 'victims of false consciousness.)[46] In fact, the melodramas of Demirkubuz remind one of some of the films of Fassbinder, where the mundane lives of the characters stand for images much larger than themselves.

Özgüven claims that the paths of Demirkubuz and Ceylan cross in *Distant*. Demirkubuz's deliberately rugged narrative that favours exposing its seams and Ceylan's meticulously polished stories aside, the characters of Ceylan are very close to the characters of Demirkubuz; they are all deceived by the city. The difference is that Demirkubuz's characters internalize their disappointment, which turns to anger, whereas the characters of Ceylan live their disappointments with the city as a tragic reconciliation and perhaps the 'rugged' and the 'polished' find their place in this context. On one side is a confrontation that is felt in the form as well, on the other a melancholy that is externalized with the precision of the form.[47]

Faith in modern Turkey has begun to be discussed more openly in cinema in recent years. *Takva / A Man's Fear of God* (2006) by Özer Kızıltan (produced by Fatih Akın) approaches the issue through the story of a modest loner, Muharrem, whose orderly life, structured around his insignificant job as a helping-hand for the sack merchant Ali and his religious activities, is disrupted when he draws the attention of an enterprising religious sect, who want to use him for their worldly dealings. Lured to the seminary and appointed as the treasurer, Muharrem witnesses bribery, nepotism and unjust privileges, which threaten his religious faith. The most prominent three temptations are money, politics and the daughter of the sheik, responsible for his wet dreams. Muharrem's oscillation between the two worlds, that inside the seminary, which seems to belong to another age, and that outside, with high-rises, fancy cars and cellular phones, reflects the two sides of Turkey where 'modernity as Westernism exists simultaneously with modernity as Easternism or where modernity as unmarked universalism coexists with a heavily marked particularism'.[48]

Religious sects are one of the most controversial issues in Turkish politics and social life. To expose wealthy religious foundations has been quite daring for Kızıltan, a self-declared atheist who worked with dervishes of various sects, both as advisers and as participants. The *zikir* (*dhikr*, the Islamic ceremony of repeating the 99 names of Allah) scenes when the dervishes oscillate in synchronized meditation are very powerful. In Istanbul there are 2,500 religious houses, Kızıltan claims, and 25,000 in the whole of Turkey, with representatives from every level of society, even members of the government,[49] although *tarikat*, the Islamic fraternities, were officially banned by Kemal Atatürk in 1925.[50]

The film has been successful nationally and internationally in terms of festival awards, although local audiences were split in their opinion, one group finding it a true rendition of the dilemmas of one man in terms of his faith and an authentic exposé of the operations of the religious sects and another considering the film touristy and orientalist in its approach. After its screening at the Antalya Golden Orange film festival in 2006, some spectators felt that the film was 'advocating' the religious sects, and this could have 'bad influences on the youth'. On

*Takva / A Man's Fear of God* (2006), dir. Özer Kızıltan.

the other hand, some Islam-oriented newspapers praised it for rising above the clichés regarding Islam. At the press conference the screenwriter of the film, Önder Çakar, defended the film, which he claimed was trying to show the necessity of balance between the love of God and the fear of God through the disintegration of a man who loses this balance.[51]

Alev Çınar points out that modernity in Turkey is 'neither exclusively Western nor Eastern, neither foreign or local, neither universal

nor particular, neither historical nor atemporal, neither old nor new, but at times it can be all of these at once, or it can emerge in the ambiguous space between these binary oppositions'.[52] New Turkish Cinema has been exploring the question of modern identity in constantly evolving Turkish society and the modern world with the works of noteworthy filmmakers discussed in this book, such as Zaim, Ceylan, Demirkubuz, Ustaoğlu, Öz, İpekçi, Çelik, Kaplanoğlu and Pirselimoğlu and new-comer Özer Kızıltan, but also Barış Pirhasan (*Adem'in Trenleri / Adam and the Devil*, 2006), Reha Erdem (*Beş Vakit / Times and Winds*, 2006), Ahmet Uluçay (*Karpuz Kabuğundan Gemiler Yapmak / Boats Out of Watermelon Rinds*, 2006), Ümit Ünal (*9*, 2002), Turgut Yasalar (*Sis ve Gece / The Fog and the Night*, 2007), Uğur Yücel (*Yazı Tura / Toss Up*, 2004) and Ulaş İnaç (*Türev / Derivative*, 2005), whose works are diverse in form and content as well as artistic position, but converge at one fundamental point, the search for authenticity and sincerity in mirroring their complex society.

# Afterword

A vibrant film industry has been established in Turkey with the new millennium. From a maximum of ten films produced annually in the early 1990s, production figures tripled in 2006 and indigenous films took over 51.7 per cent of the local box office.[1] Considering the fact that cinema competes with at least 300 television channels and that American major studios control the distribution and the exhibition not only of foreign products but of a large number of local films as well, this was no small feat.

The seeds of box-office success were sown in the stagnant 1990s, when local versions of Hollywood products began to be made as an attempt to gain an audience disillusioned by the so-called *angst* films that appeared in the post-coup years of the 1980s.[2] The stifling climate of apoliticization and the heavy hand of censorship that silenced *engagé* writers, artists and filmmakers were instrumental in the emergence of the *auteur cinema*, the best examples of which are the works of the late Ömer Kavur (*Motherland Hotel*, *The Secret Face*, etc.). However, existential stories with layered narratives and rich metaphors that required audience participation alienated the masses, whose tastes had been shaped by Yeşilçam melodramas, Hollywood popcorn movies and foreign soap operas. To save the film industry from collapsing, some filmmakers decided to follow the Hollywood formula by making films with mass appeal. *Amerikalı / The American* (1993) by Şerif Gören, *Eşkıya / The Bandit* (1996) by Yavuz Turgul and *Istanbul Kanatlarımın Altında / Istanbul Beneath My Wings* (1996) by Mustafa Altıoklar are pioneer efforts that were highly successful. In addition to technical improvements comparable to the standards of the West and the casting of celebrities, distributors adopted Western-style publicity (CDs of the theme songs, t-shirts, TV

*Vizontele Tuuba*
(2004) by Yılmaz
Erdoğan.

*G.O.R.A.* by Cem
Yılmaz (2004).

commercials, websites and the eventual VCD/DVD), ensuring maximum visibility, which contributed to box-office success. *Vizontele* (2001), about the arrival of television to a remote town in the 1970s, starring well-known comedian Yılmaz Erdoğan, broke records with 3.6 million admissions. Its sequel, *Vizontele Tuuba* (2004), which takes place shortly before the 1980 coup, was also successful. The pseudo science fiction *G.O.R.A.* (Cem Yılmaz, 2004), a parody of *Matrix*, *Fifth Element* and similar films, had a record earning of $30 million worldwide.

In 2006 four Turkish productions topped the charts: *Kurtlar Vadisi Irak / Valley of the Wolves, Iraq* with 4,256,567 viewers; *Hababam Sınıfı Üç Buçuk* with 2,067,661; *Hokkabaz / The Magician* with 1,684,282 and *Sınav / The Exam* with 1,145,014. Hollywood box-office hit *The Da Vinci Code* (Ron Howard, 2006) was number five on the list with only 1,028,928.³ An important point is that, with a few exceptions, the films that draw the largest crowds are not necessarily appreciated by film critics and the films that the critics praise do not always draw large crowds. The Turkish audience, as is the case globally, is composed mostly of the younger generation, who go to the cinema to be entertained, with popcorn in one hand, Coke in the other. The films that appeal to the majority are formulaic Hollywood products. Well-made local versions are welcome, offering the additional edge of cultural identification and exalting national pride. *Valley of the Wolves, Iraq*, which made $20 million at the box office, was not only the most viewed film of 2006 but also the only Turkish film ever to attract such a large audience. It was also released in fourteen foreign countries, including Belgium, The Netherlands, Austria, the UK, Switzerland, Denmark, Russia, Australia and the US. In Germany alone 700,000 people saw it. However, Turkish critics found the film 'mediocre', an 'unsuccessful imitation of some Hollywood movies that the US government uses for propaganda purposes', 'a film that exploits nationalistic sentiments' and 'a mega-budget movie that surpasses the limits of Yeşilçam, but shows the US and the whole West, unnecessarily, as the personifications of Satan'. On the other hand, *The Magician* (Ali Taner Baltacı and Cem Yılmaz, 2006), a road movie that is third on the list of 'most watched films', having earned $9.3 million at the box office, was praised by local critics as well,⁴ although it did not impress foreign guests at the International Istanbul Film Festival of 2007. In 2005 *My Father and Son* by Çağan Irmak, which uses the terror of the 1980 military coup to build a family melodrama, was seen by almost four million people and was praised by local critics. According to Agah Özgüç, 'the audience needed a film that could reflect the sensibilities of the 1960s Yeşilçam using modern technology. Unprecedented in the history of Turkish cinema, the film made waves by word of mouth before any advertising.'[5] The foreign audience at the Istanbul International Film Festival (2006), however, dismissed the film as an exploitative tear-jerker.

Among the films of the 2006–7 season, *International* (431,300 admissions in 32 weeks), *Takva /A Man's Fear of God* (349,530 admissions in 30 weeks) and *Bliss* (544,441 admissions in 28 weeks) were films liked by the audience, the critics and the international film festivals. However, *Destiny*, *Climates* and *Waiting for Heaven*, films that were praised by local critics and invited to foreign film festivals, were not able to achieve more than 100,000 spectators at home.[6]

*Dünyayı Kurtaran Adam'ın Oğlu / The Son of the Man Who Saves the World* aka *Turks in Space* (Kartal Tibet, 2006), in the genre of G.O.R.A., was one of the most discussed films of the year. Chastised by the critics, it got an audience of 439,000. The film is a remake of Çetin İnanç's *Dünyayı Kurtaran Adam / The Man Who Saves the World* aka *Turkish Star Wars* (1982), notorious for its bootlegged scenes from *Star Wars IV: A New Hope* and the *Star Trek* series, among others. Chosen as one of the worst ten films in the world by Turkish critics, İnanç's version has gained cult status over the years among the young audience and its VCD/DVD sales have been thriving. Cüneyt Arkın, legendary star of the original (and its screenwriter), still plays the heroic Turkish astronaut despite his advancing years. A Turkish critic wrote:

> 'A National Space Movie: *The Son of the Man Who Saves the World*' seems to have sprung from the idea that the Turks who had fought to the death with the dragons in the steppes of Central Asia have surmounted the Great Wall of China, have tamed the Byzantine Empire with the ships they slid down from the mountains and have been preparing to make history in Europe with every championship league must have a space epic as well.[7]

Another film derided by local critics that has broken box-office records is *Son Osmanlı, 'Yandım Ali'/ The Last Ottoman, 'The Knockout Ali'* (2007), a three-million-dollar budget period piece of action, drama (melodrama) and comedy inspired by a popular comic book. The film takes place around 1918 during the War of Independence and

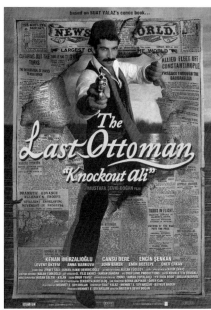

*Son Osmanlı,
'Yandım Ali' / The
Last Ottoman,
'The Knock-out
Ali' (2007), dir.
Mustafa Şevki
Doğan.*

recounts the tale of a young adventurer and womanizer who gains patriotic feelings under the influence of Mustafa Kemal's charisma and joins
the revolutionary movement. On several websites aficionados recom-
mend the movie for the action scenes with the 'world-famous Wing Tsu
master Emin Boztepe' and the execution of the notorious 'Ottoman
slap'. According to local film critic Fatih Özgüven, *The Last Ottoman*
resembles Lütfi Ö. Akad's 1950s film *İngiliz Kemal Lawrence'e Karşı /
English Kemal against Lawrence*, but in that film among those resisting
the invasion of Istanbul by the Allies one could spot ethnic Greeks as
well.[8] *The Last Ottoman*, however, shows the local Greeks as lascivious
skirt-chasers and naïve and incompetent soldiers in complicity with the
occupying British forces. Part of the success of the film with the masses
lies in its timely exhibition when the political manoeuvrings of the government and the oppositional parties on the election of a new president
resulted in clashes in the spring of 2007 between Islamist and secularist
factions, leading to street demonstrations demanding their republic to
remain 'laic' as established by the founder, Mustafa Kemal Atatürk.

   The immense popularity of this film, as well as films like *Valley of
the Wolves, Iraq* and *The Son of the Man Who Saves the World* is a good

indication of the general atmosphere in Turkey, where nationalism is on the rise. Perhaps Europe's growing reticence in accepting Turkey into the European Union is an important element that has triggered this self-defence mechanism, as has been pointed out in the Turkish media.

Orhan Pamuk asks the question he has been hearing from many since he became a writer: who do you write for?[9] This question is pertinent to cinema as well. Nuri Bilge Ceylan, one of the most important representatives of the New Turkish Cinema, won the Grand Jury Prize at the Cannes Film Festival in 2003 with *Distant*. However, the film did not do well at home. A Turkish critic narrates that when he went to the screening of *Distant* it was cancelled due to lack of audience. He declares: '*Distant* is distant to "us".' Ceylan's *Climates* was shown for only nine weeks and had 31,366 admissions. 'National cinema', US critic Jonathan Rosenbaum comments, is 'a cinema that expresses something of the soul of the nation it comes from: the lifestyle, the consciousness, the attitudes . . . For a movie belonging to a particular national cinema often means that it's likely to have a stronger impact on its home turf.'[10] Who does Nuri Bilge Ceylan make films for?

Pamuk states that writers write for those who read them, less for their own national majorities who do not read them than for the small minority of readers in the world who do, which seems also to be the case for filmmakers with a conscientious artistic agenda such as Ceylan. Suspicions about the artists' true intentions reflect the uneasiness towards the new cultural order that has established itself over the past thirty years, Pamuk argues.

> Those who find it most disturbing are the representatives of the non-Western nations who are uneasy about their national identity and unwilling to accept certain blemishes in their history. They are apprehensive of creative attempts to view history and nationalism from a non-national perspective and reproach artists who look beyond the national audiences for 'exoticizing their country for foreign consumption and inventing problems that have no basis in reality'.[11]

A good example is the case of Yeşim Ustaoğlu who has been reproached for choosing topics (the Kurdish issue in *Journey to the Sun* and the deportation of the Greeks in *Waiting For the Clouds*) that could be funded by European agencies.

On the other hand, in the West what Pamuk calls 'the parallel suspicion' exists, where many believe that local literatures should remain local. When Nuri Bilge Ceylan, Zeki Demirkubuz, Derviş Zaim, Yeşim Ustaoğlu, Semih Kaplanoğlu, Özer Kızıltan and others have been creating transnational and transcultural cinemas, perhaps such issues have become obsolete, or should have. Within international cinema, particularly in the last decade, a large body of work has been created that questions physical or metaphorical borders and 'imagined communities', and New Turkish Cinema is part of this movement. Film production itself has been internationalized and co-financing across national borders has become the norm, particularly with the establishment of the Council of Europe Fund (EURIMAGE) that aims to support European cinema against the domination of Hollywood. Turkey became a member in 1990 and this has played an important role in improving technical quality of the Turkish films and giving Turkish cinema the visibility it lacked outside its borders. In addition certain filmmakers have benefited from the Hubert Bals Fund associated with the Rotterdam Film Festival and other international script funds including those organized by the Sundance, Thessaloniki and Montpellier film festivals. Since the late 1990s Turkish films have reached international audiences through film festivals and theatrical releases in Europe and North America and/or have been shown on foreign television. With the development of such trends, the ingrained national identities of cinematic tradition have begun to yield to alternative criteria for discerning and inscribing identity.

Sceptics question the repercussions of funding from the West, such as the EURIMAGE fund. Has Turkish cinema become 'more European' since it has started receiving support from this organization, which gives priority to issues of human rights and women's emancipation, subjects on which there has been reticence in Turkey? Some of the recent films that have received such support deal with incest (*Angel's Fall*), honour killings (*Bliss*), ethnic strife (*Journey to the Sun*) and religious fanaticism (*Takva / The Man's Fear of God*). How far does the possibility of European finance affect the choice of subject matter? Turkey's EURIMAGE representative, who served in this position for fifteen years, was replaced by the Ministry of Culture in the spring of 2005 with the allegation that films that give a bad image of Turkey by foregrounding under-development and exposing negative aspects were receiving EURIMAGE support at a time when Turkey was trying to join the European Union.

During the 44th Golden Orange Film Festival in Antalya in 2007, in addition to *Bliss* two competing films, *Hidden Faces* and *Janjan*, were about honour killings and violence against women. (*Bliss* was refused government support but received EURIMAGE funding, while the other two had partners in Germany in addition to government loans.) According to Handan İpekçi of *Hidden Faces*, the subject matter rises out of the urge to interpret pressing issues and not calculations of financing possibilities.[12] Derviş Zaim asserts that the EURIMAGE fund has been instrumental in the realization of certain projects that due to their subject matter would have had slight chance of securing funds within Turkey. *Journey to the Sun*, *Hejar* and *Home Coming* are some of these films, although many films of different 'views, styles, subjects and artistic conventions and formats' have also received funding. Zaim interviewed a variety of filmmakers on this topic. Yeşimoğlu and Ceylan, representatives of New Turkish Cinema, did not agree that EURIMAGE funded only political projects. However, in the conservative and nationalist circles the viewpoint was quite different. Veteran filmmaker Halit Refiğ believed that all Turkish films that were recognized in the West were anti-nationalist; the Westerners wanted to see Turks in clichés – Asian, backward and followers of a primitive religion – and believed that their audience would only appreciate films that endorse the existing clichés. From the middle generation, Ali Özgentürk, a disciple of Yılmaz Güney, raised another important question: if he made an adaptation of Shakespeare, would he attract interest in the West? Erden Kıral pointed out that the considerations for recognition in the West could even lead some creators to 'self-Orientalism'. According to producer Ali Akdeniz and filmmaker Reis Çelik, this perspective was valid for the work of Ferzan Özpetek, a filmmaker living in Italy who has brought Eastern eroticism and homosexuality to the West with *Hamam / The Turkish Bath* (1997) and followed the same trend with *Harem / Harem Suare* (1999). Ceylan agreed that the West expected certain types of films from Turkey, but he did not think that content was the only crucial issue. *Yol* was awarded at the Cannes Film Festival because it was a good film. For Ceylan originality, rather than exoticism, was the decisive factor.[13]

In addition to foreign funds, the Ministry of Culture invests $12.5 million annually in loans for film production. (The average budget of a Turkish film is $500,000–$1,000,000.) A new government initiative stipulates that films that win international prizes or slots in A Class international festivals will evade the penalty (refusal of future funding for three

Ferzan Özpetek: living in Italy has brought Eastern eroticism and homosexuality to the West with *Hamam / The Turkish Bath* (1997).

years) in case they are not able to pay back their loans. Aydın Sayman (*Janjan*) points out that receiving the government loan requires guarantees similar to bank loans: a guarantee letter from the bank, mortgage and guarantor(s). In 2005, out of the 42 projects that could have received the loan, 30 could not fulfil these conditions. At the Ministry of Culture, the minister, the under-secretary and the supervisor are changed too often to establish a policy for the cinema sector and implement regulations to support and protect national cinema. Often bureaucrats unfamiliar with the cinema sector hold such positions. Although most of the existing regulations are comparable to those in EU countries, some are not feasible in practicality. For instance, films that receive government loans are obliged to be completed during the year the loan is granted. Considering the loans are customarily received around mid-year, such regulation is contrary to the nature of filmmaking, according to Aydın Sayman; difficulties that may delay the shooting aside, at present it is not possible to make a film with a story that would stretch over seasons.[14]

Producers often rely on private resources, which have been reduced in the last few years. Once the main sponsor, Efes Pilsen (a beer company) has stopped funding films. Only small sponsors are available, such as a textile company that may take care of the costumes or a transportation company that may offer their vehicles. If Kodak film is used, Kodak covers the poster expenses, etc.[15] Filmmakers such as Abdullah Oğuz

(*Bliss*) work in the commercial sector (advertising and TV series) to be able to finance cinema projects. Luring television celebrities is a guarantee of box-office success, a trend that Yavuz Turgul established with *The Bandit*. Handan İpekçi explained during our interview that the government loan, a grant from the United Nations and a monetary award from the Thessaloniki Script Competition covered only 30 per cent of the budget of *Hidden Faces*. Most of the crew worked voluntarily, waiting for box-office gains.[16] Ahmet Boyacıoğlu, a staunch representative of the industry in international relations and the director of the Festival of European Films on Wheels, laments the lack of such government support as the filmmakers of EU countries benefit from. 'Do the young filmmakers today have to mortgage their grandmother's real estate to realize their projects?' he asks.[17]

Critics and filmmakers such as Demirkubuz point out that countless mediocre TV series that constantly repeat themselves set standards that are detrimental to the development of Turkish cinema, the artistic quality of which has not grown in proportion to production numbers. One of the weaknesses of contemporary films is the lack of good stories, ironic for a country that has remarkable potential in this respect. Many filmmakers choose modern stories from other cultures rather than delving into the richness of their own culture and the dynamics of local daily experiences, social or political. Scriptwriting has not developed professionally, despite cinema sections in several universities around the country. Another aspect is that not many filmmakers try their hands in genre cinema, or do it without research. Detective or horror films suffer from bad scripts. Even the genre of melodrama, of which Yeşilçam had given such good examples, Göral argues, is mediocre, except perhaps for *My Father and My Son*. As for comedies, mature comedies are so obscure that it is difficult to decipher what they parody; a good example is *Maskeli Beşler / The Masked Five* (2006) by Murat Aslan, and the so-called teenage comedies such as *Çılgın Dersane / Wild Classroom* (2007) by Faruk Aksoy are 'kitsch and trash'. 'Our cinema sector is composed of filmmakers whose creativity has been curbed by the self-censorship they have mastered; the new generation has developed a malady that can be identified as "distribution/exhibition syndrome" and the filmmakers with commercial inclinations suffer from the greed to make money easily.'[18]

There are some who succeed in the commercial sector, such as Yavuz Turgul and Abdullah Oğuz, with films that maintain high standards, and some who receive international acclaim with self-reflexive films of remarkable artistic accomplishment, Nuri Bilge Ceylan, Zeki Demirkubuz, Semih Kaplanoğlu and Derviş Zaim to name a few. Burçak Evren comments that the second group has appeared in a transition period of stalemate for Turkish cinema following the establishment of the American majors during 1987–8, which, benefiting from the Foreign Capital Act, took over the distribution and exhibition market. The 'independent filmmakers', as Evren calls the group that started to make films after 1990, have tried to surpass the boundaries of traditional filmmaking economically, ideologically and aesthetically. Their small budget films were like a silent rebellion against the hegemony of Hollywood. One of the changes they brought was to channel capital from outside into the cinema sector. Despite risks involved, they shouldered single-handedly the roles of producer, director, screenwriter, cameraman and if necessary actor. For the first time in Turkish cinema actors were chosen for the film and not the film for the actors. Using unknown faces they resisted the classical Yeşilçam tradition of attributing the commercial success of a film to its actor(s). They also displayed remarkable freedom of narrative choice. But they gradually began to repeat themselves and furthermore, lacked a common subject, theme or ideology. The style of personal and individual cinema that they deliberately chose, focused on the interior and offered the possibility of several readings, was awarded at national film festivals and praised by the press, but could not find the same support from the masses.[19]

The dilemma of young filmmakers is that they do not know how to make films with mass appeal, according to Agah Özgüç, 'films that would target different audiences'. The artistic aspect is important, but in the past, for instance, Metin Erksan's *Acı Hayat / Bitter Life* (1962) (a 'black passion' film that is considered within the social realist movement), broke box-office records but it was also a very good film, considered one of the best love films ever made. Memduh Ün's *Üç Arkadaş / Three Friends* (1958) was a good film (said to owe its success to the collaboration of several professionals) that also appealed to the masses. Ertem Eğilmez's *Arabesk / Arabesque* reached audiences from different backgrounds during a period when cinemas were closing. *Amerikalı* and *The Bandit* are films that have attracted the audiences. 'Today, Turkish cinema lacks good stories. The films of the new generation reflect their personal anxieties from their point of view, but do not reach the audience. Mentioning 'Yeşilçam sensibility' is a taboo these days, but Yeşilçam knew how to appeal to the audience. Furthermore, some of the new generation film-makers are successful with their first or second films but are not able to maintain the same level, such as Serdar Akar with *Gemide / On Board* (1998) and Zeki Demirkubuz with *Innocence*.'[20]

In an interview, Deniz Yavuz, secretary general of the Film Critics' Association (SİYAD), comments that the reason why local films have not improved in quality parallel to the increase in production numbers is that the same filmmakers make similar box-office films that do not appeal to cinéphiles. The average filmgoer has the budget to go to the cinema once a fortnight; therefore the increase in the number of productions may not mean an automatic increase in the number of tickets sold. The audience increased from 27 million in 2006 to 33 million in 2007, but this was possible only with four or five commercial films. Yavuz thinks that if Demirkubuz, Ceylan or Zaim made films with a bigger budget and better technical quality they would attract larger audiences than they do at present. He also suggests that the 10 per cent of the profit from the box office, which the state appropriates, should be given to the film sector; the films to be supported should be determined more rapidly and sponsorship that is based on family or friendship ties should be institutionalized.[21]

Similar to the trend in many countries, there has been a steady increase in the number of cinemas as well as individual cinema halls with the opening of multiplexes inside shopping centres (from 279 cinemas and 292 halls in 1992 to 458 cinemas and 1,299 halls in 2006). On the other hand, in the last two years, 40 neighbourhood cinemas have closed and closures will increase, according to cinema owner Mehmet Soyarslan, unless the Ministry of Culture extends support. Turkey has about 25 million potential viewers; this number does not increase in proportion to the increase in the number of cinema halls, which reached 1,346 in 2007. Since the multiplex chains prefer mainstream cinema with box-office guarantees, in the future it will be much more difficult for local films to secure exhibition space, claims Soyarslan.[22]

How can Turkish films become part of international distribution?, Zaim asks. Unless it has been produced in partnership with a reputable Western producer, the first condition for a Turkish film to be considered for foreign sales is its participation in the official programme of important festivals. Favourable reviews in the major media outlets are also instrumental in securing sales and distribution. Unfortunately, it is rare for Turkish films to be chosen for the main programme of prestigious festivals such as Cannes and Venice. With few exceptions, Turkish cinema seems to be categorized as a cinema that usually appears in the sidebars. Two Demirkubuz films, *Confession* (2001) and *Fate* (2001), were screened in the Un Certain Regard section of the Cannes Film Festival and did not attract many buyers. Erden Kıral's *On the Way* (2005), screened in the Orizzonti section of the Venice Film Festival, did not find a buyer despite his previous festival success. Turkish cinema's lack of experience in sales and distribution at the international level, insufficient marketing budgets, lack of support from government organizations and the lack of interest in general in so-called art cinema contribute to the limited success of such films with international sales, but the image of the country is equally important, Zaim points out, in attracting foreign buyers.[23]

Turkish society has been rapidly modernized in tune with global technological advancements. Traditional values are challenged and the future is uncertain. The hegemony of Hollywood, competition from television and the DVD/VCD market, globalization, inflation, various forms of censorship and general lack of audience support are not issues unique to Turkish cinema. Filmmakers such as Demirkubuz and Ceylan have demonstrated that good films do not need mega-budgets, and the films of Ataman, Ustaoğlu, Öz and İpekçi, among others, are testimony to the fact that oppression from 'above' will not deter conscientious artists. More than the visible and invisible difficulties that threaten the industry, what will determine the future of Turkish cinema is the authenticity and originality of its filmmakers, who, after decades of political unrest, rapid changes in society and the heavy hand of censorship, have continually succeeded in proposing alternative and personal perspectives on their realities.

# Film Credits

**40m² of Germany / 40m² Deutschland**, 1986, 80 mins, colour
Director, Producer and Scriptwriter: Tevfik Başer; Production: Film Production/ Studio Hamburg Film Production; Cinematographer: İzzet Akay; Editor: Renate Merck; Music: Klaus Bantzer; Cast: Özay Fecht, Yaman Okay, Demir Gökgöl, Mustafa Gölpınar, Grit Mackentanz, Marita Petersen, Reinhold Fama, Kay Miller

**Abdullah of Minye / Minyeli Abdullah**, 1989, 118 mins, colour
Director: Yücel Çakmaklı; Production: Feza Film; Producer: Mehmet Tanrısever; Scriptwriter: Bülent Oran (based on a story by İsmail Hekimoğlu); Cinematographer: Hüseyin Özşahin; Editor: Turgut İnangiray; Music: Ahmet Güvenç; Cast: Perihan Savaş, Berhan Şimşek, Haluk Kurdoğlu, Nazan Saatçi, Lütfü Seyfullah, Can Özsobay

**Angel's Fall / Meleğin Düşüşü**, 2004, 98 mins, colour
Director and Scriptwriter: Semih Kaplanoğlu; Producer: Semih Kaplanoğlu; Panayiotis Payazoglu, Yorgos Lykiardopoulos and Lilette Botassi; Production: Kaplan Film; Cinematographer: Eyüp Boz; Editor: Ayhan Ergürsel, Semih Kaplanoğlu and Susan Hande Güneri; Cast: Tülin Özen, Budak Akalın, Musa Karagöz, Engin Doşan, Yeşim Ceren Bozoğlu, Özlem Turhal, Can Kolukısa

**The Anxiety / Endişe**, 1974, colour
Director: Şerif Gören; Producer and Scriptwriter: Yılmaz Güney; Production: Güney Film; Cinematographer: Kenan Ormanlar; Music: Attila Özdemiroğlu, Sanar Yurdatapan; Cast: Erkan Yücel, Kamran Usluer, Adem Tolay, Ayşe Emel Mesçi Kuray, Nizam Ergüden, Mehmet Eken, İnsel Ardan, Yaşar Gökoğlu, Ahmet Bayrak

**Atıf Hodja of İskilip – Butterflies Fly to Eternity / İskilipli Atıf Hoca – Kelebekler Sonsuza Uçar**, 1993, 110 mins, colour
Director and Scriptwriter: Mesut Uçakan; Producer: Mustafa Çelik; Production: Dost Film; Cinematographer: Ümit Ardabak; Music: Özhan Eren; Cast: Yılmaz Zafer, Haluk Kurtoğlu, Nilüfer Aydan, Baki Tamer, Gülay Pınarbaşı, Arzu Atalay

**Balcony / Denize Hançer Düştü**, 1992, 94 mins, colour
Director (and Scriptwriter and Producer): Mustafa Altıoklar, Production: Negatif Film, Cinematographer: Uğur İçbak, Editor: Hilmi Güver, Music: Mete Sakpınar, Cast: Nur Sürer, Yasemin Alkaya, Yaman Okay, Zühtü Erkan

**The Bandit / Eşkıya**, 1996, 212 mins, colour
Director and Scriptwriter: Yavuz Turgul; Producer: Mine Vargi; Production: Filma-Cass, Artcam International and Geopoly; Cinematographer: Uğur İçbak; Editor: Onur Tan, Selahattin Turgut; Art Director: Mustafa Ziya Ülkenciler; Music: Erkan Oğur; Cast: Şener Şen, Uğur Yücel, Kamran Usluer, Yeşim Salkım, Kayhan Yıldızoğlu, Şermin Şen Hürmeriç, Jeyan Mahfi Ayral

**Big Man, Small Love** aka **Hejar / Büyük Adam, Küçük Aşk** aka **Hejar**, 2001, 120 mins, colour
Director (and Producer and Scriptwriter): Handan İpekçi; Production: Yeni Yapım Film Ltd, Hyperion S.A., Focus Film; Cinematographer: Erdal Kahraman; Editor: Nikos Kanakis; Music: Serdar Yalçın and Mazlum Çimen; Cast: Şükran Güngör, Dilan Erçetin, Füsun Demirel, Yıldız Kenter, İsmail Hakkı Şen

**The Birds of Nostalgia** aka **Migrating Birds** aka **Birds of Exile / Gurbet Kuşları**, 1964, 90 mins, black and white
Director: Halit Refiğ; Producer: Recep Ekicigil; Production: Artist Film; Scriptwriters: Orhan Kemal and Halit Refiğ (based on a play by Turgut Özakman); Cinematographer: Çetin Gürtop; Art Director: Danyal Topatan; Cast: Tanju Gürsu, Filiz Akın, Özden Çelik, Pervin Par, Cüneyt Arkın, Sevda Ferdağ, Önder Somer, Hüseyin Baradan, Mğmtaz Ener, Gülbin Eray, Danyal Topatan, Muadelet Tibet

**Bliss / Mutluluk**, 2007, 126 mins, colour
Director: Abdullah Oğuz; Producer: Abdullah Oğuz and George Lykiardopoulos; Production: ANS Productions; Scriptwriter: Kubilay Tunçer, Elif Ayan and Abdurrahman Oğuz (based on *Mutluluk / Bliss* by Zülfü Livaneli); Cinematographer: Mirsad Heroviç; Editor: Levent Çelebi and Abdullah Oğuz; Music: Zülfü Livaneli; Cast: Talat Bulut, Özgü Namal, Murat Han, Mustafa Avkıran, Emin Gürsoy, Şebnem Köstem, Meral Çetinkaya, Erol Babaoğlu

**Block C / C Blok**, 1994, 95 mins, colour
Director, Producer and Screenwriter: Zeki Demirkubuz; Production: Mavi Film;
Cinematographer: Ertunç Şenkay; Editor: Nevzat Dişaçık; Music: Serdar Keskin; Cast:
Fikret Kuşkan, Serap Aksoy, Zuhal Gencer, Selçuk Yöntem, Ülkü Duru

**The Blood Money / Diyet**, 1975, 90 mins, colour
Director (and Scriptwriter): Lütfi Ö. Akad; Producer: Hürrem Erman; Production:
Erman Film; Cinematographer: Gani Turanlı; Art Director: Erol Keskin; Music: Arif
Erkin; Cast: Hülya Koçyiğit, Hakan Balamir, Erol Günaydın, Güner Sümer, Atıf Kaptan,
Turgut Savaş, Güney Güner, Yaşar Şener, Murat Tok, Osman Alyanak, Uğur Kıvılcım

**The Blue Exile / Mavi Sürgün**, 1993, 108 mins, colour
Director: Erden Kıral; Producer: Kenan Ormanlar; Production: Elly Scheller-Ormanlar;
Scriptwriters: Erden Kıral; Kenan Ormanlar, Elly Scheller-Ormanlar; Cinematographer:
Kenan Ormanlar; Music: Timur Selçuk; Editor: Karin Fischer; Sound: Simon Happ;
Costume: Zepür Hanımyan; Cast: Can Togay, Hanna Schygulla, Özay Fecht, Ayşe
Romey, Tatiana Papamoshou, Halil Ergün

**The Bride / Gelin**, 1973, 92 mins, colour
Director and Scriptwriter: Lütfi Ö. Akad; Producer: Hürrem Erman; Production: Erman
Film; Cinematographer: Gani Turanlı; Editor: Ismail Kalkan; Music: Yalçın Tura; Cast:
Hülya Koçyiğit, Kerem Yılmazer, Kamran Usluer, Aliye Rona, Nazan Adalı, Ali Şen,
Kahraman Kıral, Seden Kızıltunç

**The Bus / Otobüs**, 1974, 87 mins, colour
Director (and Scriptwriter and Editor): Tunç Okan; Producer: Arif Keskiner and Tunç
Okan, Cengiz Ergun; Production: Pan Film; Cinematographer: Güneş Karabuda; Music:
Zülfü Livaneli, Pierre Favre, Leon Françoli; Cast: Tunç Okan, Tuncel Kurtiz, Björn
Gedda, Aras Ören, Nuri Sezer, Hasan Gül, Sümer Işgör, Ünal Nurkan, Nadir Sütemen

**The Bus Passengers / Otobüs Yolcuları**, 1961, 99 mins, black and white
Director: Ertem Göreç; Producer: Nusret İkbal; Production: Be-Ya Film; Scriptwriter:
Vedat Türkali; Cinematographer: Turgut Ören, Music: Yalçın Tura; Cast: Ayhan Işık,
Türkan Şoray, Senih Orkan, Salih Tozan, Suna Pekuysal, Ahmet Tarık Tekçe, Reha
Yurdakul, Atıf Kaptan, Suphi Kaner, Avni Dilligil, Diclehan Baban

**Chinese are Coming / Çinliler Geliyor**, 2007, 98 mins, colour
Director: Zeki Ökten; Producer: Zafer Çelik, Temel Kerimoğlu and Baha Serter;
Production: Kara Film, Scriptwriter: Fatih Altınöz; Cinematographer: Gökhan Atılmış;
Editor: Nevzat Dişiaçık; Music: Cafer İşleyen and Selim Bölükbaşı; Cast: Cüneyt Türel,

Bülent Kayabaş, Gürgen Öz, Nilgün Belgün, Şenay Gürler, Salih Kalyon

## Climates / İklimler, 2006, 101 mins, colour

Director and Scriptwriter: Nuri Bilge Ceylan; Producer: Zeynep Özbatur; Production: Pyramide, NBC Film and IMAJ; Cinematographer: Gökhan Tiryaki; Editors: Nuri Bilge Ceylan, Ayhan Ergürsel; Cast: Ebru Ceylan, Nuri Bilge Ceylan, Nazan Kesal, Mehmet Eryılmaz, Arif Aşçı, Can Özbatur, Fatma Ceylan, Semra Yıldız, Abdullah Demirkubuz, Feridun Koç, Ceren Olcay, Zeker Saka

## Clouds of May / Mayıs Sıkıntısı, 1999, 131 mins (long version) and 117 mins (short version), colour

Director, Producer, Scriptwriter and Cinematographer: Nuri Bilge Ceylan; Production: NBC Film; Editor: Ayhan Ergürsel, Nuri Bilge Ceylan; Music: J. C. Bach, Handel and Schubert; Cast: M. Emin Ceylan, Muzaffer Özdemir, Fatma Ceylan, Muhammed Zımbaoğlu, Mehmet Emin Toprak, Sadık İncesu

## Confession / İtiraf, 2001, 90 mins, colour

Director, Producer, Scriptwriter, Cinematographer, Editor: Zeki Demırkubuz; Production: Mavi Film; Cast: Taner Birsel, Başak Köklükaya

## Crossing the Bridge: The Sound of Istanbul, 2005, 90 mins, black and white and colour

Director (and Cinematographer and Scriptwriter): Fatih Akın; Producer: Fatih Akın, Sandra Harzer, Christian Kux, Klaus Maeck, Tina Mersmann, Andreas Thiel; Production: Corazon International, NDR, intervista digital media; Cinematography: Herve Dieu; Editor: Andrew Bird; Cast: Alexander Hacke, Baba Zula, Orient Expressions, Duman, Replikas, Erkin Koray, Ceza, Istanbul Style Breakers, Mercan Dede, Selim Sesler, Brenna MacCrimmon, Siyasiyabend, Orhan Gencebay, Müzeyyan Senar, Sezen Aksu

## Dad Is in the Army / Babam Askerde, 1994, 86 mins, colour

Director (and Producer and Scriptwriter): Handan İpekçi; Production: Yeni Yapımlar Ltd; Cinematographer: Tevfik Şenol; Editor: Nevzat Dişiaçık; Art Director: Ayşe Akıllıoğlu; Music: A. Sinan Hatipoğlu; Cast: Gülnihal Yazıcı, Yunus Gencer, Zühal Gencer Erkaya, Nurettin Şen, Nuran Bozkurt, Yasemin Alkaya, Hülya Karakaş, Mehmet Atak, Murat Daltaban, Ceylan Öcal, Ali Sürmeli, Füsun Demirel, Selçuk Uluergüven, İsmail Hakkı Şen, Tanju Yücel, Saim Yavuz

## The Day of the Eclipse of the Sun / Güneşin Tutulduğu Gün, 1983, colour

Director: Şerif Gören; Production: Anadolu Filmcilik; Scriptwriter: Barış Pirhasan,

Turgay Aksoy; Cinematographer: Ertunç Şenkay; Cast: Müjde Ar, Bülent Bilgiç, Selahattin Fırat, Gülşen Girginkoç, Günay Girik, Fatoş Çelik, Fatma İpek, Tuncay Akça, Gülşen Girgin

### Destiny / Kader, 2006, 104 mins, colour
Director, Producer, Scriptwriter, Cinematographer and Editor: Zeki Demirkubuz; Production: Mavi Film; Music: Edward Artemiev; Cast: Vildan Atasever, Ufuk Bayraktar, Müge Ulusoy, Engin Akyürek, Ozan Bilen, Settar Tanrıöğen, Erkan Can

### Distant / Uzak, 2002, 110 mins, colour
Director (and Producer, Cinematographer and Scriptwriter): Nuri Bilge Ceylan; Production: NBC Film; Editor: Nuri Bilge Ceylan and Ayhan Ergürsel; Art Director: Ebru Ceylan; Music: Mozart (c.364); Cast: Muzaffer Özdemir, Mehmet Emin Toprak, Zuhal Gencer Erkaya, Nazan Kırılmış, Feridun Koç, Fatma Ceylan, Ebru Ceylan

### A Dry Summer / Susuz Yaz, 1963, 90 mins, black and white
Director: Metin Erksan; Scriptwriter: Metin Erksan, Kemal İnci, İsmet Soydan (based on a work by Necati Cumalı); Producer: Metin Erksan and Ulvi Doğan; Production: Hitit Film, Erksan Film, Doğan Film; Cinematographer: Ali Uğur; Music: Ahmet Yamacı, Manos Hadjidakis; Cast: Ulvi Doğan, Hülya Koçyiğit, Erol Taş, Hakkı Haktan, Yavuz Yalınkılıç, Zeki Tüney, Alaattin Altıok

### The Edge of Heaven / Auf der Anderen Seite / Yaşamın Kıyısında, 2007, 122 mins, colour
Director (and scriptwriter): Fatih Akin; Producer: Fatih Akin, Andreas Thiel, Klaus Maeck Production: Corazon Int, Anka Film; Cinematographer: Rainer Klausman; Editor: Andrew Bird; Music: Shantel; Cast: Nurgül Yeşilçay, Tuncel Kurtiz, Baki Davrak, Patrycia Ziolkowska, Nursel Köse, Hanna Schygulla

### Elegy / Ağıt, 1971, 82 mins, colour
Director (and Producer/Scriptwriter): Yılmaz Güney; Production: Akün Film, Güney Film; Cinematographer: Gani Turanlı; Music: Arif Erkin; Cast: Yılmaz Güney, Hayati Ham-zaoğlu, Bilal İnci, Atilla Olgaç, Yusuf Koç, Şahin Dilbaz, Şermin Hümeriç, Nizam Ergüden

### Elephants and Grass / Filler ve Çimen, 2000, 115 mins, colour
Director and Scriptwriter: Derviş Zaim; Producer: Ali Akdeniz; Production: Pan Film Filmcilik Ltd; Cinematographer: Ertunç Şenkay; Editor: Mustafa Preşeva; Music: Serdar Ateşer; Cast: Haluk Bilginer, Senem Çelik, Ali Sürmeli, Bülent Kayabaş, Uğur Polat, Taner Barlas, Taner Birsel, Arif Akkaya

## The Enemy / Düşman, 1979, 125 mins, colour

Director: Zeki Ökten; Producer and Scriptwriter: Yılmaz Güney; Production: Güney Film; Cinematographer: Çetin Tunca; Music: Yavuz Top; Cast: Aytaç Arman, Güngör Bayrak, Hikmet Çelik, Güven Şengil, Kamil Sönmez, Hüseyin Kutman, Muadalet Tibet, Şevket Altuğ, Fehabet Atilla, Hasan Ceyhan, Fehmi Yaşar, Macit Koper, Lütfi Engin

## Far Away / Dur / Uzak, 2005, 75 mins, colour

Director (and Producer, Cinematographer and Editor): Kazım Öz; Production: kolektifa sinema ya mezopotamya

## Fate / Yazgı, 2001, 120 mins, colour

Director, (and Scriptwriter, Editor and Producer): Zeki Demirkubuz; Production: Mavi Filmcilik; Cinematographer: Ali Utku; Cast: Serdar Orçin, Zeynep Tokuş, Engin Günaydın, Demir Karahan

## The Father / Baba, 1971, 96 mins, colour

Director (and Scriptwriter): Yılmaz Güney; Producer: İrfan Ünal; Production: Akün Film; Cinematographer: Gani Turanlı; Music: Metin Bükey, Yalçın Tura; Sound: Necip Sarıcıoğlu; Cast: Yılmaz Güney, Müşerref Tezcan, Aytaç Arman, Ferudun Çölgeçen, Nedret Güvenç, Nimet Tezel, Mehmet Büyükgüngör, Yeşim Tan, Muammer Özalan, Güven Şengil, Faik Coşkun, Osman Han, Ali Seyhan, Mehmet Yağmur, Mustafa Yavuz, Ahmet Karaca, Cemal Tezen, Oktay Demiriş, Saliha Demiriş

## Four Women in the Harem / Haremde Dört Kadın, 1965, 110 mins, black and white

Director: Halit Refiğ; Producer: Nüzhet-Özdemir Birsel; Production: Birsel Film; Scriptwriter: Kemal Tahir, Halit Refiğ; Cinematographer: Memduh Yükman and Mike Rafaelyan; Art Director: Stavro Yuanidis; Music: Metin Bükey; Cast: Cüneyt Arkın, Pervin Par, Tanju Gürsu, Nilüfer Aydan, Sami Ayanoğlu, Birsen Menekşeli, Ayfer Feray, Devlet Devrim, Önder Somer, Hüseyin Baradan, Gülbin Eray, Zeki Alpan

## Fratricide / Brudermord, 2005, 90 mins, colour

Director (and Scriptwriter): Yılmaz Arslan; Producers: Eric Tavitian, Eddy Geradon-Luyckx, Donato Rotunno, Yılmaz Arslan; Production: Tarantula, Yılmaz Arslan Film Production; Cinematographer: Jean-Francois Hensgens; Editor: Andre Bendocchi-Alves; Sound Engineer: Laurent Benaim; Music: Evgueni Galperine; Cast: Xewat Gectan, Erdal Çelik, Nurettin Çelik, Bülent Büyükaşık, Xhiljona Ndoja, Oral Uyan

## The Friend / Arkadaş, 1974, 90 mins, colour

Director (and Scriptwriter and Producer): Yılmaz Güney; Production: Güney Film;

Cinematographer: Çetin Tunca; Music: Attila Özdemiroğlu, Şanar Yurdatapan; Cast: Yılmaz Güney, Kerim Afşar, Azra Balkan, Civan Canova, Melike Demirağ, Nizam Ergüden, Semra Özdamar

### Gülüşan, 1986, 79 mins, colour
Director and Scriptwriter: Bilge Olgaç; Producer: Şeref Gür; Production: Şeref Film; Cinematographer: Hüseyin Özşahin; Music: Timur Selçuk; Cast: Halil Ergün, Yaprak Özdemiroğlu, Meral Orhonsoy, Güler Ökten

### Head-on / Gegen die Wand / Duvara Karşı, 2003, 121 mins, colour
Director and Scriptwriter: Fatih Akın; Producers: Andreas Schreitmüller and Stefan Schubert; Production: Bavaria Film International, Corazon International, NDR, Panfilm, Wüste Film, Arte; Cinematographer: Reiner Klausmann; Editor: Andrew Bird; Music: Klaus Maeck; Cast: Birol Üner, Sibel Kekilli, Catrin Striebeck, Meltem Cümbül, Zarah McKenzie, Stefan Gebelhoff, Francesco Fiannaca, Demir Gökgöl, Yılmaz Güner, Birsen Güner

### The Herd aka The Flock / Sürü, 1978, 118 mins, colour
Director: Zeki Ökten; Producer: Yılmaz Güney; Production: Güney Film; Scriptwriter: Yilmaz Güney; Cinematographer: Izzet Akay; Editor: Özdemir Aritan; Art Director: Rauf Ozangil, Sabri Aslankara; Music: Zülfü Livaneli; Cast: Tarik Akan, Melike Demira ğ, Tuncel Kurtiz, Şenel Gökkaya, Meral Niron, Erol Demiröz, Yaman Okay, Savaş Yurttaş

### Her Name Is Vasfiye / Adı Vasfiye, 1986, 88 mins, colour
Director: Atıf Yılmaz; Producer: Cengiz Ergun; Production: Promete Film; Scriptwriter: Barış Pirhasan (based on stories by Necati Cumalı); Cinematographer: Orhan Oğuz; Art Director: Şahin Kaygun; Music: Atilla Özdemiroğlu; Cast: Müjde Ar, Aytaç Arman, Yılmaz Zafer, Macit Koper, Levent Yılmaz, Erol Durak, Suna Tanrıverdi, Oktay Kutluğ

### He's in the Army Now / O Şimdi Asker, 2002, 119 mins, colour
Director: Mustafa Altıoklar; Producer: Abdullah Oğuz; Production: ANS Yapım Yayın Reklamcılık; Scriptwriter: Levent Kazakö Mustafa Altıoklar; Cinematographer: Soykut Turan; Editor: Erol Adilçe; Music: Jingle House; Cast: Özcan Deniz, Ali Poyrazoğlu, Yavuz Bingöl, Gökhan Özoğuz, Mehmet Günsur, Pelin Batu, Seray Sever

### Home, 2002, 70 mins, colour
Director and Scriptwriter: Phyllis Katrapani; Producer: Jeannine Gagné and Phyllis Katrapani; Production: Amazon Film and Ile Blanche; Cinematographer: Phyllis Katrapani and Michel Lamothe; Editor: Louise Dugal; Music: Ned Bouhalassa; Cast: François Papineau, Jacinthe Laguë and Atanas Katrapani with participation of Eva Kyzirides, Myriam Saad, Patricia Diaz, Theo Diamantis, Jorge Martinez, Bachir Bensaddek

## The Hope / Umut, 1970, 100 mins, black and white

Director (and Producer): Yılmaz Güney; Production: Lale Film, Güney Film; Scriptwriter: Yılmaz Güney and Şerif Gören; Cinematographer: Kaya Ererez; Editor: Celal Köse; Music: Arif Erkin; Cast: Yılmaz Güney, Gülsen Alnıaçık, Tuncel Kurtiz, Osman Olyanak

## The Hopeless Ones / Umutsuzlar, 1971, colour

Director (and Scriptwriter): Yılmaz Güney; Producer: İrfan Ünal; Production: Akün Film; Cinematographer: Gani Turanlı; Art Director: Secat Kırmacı; Music: Yalçın Tura; Cast: Yılmaz Güney, Filiz Akın, Refik Kemal Arduman, Şükriye Atav, Mehmet Büyükgüngör, İhsan Gedik, Hayati Hamzaoğlu

## The Horse / At, 1981, 116 mins, colour,

Director (and Producer): Ali Özgentürk; Production: ZDF, Kentel Film and Asya Film; Scriptwriter: Işıl Özgentürk; Cinematographer: Kenan Ormanlar; Music: Okay Temiz; Editor: Yılmaz Atadeniz; Cast: Genco Erkal, Harun Yeşilyurt, Güler Ökten, Ayberk Çölok, Yaman Okay, Macit Koper, Selçuk Uluergüven, Erol Demiröz, Bektaş Altınok, Sıdıka Duruer, Suna Selen, Lütfi Engin, Erdal Gülver, Gülsen Tuncer, Gönül Dönmez, Filiz Katrapani

## Horse, Woman, Gun / At, Avrat, Silah, 1966, black and white

Director (and Scriptwriter): Yılmaz Güney; Producer: Hasan Kazankaya; Production: Kazankaya Films; Cinematographer: Vedat Akdimen; Cast: Yılmaz Güney, Nebahat Çehre, Tuncel Kurtiz, Cahide Sonku, Mümtaz Ener, Danyal Topatan, Tuncel Kurtiz, Sedef Türkay, Sami Tunç

## How Can Asiye Be Saved? / Asiye Nasıl Kurtulur?, 1986, 105 mins, colour

Director: Atıf Yılmaz; Producer: Cengiz Ergun; Production: Odak Film, Scriptwriter: Barış Pirhasan; Cinematographer: Kenan Davutoğlu; Editor: Mevlut Koçak; Music: Sarper Özsan; Sound: Ertan Aktaş; Cast: Müjde Ar, Ali Poyrazoğlu, Hümeyra, Nuran oktar, Yaman Okay, Güler Ökten, Füsun demirel, Fatoş Sezer, Yavuzer Çetinkaya,

## If Dreams Could Come True / Rüyalar Gerçek Olsa, 1972, colour

Director (and Producer): Hulki Saner; Production: Saner Film; Scriptwriter: Oksal Pekmezoğlu; Cinematographer: Çetin Tunca; Music: Emel Sayın; Cast: Engin Çağlar, Müjdat Gezen, Esen Püsküllü, Kayhan Yıldızoğlu, Hulusi Kentmen

## In the Bar / Barda, 2006, 92 mins, colour

Director (and Producer and Scriptwriter): Serdar Akar; Production: Filmakar; Cinematographer: Mehmet Aksın; Editor: Aziz İmamoğlu; Music: Selim Demirdelen;

Cast: Nejat İşler, Hakan Boyav, Serdar Orçin, Erdal Beşikçioğlu, Volga Sorgu, Doğu Alpan, Burak Altay, Melis Birkan, Meltem Parlak

## In the Name of the Law / Kanun Namına, 1952, 95 mins, black and white

Director: Lütfi Ö. Akad; Producer: Osman Seden; Production: Kemal Film; Scriptwriter: Osman Seden; Cinematographer: Enver Burçkin; Cast: Ayhan Işık, Gülistan Güzey, Muzaffer Tema, Pola Morelli, Settar Körmükçü, Neşe Yulaç, Nubar Terziyan, Muhterem Nur, Talat Artemel, Muazzez Arçay

## Innocence / Masumiyet, 1997, 110 mins, colour

Director and Scriptwriter: Zeki Demirkubuz; Producer: Zeki Demirkubuz and Nihal G. Koldaş; Production: Mavi Film; Cinematographer: Ali Utku; Editor: Mevlüt Koçak, Music: Cengiz Onural; Cast: Haluk Bilginer, Derya Alabora, Güven Kıraç

## Innowhereland / Hiçbiryerde, 2002, 90 mins, colour

Director and Scriptwriter: Tayfun Pirselimoğlu; Producers: Zeynep Özbatur, Kadri Yurdatap, Gudrun Ruzickova-Steiner; Production: Mine Film and Media Luna; Cinematographer: Colin Mounier; Editors: Şevket Uysal and Hamdi Deniz; Music: Cengiz Onural; Sound: Nuh Mete Deniz; Art Director: Natali Yeres; Cast: Zühal Olcay, Mizhael Mendl, Parkan Özturan, Meral Okay, Ruhi Sarı, Cezmi Baskın, Devin Özgür Çınar

## International / Beynelmilel, 2006, 106 mins, colour

Directors (and Scriptwriters): Sırrı Süreyya Önder and Muharrem Gülmez; Producer: Necati Akpınar; Production: BKM Film; Cinematographer: Gökhan Atılmış; Editor: Engin Öztürk; Music: Kalan Müzik, Aytekin G. Ataş, Sırrı Süreyya Önder and Tolga Kılıç; Cast: Cezmi Baskın, Özgü Namal, Umut Kurt, Bahri Beyat, Meral Okay, Nazmi Kırık, Dilber Ay, Oktay Kaynarca

## Istanbul Beneath My Wings / Istanbul Kanatlarımın Altında, 1996, 120 mins, colour

Director and Scriptwriter: Mustafa Altıoklar; Producer: Üstün Karabol; Production: Ümit Sanat Ürünbleri Ltd.; Cinematographer: Uğur İçbak; Music: Tuluyhan Uğurlu, Cast: Beatriz Rico, Ege Aydan, Okan Bayülgenü Haluk Bilginer, Zuhal Olcay, Burak Sergen, Savai Ay

## Ithaca / Ithaque, 1997, 35 mins, black and white

Director, Producer, Scriptwriter and Editor: Phyllis Katrapani; Production: Ile Blanche; Cinematographer: Phyllis Katrapani and Michel Lamothe; Music: Erich Kory; Cast: Atanas Katrapani

**Journey to the Sun / Güneşe Yolculuk**, 1999, 104 mins, colour
Director and Scriptwriter: Yeşim Ustaoğlu; Producer: Behrooz Hashemian; Production: Ifr, The Film Company Amsterdam, Medıas Res Berlin, Fabrica, Arte / ZDF; Cinematographer: Jacek Petrycki; Editor: Nicolas Goster; Music: Vlato Stefanovski; Cast: Nevruz Baz, Nazmi Kırık, Mizgin Kapazan, Nigar Aktar, İskender Bağcılar, Ara Güler

**The Land / Ax / Toprak**, 1999, 27 mins, colour
Director (and Editor): Kazım Öz, Production: Mezopotamya Sinema Yapımı3 Film Prodüksüyon; Scriptwriter: MKM Cinema Department (Group Work); Cinematographer: Ahmet Demir, Art Director: Özkan Küçük; Music: Mustafa Biber, Yasin Boyraz; Cast: Hikmet Karagöz and players from Theatre Jiyana Nu

**The Law of the Borders / Hudutların Kanunu**, 1966, 68 mins, black and white
Director: Lütfi Ö. Akad; Producer: Kadir Kesemen; Production: Dadaş Film; Scriptwriter: Yılmaz Güney and Lütfi Ö. Akad; Cinematographer: Ali Uğur; Music: Nida Tüfekçi; Cast: Yılmaz Güney, Pervin Par, Erol Taş, Tuncel Kurtiz, Osman Alyanak, Atilla Ergün, Kadir Savun, Muharrem Gürses, Tuncer Necmioğlu, Aydemir Akbaş, Hikmet Olgun, Danyal Topatan

**Let There Be Light / Işıklar Sönmesin**, 1996, 90 mins, colour
Director: Reis Çelik; Producer: Ferdi Eğilmez; Production: Arzu Film; Scriptwriter: Cemal Şan and Reis Çelik; Cinematographer: Aytekin Çakmakçı; Editor: İsmail Kalkan; Music: Maslum Çimen; Cast: Berhan Şimşek, Tarık Tarcan, Sermin Karaali, Tuncel Kurtiz

**Licensed to Love / Vesikalı Yarim**, 1968, 90 mins, black and white
Director: Lütfi Ö. Akad; Producer: Şeref Gür; Production: Şeref Film; Scriptwriter: Safa Önal; Cinematographer: Alı Uğur; Music: Metin Bükey; Cast: Türkan Şoray, İzzet Günay, Ayfer Freay, Aydemir Balkan, Semih Sezerli, Hakkı Haktan, Behçet Nacar, Selahattin İçsel

**Lola and Bilidikid / Lola ve Bilidikid / Lola und Bilidikid**, 1998, 93 mins, colour
Director and Scriptwriter: Kutluğ Ataman; Producer: Zeynep Özbatur, Mastin Hagemann and James Schamus; Production: CandO Prodiksiyon; Cinematographer: Chris Squires; Editor: Eva J. Lind; Music: Arpad Bondy; Cast: Gandi Mukli, Erdal Yıldız, Baki Davrak, Inge Keller, Celal Perk, Mesut Özdemir, Murat Yılmaz, Hakan Tandoğan, Cihangir Gümüştürkmen, Ulrich Simontowitz, Hasan Ali Mete, Willi Heren, Mario İrrek

## A Man's Fear of God / Takva, 2006, 96 mins, colour

Director: Özer Kızıltan; Producer: Sevil Demirci and Fatih Akın; Production: Yeni Sinemacılar; Cinematographer: Soykut Turan; Editor: Andrew Bird and Niko; Music: Gökçe Akçelik; Cast: Erkan Can, Güven Kıraç, Meray Ülgen, Duygu Şen, Settar Tanrıöğen, Öznur Kula, Erman Saban, Engin Günaydın

## Moon Time / Ay Vakti, 1993, 100 mins, colour

Director (and Scriptwriter): Mahinur Ergun; Producer: Kadri Yurdatap; Production: Mine Film; Cinematographer: Uğur İçbak; Editor: Nevzat Dişiaçık; Music: Can Hakgüder; Cast: Müşfik Kenter, Zuhal Olcay, Füsun Demirel, Mehmet Kartal, Serra Yılmaz

## Mrs Salkım's Diamonds / Salkım Hanımın Taneleri, 1999, 137 mins, colour

Director: Tomris Giritlioğlu; Producer: Şükrü Avşar; Production: Avşar Film; Scriptwriter: Etyen Mahçupyan and Taner Baran (based on a novel by Yılmaz Karakoyunlu); Cinematographer: Yavuz Türkeri and Ercan Yılmaz; Editor: Mevlut Koçak; Music: Tamer Çıray; Cast: Zuhal Olcay, Hülya Avşar, Uğur Polat, Zafer Algöz, Kamuran Usluer, Derya Alabora, Güven Kıraç, Murat Daltaban, Nurseli İdiz

## Mud / Çamur, 2003, 98 mins, colour

Director (and Scriptwriter): Derviş Zaim; Producer: Derviş Zaim, Marco Muller, Panicos Chrysanthou; Production: Downtown Pictures, Marathon Film Yapımcılık and Aritmages; Cinematographer: Feza Çaldıran; Editor: Francesca Calvelli; Music: Michael Galasso, Koulis Theodorou; Cast: Taner Birsel, Yelda Reynaud, Mustafa Uğurlu

## The Muleteers / Katırcılar, 1987, colour

Director: Şerif Gören; Producer: Kadir Turgut, Ferit Turgut; Production: Uzman Fılm; Scriptwriter: Hüseyin Kuzu, Halit Türkyazıcı, Fuat Çelik; Cinematographer: Erdal Kahraman; Music: Bora Ayanoğlu; Cast: Ayşegül Aldinç, Bülent Bilgiç, Necmettin Çobanoğlu, Halil Ergün, Mehmet Esen, Kadir İnanır, Raci Kiper

## My Dark-eyed One / Kara Gözlüm, 1970, black and white

Director: Atıf Yılmaz; Producer: İrfan Ünal; Production: Akün Film; Scriptwriter: Bülent Oran; Cinematographer: Orhan Kapkı; Art Director: Secat Kırmacı; Music: Orhan Gencebay, Metin Bükey; Cast: Türkan Şoray, Kadir İnanır, Ali Şen, Aziz Basmacı, Diclehan Baban, Mualla Sürer, Müjdat Gezen, Turgut Boralı, Aynur Aydan, Mürüvvet Sim, Talia Salta, Rıza Tüzün, Kudret Karadağ

**My Daughter, Ayşe / Kızım Ayşe**, 1974, 100 mins, colour

Director and Producer: Yücel Çakmaklı; Production: Elif Film; Scriptwriter: Yücel Çakmaklı, Berrin Giz, Atilla Gökbürü; Production: Elif Film; Cinematographer: Mike Rafaelyan; Cast: Yıldız Kenter, Necla Nazır, Tülin Örsek, Şükran Güngör, Nazan Adalı, Hamit Yıldırım, Mahmut Hekimoğlu, Turgut Boralı, Selçuk Özer

**The Night, Angel and Our Gang / Gece, Melek ve Bizim Çocuklar**, 1994, 105 mins, colour

Director: Atıf Yılmaz; Producer: Metin Erarabacı; Production: Yeşilçam Filmcilik; Scriptwriter: Yıldırım Türker; Cinematographer: İzzet Akay; Music: Uzay Hepari; Cast: Deniz Türkali, Derya Arbaş, Uzay Hepari, Deniz Atamtürk, Kaan Girgin, Mehmet Teoman

**Oh, Beautiful Istanbul / Ah, Güzel Istanbul**, 1966, 97 mins, black and white

Director: Atıf Yılmaz; Producer: Nusreet İkbal; Production: Be-Ya Film; Scriptwriter: Safa Önal; Cinematographer: Gani Turanlı; Editor: İsak Dilman; Music: Metin Bükey; Cast: Sadri Alışık, Ayla Algan, Diclehan baban, Feridun Çölgeçen, Danyal Topatan

**On the Way / Yolda**, 2005, 90 mins, colour

Director (and Scriptwriter): Erden Kıral; Producers: Erden Kıral, Georgy Cholakov and Pavlina Jeleva; Production: Deniz Film; Cinematographer: Zekeriya Kurtuluş; Editor: Şerif Gören; Music: Taner Ayan and Arıkan Sırakaya; Cast: Halil Ergün, Yeşim Büber, Serdar Orçin

**Pain / Acı**, 1971, 85 mins, colour

Director (and Scriptwriter): Yılmaz Güney; Producer: Namı Dilbaz; Production: Özleyiş Film; Cinematographer: Gani Turanlı; Music: Metin Büket; Cast: Mehmet Büyükgüngör, Fatma Girik, Yılmaz Güney, Hayati Hamzaoğlu, Oktay Yavuz

**The Photograph / Fotoğraf**, 2001, 66 mins, colour

Director and Scriptwriter: Kazım Öz; Production: Mezopotamya Kültür Merkezi; Cinematographer: Ercan Özkan; Music: Mustafa Biber; Cast: Feyyaz Duman, Nazmi Kırık, Mizgin Kapazan, Zülfiye Dolu

**The Poor** aka **The Suffering Ones / Zavallılar**, 1974, 72 mins, colour

Directors (and Scriptwriters): Yılmaz Güney and Atıf Yılmaz; Producer: Yılmaz Güney; Production: Güney Film; Cinematographer: Kenan Ormanlar and Gani Turanlı; Music: Şanar Yurdatapan and Atilla Özdemiroğlu; Cast: Yılmaz Güney, Yıldırım Önal, Güven Sengil, Nuran Aksoy, Göktürk Demirezen, Birtane Güngör, Seden Kızıltunç, Mehmet Şahiner, Hülya Şengül, Kamran Usluer

**The Revenge of the Serpents / Yılanların Öcü**, 1961, 110 mins, black and white
Director: Metin Erksan, Producer: Nusret İkbal; Production: Be-Ya Film; Scriptwriter: Metin Erksan (based on a novel by Fakir Baykurt); Cinematographer: Mengü Yeğin; Music: Yalçın Tura; Cast: Fikret Hakan, Nurhan Nur, Kadir Savun, Erol Taş, Ali Şen, Aliye Rona

**A Season in Hakkari / Hakkari'de Bir Mevsim**, 1983, 113 mins, colour
Director: Erden Kıral; Production: Data Inc. Kentel Film; Cinematographer: Kenan Ormanlar; Scriptwriter: Onat Kutlar; Editor: Yılmaz Atadeniz; Sound: Cemal Kıvanç; Music: Timur Selçuk; Cast: Genco Erkal, Erkan Yücel, Şerif Sezer, Rana Cabbar, Erol Demiröz, Berrin Koper, Macit Koper

**Seyyit Han** aka **The Bride of the Earth / Seyyit Han** aka **Toprağın Gelini**, 1968, 78 mins, black and white
Director (and Producer and Scriptwriter): Yılmaz Güney; Production: Güney Filmcilik; Cinematographer: Gani Turanlı; Music: Nedim Otyam; Cast: Yılmaz Güney, Nebahat Çehre, Hayati Hamzaoğlu, Nihat Ziyalan, Danyal Topatan, Sami Tunç, Hüseyin Zan, Çetin Başaran

**Silky / Ipekçe**, 1987, 102 mins, colour
Director and Scriptwriter: Bilge Olgaç; Production: Varlık Film; Cinematographer: Aytekin Çakmakçı; Editor: Nevzar Dişiaçık; Music: Serdar Yalçın; Cast: Perihan Savaş, Berhan Şimşek, Gülsen Tuncer, Oktar Durukan

**Siyabend and Xece / Siabend u Xece**, 1992, 100 mins, colour
Director: Şahin Gök; Producer: Senar Turgut; Production: Senar Film; Scriptwriter: Hüseyin Erdem; Cınematographer: Kamal Saydo, Georg Berg; Editor: Margot Löhlein; Music: Ken B. Wood, W. Fuhr, T. Daun; Cast: Tarik Akan, Mine Çayiroğlu, Yaman Okay, Yılmaz Erdoğan

**The Small Town / Kasaba**, 1997, 82 mins, black and white
Director, Scriptwriter, Cinematographer and Producer: Nuri Bilge Ceylan; Production: NBC Film; Editor: Ayhan Ergürsel, Nuri Bilge Ceylan; Music: Ali Kayacı (clarinet improvisation); Cast: Mehmet Emin Toprak, Havva Sağlam, Fatma Ceylan, Mehmet Emin Ceylan, Sercihan Alioğlu, Semra Yılmaz, Latif Altıntaş, Muzaffer Özdemir

**Somersault in a Coffin / Tabutta Rövaşata**, 1996, 75 mins, colour
Director (and Scriptwriter): Derviş Zaim; Producer: Ezel Akay, Derviş Zaim; Production:

IFR; Cinematographer: Mustafa Kuşçu; Editor: Mustafa Presheva; Music: Baba Zula –
Yansımalar; Sound Designer: Ender Akay; Sound Editors: Selim Kocabaşı, Ufuk Çoban;
Art Director: Aslı Kurnaz; Cast: Ahmet Uğurlu, Tuncel Kurtiz, Ayşen Aydemir, Şerif Erol,
Fuat Onan, Ahmet Çadırcı, Mahmut Benek, Nadı Güler, Figen Evren, Barış Çelikoğlu,
Hasan Uzma

## A Song for Beko / Stranek Ji Bo Beko / Beko'nun Türküsü / Ein Lied Für Beko, 1992, 110 mins, colour

Director: Nizamettin Ariç; Producer: Margarita Woskanjan; Scriptwriter: Nizamettin
Aric and Christine Kernich; Cinematographer: Thomas Mauch; Music: Nizamettin
Ariç; Cast: Nizamettin Ariç, Bezara Arsen, Lusika Hesen, Emale Jora

## Spoon Enemy aka A Wedding Room / Kaşık Düşmanı, 1984, 104 mins, colour

Director and Scriptwriter: Bilge Olgaç; Producer: Mehmet Ali Yılmaz; Production: Tek
Film; Cinematographer: Ümit Gülsoy; Music: Mutlu Torun; Cast: Perihan Savaş, Halil
Ergün, Mesut Engin, Ayşegül Ünsal, Aliye Rona, İsmet Ay, Seden Kızıltunç, Mesut
Engin, Ayşegül Ünsal, Menderes Samancılar, Ali Yaylı

## A Stranger in Town / Şehirdeki Yabancı, 1962, 80 mins, black and white

Director: Halit Refiğ; Producer: Nusret İkbal; Production: Be-Ya; Scriptwriter: Vedat
Türkali and Halit Refiğ; Cinematographer: Mengü Yeğin, Çetin Gürtop; Cast: Nilüfer
Aydan, Göksel Arsoy, Talat Gözba Reha Yurdakul, Ali Şen, Erol Taş, Hasan Ceylan,
Orhan Çubukçu, Abdullah Ataç, İclal Genç, Nusret Özkaya, Ateş Tekin

## A Taste of Love / Bir Yudum Sevgi, 1984, 96 mins, colour

Director: Atıf Yılmaz; Production: Yeşilçam Filmcilik; Scriptwriter: Latife Tekin, Atıf
Yılmaz, Fehmi Yaşar; Cinematographer: Çetin Tunca; Editor: Nevzat Dişiacık; Music:
Yalçın Tura; Sound: Erkan Aktaç; Cast: Kadir İnanır, Hale Soygazi, Macit Koper, Meral
Çetinkaya, Dursun Ali Sağıroğlu, Füsun Demirel, Serra Yılmaz

## The Third Page / Üçüncü Sayfa, 2000

Director, Scriptwriter and Producer: Zeki Demirkubuz; Production: Mavi Film;
Cinematographer: Ali Utku; Editor: Nevzat Dişiacık; Cast: Ruhi Sarı, Başak Köklükaya,
Cengiz Sezivi, Serdar Orçin, Emrah Elçiboğa, Naci Taşdöven

## Those Awakening in the Dark / Karanlıkta Uyananlar, 1964, 115 mins, black and white

Director: Ertem Göreç; Producer: Beklam Algan, Lütfi Ö. Akad; Production: Filmo
Ltd.; Scriptwriter: Vedat Türkali; Cinematographer: Turgut Ören and Mahmut Dem'r;

Music: Nedim Otyam, Cast: Fikret Hakan, Ayla Algan, Beklan Algan, Kenan Pars, Tülin Elgin, Tolga Tigin, Mümtaz Ener, Ersun Kazançel, Hakkı Haktan

## Traces / İz, 1994, 118 mins, colour
Director: Yeşim Ustaoğlu; Producer: Kadri Yurdatap; Production: Mine Film; Cinematographer: Uğur İçbak; Scriptwriter: Tayfun Pirselimoğlu; Editor: Thomas Balkenhol; Music: Aydın Esen; Cast: Aytaç Arman, Nur Sürer, Derya Alabora

## Two Girls / İki Genç Kız, 2005, 107 mins, colour
Director and Scriptwriter: Kutluğ Ataman; Producer: Gülen Güler; Production: Yalan Dünya Film Yapım ve Dağıtım Ltd.; Cinematographer: Emre Erkmen; Editor: Zeynep Zilelioğlu, Aziz Günhan İmamoğlu / Lev Q; Music: Replikas; Cast: Hülya Avşar, Feride Çetin, Vildan Atasever, Tuğçe Tamer, Sezgi Mengi, Uğur Baltepe, Cengiz Sezici

## Valley of the Wolves, Iraq / Kurtlar Vadisi Irak, 2005, 122 mins, colour
Director: Serdar Akar; Producer: Raci Şaşmaz; Scriptwriter: Bahadır Özdener, Raci Şaşmaz; Cinematographer: Selahattin Sancaklı; Editor: Kemalettin Osmanlı; Music: Gökhan Kırdar, Loopus; Cast: Necati Şaşmaz, Billy Zane, Ghassan Massoud, Gürkan Uygun, Bergüzar Korel, Kenan Çoban, Erhan Ufak, Diego Serrano, Gary Busey, Spencer Garrett, Tito Ortiz, Nusret Senay, Tayfun Eraslan, İsmet Hürmüzlü, Jihad Abdou

## Waiting for the Clouds / Bulutları Beklerken, 2004, 92 mins, colour
Director: Yeşim Ustaoğlu; Producer: Yeşim Ustaoğlu, Behrooz Hashemian; Production: Ustaoğlu Filmcilik; Scriptwriter: Yeşim Ustaoğlu, Petros Markaris based on *Tamama* by George Andreadis; Cinematographer: Jacek Petrycki; Editor: Timo Linasolle, Nicolas Gaster; Music: Michael Galasso; Cast: Rüçhan Çalışkur, Rıdvan Yağcı, İsmail Baysan, Dimitris Kamberides, Suna selen, Feride Karaman, Jannis Georgiadis

## Waiting for Heaven / Cenneti Beklerken, 2006, 107 mins, colour
Director (and Scriptwriter): Derviş Zaim; Producer: Derviş Zaim, Baran Seyhan, Elif Dağdeviren, Bülent Helvacı and Denes Szekeres; Production: Marathon Film, Sarmaşık Sanatlar, Hermes Film, Tivoli Film; Cinematographer: Mustafa Kuşçu; Editor: Ulaş Cihan Şimşek; Music: Rahman Altın; Cast: Serhat Tutumluer, Mesut Akusta, Melisa Sözen, Mehmet Ali Nuroğlu, Rıza Sönmez

## Walking After Midnight / Düş Gezginleri, 1992, 110 mins, colour
Director, Producer and Scriptwriter: Atıf Yılmaz; Production: Yeşilçam Filmcilik; Cinematographer: Ertunç Şenkay; Editor: Mevlut Koçak; Music: Selim Atakan; Cast: Meral Oğuz, Lale Mansur, Yaman Okay, Selçuk Özer, Deniz Türkali

**The Wall / Duvar / Le Mur**, 1983, 117 mins, colour
Director and Scriptwriter: Yılmaz Güney; Producer: Marin Karmitz; Production: MK2 Diffusion; Cinematographer: İzzet Akay; Editor: Sabine Mamou; Music: Ozan Garip Şahin, Setrak Bakırel; Cast: Tuncel Kurtiz, Ayşe Emel Mesçi, Nicolas Hossein, İsabelle Tissandier, Ahmet Ziyrek, Ali Berktay, Selahattin Kuzuoğlu, Jean Pierre Colin, Jacques Dimanche, Ali Dede Altıntaş, Sema Kuray, Zeynep Kuray, Malik Berrichi

**The Way / Yol**, 1981, 111 mins, colour,
Director: Şerif Gören; Producer (and Editor): Yılmaz Güney; Production: Güney Film and Cactus Film; Scriptwriter: Yılmaz Güney; Cinematographer: Erdoğan Engin; Music: Sebastian Argol (Zülfü Livaneli), Kendal; Cast: Tarık Akan, Şerif Sezer, Halil Ergun, Meral Orhansoy, Necmettin Çobanoğlu, Semra Uçar, Hikmet Çelik, Sevda Aktolga, Tuncay Akça, Hale Akınlı, Turgut Savaş, Hikmet Taşdemir, Engin Çelik, Osman Bardakçı, Enver Güney, Erdoğan Seren

**The Wedding / Düğün**, 1974, 84 mins, colour
Director and Scriptwriter: Lütfi Ö. Akad; Producer: Hürrem Erman; Production: Erman Film; Cinematographer: Gani Turanlı; Music: Metin Bükey; Cast: Hülya Koçyiğit, Kamuran Usluer, Turgut Boralı, Ahmet Mekin, Erol Günaydın, Altan Günbay, Hülya Şengül, İlknur Yağız, Sırrı Eliyaş

**Within Reach / Elimizin Altında**, 2006, 51 mins, colour
Director (and Producer, Scriptwriter, Cinematographer and Editor): Phyllis Katrapani; Production: Ile Blanche; Editor: Kara Blake, Louise Dugal

# References

## Introduction

1 Deniz Kandiyoti, 'Introduction: Reading the Fragments', in Deniz Kandiyoti and Ayşe Saktanber, eds, *Fragments of Culture: The Everyday of Modern Turkey* (London and New York, 2002), pp. 1–2.

2 Anthony Vidler, *The Architectural Uncanny: Essays in the Modern Unhomely* (Boston, MA, 1992).

3 Sigmund Freud, *The Uncanny* (1919), trans. David McLintock (London, 2003).

4 Pelin Tan, 'Istanbul's Gated Communities', *Bidoun*, VI (Winter 2005).

5 Anthony Vidler, *Warped Space: Art, Architecture and Anxiety in Modern Culture* (Cambridge, 2000).

6 In German *das Nicht-zuhause-sein*, in Martin Heidegger, *Being and Time*, trans. John Macquarrie and Edward Robinson (Oxford, 1997), p. 233.

7 Anke Dürr and Marianne Wellershoff, 'Turkey is Neither Eastern Nor Western: Or Is It Both?', interview with Fatih Akın in *Der Spiegel* (6 June 2005): www.spiegel.de/international/zeitgeist/0,1518,508521,00.htm.

8 Şerif Mardin, 'Culture in Geopolitics', www.ourworld.compuserve.com/home pages/usazerb/125.htm.

9 Nilüfer Göle, 'Europe: A Common Dream?', www.signandsight.com/features.514.html (15 December 2005).

10 Ibid.

11 Yeşim Ustaoğlu, personal interview (Ankara, May 2004).

12 Melissa Butcher, *Transnational Television, Cultural Identity and Change* (New Delhi, Thousand Oaks, CA, and London, 2003), p. 16.

13 Vytautas Kavolis, 'The Logics of Selfhood and Modes of Order – Civilizational Structures for Individual Identities', in Roland Robertson and Burkart Holzner, eds, *Identitiy and Authority: Explorations in Theory and Society* (Oxford and New York, 1980), p. 41.

14 Jacques Derrida, *The Other Heading: Reflections on Today's Europe*, trans. P. Brault and M. B. Nass (Bloomington, IN, 1992), pp. 9–10.

15 Şuayip Adlığ, a Kurdish producer and a close aide of Yılmaz Güney; personal interview (Montreal, September 2006).

16  Antonio Gramsci, *Selections from the Prison Notebooks* (London, 1971).
17  Turgut Özal was prime minister (1983–9) and president (1989–93).
18  Gönül Dönmez-Colin, 'Cours après le billet vert', *Le Monde diplomatique,* (October 2000), p. 30.
19  Zülfü Livaneli, *Mutluluk* (Istanbul, 2005), p. 20.
20  Ibid., p. 58.
21  In Gönül Dönmez-Colin, *Cinemas of the Other: A Personal Journey with Filmmakers from the Middle East and Central Asia* (Bristol, 2006), p. 142.
22  Yılmaz Güney, *Sürü* (Istanbul, 1994), p. 27.

## 1  In Search of Identity

1  Alim Şerif Onaran, *Türk Sineması*, vol. 1 (Ankara, 1994), p. 16.
2  A film bearing the same title, an adaptation from the operetta of Tekfor Nalyan-Dikran Çuhacıyan, was started in 1916 by Weinberg, but shooting was stopped when one of the leading actors died. Ertuğrul's version is a remake.
3  The screenwriter of both *Leblebici Horhor Ağa* and *The Girl From the Marshes* is Nazım Hikmet, who did not find the stories offered to him 'realistic and serious enough' to bear his signature (Oğuz Makal 'Nazım Hikmet Sinemada', www.nazimhikmet.org.tr/sinemasiz.asp.
4  Gülseren Güçhan, *Toplumsal Değişme ve Türk Sineması* (Ankara, 1992), p. 75.
5  Atilla Dorsay, 'An Overview of Turkish Cinema from its Origins to the Present Day', in Günsel Renda and C. Max Kortepeter, eds, *The Transformation of Turkish Culture: The Atatürk Legacy* (Princeton, NJ, 1986), p. 116.
6  Nazım Hikmet, *Bursa Cezaevinden Va-Nu'lara Mektuplar, 1945–47* (Istanbul, 1970), pp. 28–9.
7  Engin Ayça, 'Yeşilçam'ın Masal Büyüsü', *Cumhuriyet Dergi* (8 October 2000), pp. 6–8.
8  Seçil Büker, 'The Film Does not End with an Ecstatic Kiss', in Deniz Kandiyoti and Ayşe Saktanber, eds, *Fragments of Culture: The Everyday of Modern Turkey* (London and New York, 2002), p. 159.
9  Ayça, 'Yeşilçam'ın Masal Büyüsü'.
10  Mahmut Makal, *Our Village*, trans. Sir Wyndham Deedes, in *New World Writing* (New York, 1954), p. 270.
11  Büker, 'The Film Does not End with an Ecstatic Kiss', p. 153.
12  Metin Erksan, one of the true artists of Turkish cinema, who received the Golden Bear with *Susuz Yaz / The Dry Summer* (1963) at the Berlin Film Festival, would break this mould successfully with *Sevenler Ölmez / Lovers Don't Die* (1970), where all characters, the good and the bad, die before the curtain falls.
13  Christine Gledhill, 'The Melodramatic Field: An Investigation', in Christine Gledhill, ed., *Home Is Where the Hearth Is* (London, 1987), p. 24.
14  Arus Yumul, 'Türk Sinemasında Aşk ve Ahlak', in Deniz Derman, ed., *Türk Film Araştırmalarında Yeni Yönelimler*, Sinema Dizisi 2 (Istanbul, 2001), pp. 47–54.
15  Hilmi Maktav, 'Vatan Millet Cinema', *Birikim*, CCVII (July 2006), pp. 71–83.
16  Murat Belge, *Linç Kültürünün Tarihsel Kökeni: Milliyetçilik*, interview with Berat Günçıkan (Istanbul, 2006), p. 109.

17 Maktav, 'Vatan Millet Cinema'.

18 Ibid.

19 Aslı Daldal, *Arts, Politics and Society: Social Realism in Italian and Turkish Cinemas* (Istanbul, 2003), p. 40.

20 A contract was signed twelve years later in 1975, after four months of negotiation.

21 *Yeni Sinema* (July 1967), p. 34.

22 Alim Şerif Onaran, *Türk Sineması*, vol. I (Ankara, 1994).

23 Mukadder Çakır Aydın,'1960lar Turkiye'sinde Sinemadaki Akimlar', 25. *Kare*, XXI (October–December 1997).

24 Yılmaz Güney, *Sürü* (Istanbul, 1994), pp. 27–9.

25 Although Istanbul Technical University (ITÜ) is credited for the first broadcast, in 1952, regular broadcasting was started only on 31 January 1968 by Turkish Radio and Television (TRT).

26 Vedat Türkali, *Tüm Yazıları Konuşmaları* (Istanbul, 2001).

27 Burçak Evren, *Türk Sinemasında Yeni Konumlar* (Istanbul, 1990), p. 7.

28 Abdurrahman Şen, *Cemre: Kültür, Sanat ve Edebiyat Üzerine Politik Yazılar* (Istanbul, 1990).

29 Mesut Uçakan, personal interview (Istanbul, July 1993).

30 *EP*, 20 (Istanbul, 1993).

31 Maktav, 'Vatan Millet Cinema'.

32 Bengi Heval Öz, 'Filmime Dokunma: Sansür Yine Utandırdı', *Cumhuriyet Dergi*, DCCIX (28 April 2002), pp. 1, 8–10.

33 Feride Çiçekoğlu, '"Devlet sanatçısına Tecavüz Edilemez"', *Cumhuriyet Dergi*, CDXXVIII (5 June 1994), pp. 8–9.

34 Agah Özgüç, personal interview (Antalya, October 2007).

35 Maktav, 'Vatan Millet Cinema'.

36 Özgüç, personal interview.

37 Nilgün Toptaş, 'İşkence Filminden Masum Yüzler', *Radikal* (23 October 1999).

38 Öz, 'Filmime Dokunma', p. 9.

39 Maktav, 'Vatan Millet Cinema'.

40 Özgüç, personal interview.

41 Robert Stam, *Film Theory: An Introduction* (Oxford, 2000).

42 Anne Tereka Ciecko, 'Theorizing Asian Cinema(s)', in Anne Tereka Ciecko, ed., *Contemporary Asian Cinema: Popular Culture in a Global Frame* (Oxford and New York, 2006), p. 13.

43 Wimal Dissanayake, 'Cultural Identity and Asian Cinema: An Introduction', in Wimal Dissanayake, ed., *Cinema and Cultural Identity: Reflections on Films from Japan, India and Cinema* (Lanham and London, 1988), pp. 1–6.

44 Ibid.

## 2 Migration, Dis/Misplacement and Exile

1 Latife Tekin, 'Camileri Kibrit Kutusu', in Barbaros Altuğ, ed., *Yazarların İstanbulu* (Istanbul, 2007), pp. 154–5.

2 Elif Şafak, *Araf* [Turkish version] (Istanbul, 2003), pp. 9–10.

3  İbrahim Türk, *Halit Refiğ: Düşlerden Düşüncelere Söyleşiler* (Istanbul, 2001), p. 152.

4  Film Ekibi, 'Duygu Sağıroğlu ıle Söyleşi', *Yeni Film*, III (October–December 2003) p. 106.

5  Gülseren Güçhan, *Toplumsal Değişme ve Türk Sineması* (Ankara, 1992), pp. 127– 8.

6  Aslı Daldal, *Art, Politics and Society: Social Realism in Italian and Turkish Cinemas* (Istanbul, 2003), p. 188.

7  Gönül Dönmez-Colin, *Women, Islam and Cinema* (London, 2004), pp. 56–7.

8  Ibid., pp. 137–9.

9  Agah Özgüç, 'Film Karelerinde Yaşayan Eski Istanbul', *Cumhuriyet Dergi*, CDXIV (27 February 1994), p. 17.

10  Gülten Akın, 'At filminin Ozanca Görünümü', in Ali Özgentürk, *At* (Istanbul, 1983), p. 18.

11  Edward W. Said, *Culture and Imperialism* (New York, 1994).

12  Filiz Çiçek, 'Lola and Bilidikid', *Scope*, IV (February 2006).

13  Orhan Pamuk, 'My First Passport: What does it Mean to Belong to a Country?' *New Yorker* (16 April 2007), p. 56.

14  Laura U. Marks, *The Skin of the Film: Intercultural Cinema, Embodiment and the Senses* (Durham and London, 2000).

15  Lars-Olav Beier and Matthias Matussek, 'From Istanbul to New York: *Der Spiegel*, interview with Fatih Akin', *Der Spiegel* (28 September 2007) www.spiegel.de/international/zeitgeist/0,1518,508521,00.htm.

16  Hamid Naficy, *The Making of Exile Cultures: Iranian Television in Los Angeles* (Minneapolis, 1993), p. 237.

17  Raphael Bassan, 'Bay Okan: LE BUS', in Guy Hennebelle, ed., *CinémAction: Cinemas de l'Emigration*, VIII (Summer 1979), pp. 186–7.

18  Yves Thoraval and Guy Hennebelle, 'La "folle équipée" de clandestins turc en Suéde, racontée par Bay Okan: LE BUS', in Hennebelle, *CinémAction*, pp. 187–90.

19  German critic Georg Seesslen claims that in an epoch when no filmmakers from the immigrant communities had yet appeared, such films were 'melodramatic appeals to German society', rather than authentic portrayals of immigrant life, and that *Shirin's Wedding* had its share of 'head-scarf and gangster clichés': 'Of Aliens and Alienation: Portrayals of Immigration in Films from the 1970s to 80s', www.goethe.de/kue/flm/thm/en47136.htm (accessed 3 February 2008).

20  Tevfik Başer, 'Beni İlgilendiren Bu Durumu Yaşayan Kadınlar', *2000'e Doğru* (14–21 March 1987), p. 53, quoted in Oğuz Makal, Sinemada Yedinci Adam (Izmir, 1987), p. 103.

21  Deniz Göktürk, '*Turkish Delight – German Fright: Migrant Identities in Transnational Cinema*', www.transcomm.ox.ac.uk/workingpages.htm.

22  Cumhur Canbazoğlu, 'Almanların Kalıplarını Kırmak Zor' [interview], *Cumhuriyet Gazetesi* (13 January 1998), p. 14.

23  Tuncay Kulaoğlu, 'İki Kültür Arasında Sinema', *Cumhuriyet Gazetesi* (20 August 2002), www.cumhuriyet.com/cumhuriyet/m/c1507.html.

24  Çiçek, 'Lola and Bilidikid'.

25  Press conference, Golden Orange Film Festival, Antalya (October 2007).

26  Vecdi Sayar, 'Cannes'ın Kıyısında', *Cumhuriyet Gazetesi* (25 May 2007).

27 Press conference, Locarno International Film Festival (August 2005).

28 Hamid Naficy, ed., *Home, Exile, Homeland: Film, Media and the Politics of Place* (New York and London, 1999), p. 6.

29 Phyllis Katrapani, 'Sand Between the Fingers', unpublished MA thesis, University of Montreal, 2006.

30 Gönül Dönmez-Colin, 'Mavi Sürgün / The Blue Exile', *Cinemaya: The Asian Film Quarterly*, XXII (Winter 1993–4), pp. 24–5.

31 Gönül Dönmez-Colin, *Cinemas of the Other: A Personal Journey with Filmmakers from the Middle East and Central Asia* (Bristol, 2006), p. 97.

32 Ibid., p. 107.

33 Gönül Dönmez-Colin, 'Yolda', *Osian's Cinemaya; The Asian Film Quarterly*, I/1–2 (2005), p. 42.

34 Alfreda Benge, 'Güney, Turkey and the West: An Interview', *Race & Class*, XXVI/3 (1985), pp. 31–46.

## 3 Denied Identities

1 Hrant Dink, 'Biraz Farklınsanlar . . . azınlıklar', *Birikim*, special issue, 'Etnik Kimlikler ve Azınlıklar', LXXI–LXXII (March/April 1995), p. 152. (Hrant Dink, editor of the Armenian journal AGOS, was murdered in January 2007, supposedly by a young Turkish nationalist.)

2 *Bana kendi dilinde bir şarkı söyle*
   *Kimin adına olursa olsun*
   *Yeterki çığlığın senin olsun*
   *Belki anlamam dediğini ama,*
   *Kendi dilinde olsun*
   from a poem by Yılmaz Güney, in *Devrim: Yılmaz Güney Biyografisi*, www.drejx. blogcu.com/2617665.

3 Benedict Anderson, *Imagined Communities* (London and New York, 2006), pp. 6–7.

4 Ibid., p. 145.

5 Vassaf is referring to Elif Şafak, who was brought to trial in connection with statements uttered by Armenian characters in her book *The Bastard of Istanbul*, and to other writers including Orhan Pamuk.

6 Gündüz Vassaf, 'Türkler Irkçı mı?', *Radikal* (21 October 2007).

7 Cumhur Cambazoğlu, 'Sorunlarımızın Dili Yoktur' [Yılmaz Erdoğan interview], *Cumhuriyet Gazetesi* (28 January 2001).

8 Öz is referring to the following films shown at the national film festival in Antalya in 2001: *Dansöz / Dancer* (Savaş Ay) about the Gypsies; *Maruf* (Serdar Akar) about the Assyrians; *O da Beni Seviyor / Summer Love* (Barış Pirhasan) about the Alevis; and *Hejar* (Handan İpekçi) about the Kurds.

9 Kazım Öz, personal interview (Istanbul, April 2007).

10 Ibid.

11 Pierre Bourdieu, *Language and Symbolic Power*, ed. John B. Thompson, trans. Gino Raymond and Matthew Adamson (Cambridge, MA, 1991).

12 Kazım Öz, personal interview.

13  Ibid.

14  Reis Çelik, personal interview (Istanbul, April 2006).

15  Ibid.

16  Gönül Dönmez-Colin, '*Iz* / *Traces*', *Cinemaya; The Asian Film Quarterly*, XXX (Autumn 1995), p. 31.

17  Oral Çalışlar, 'Sinemamız Adına Yeni *Umut*', *Cumhuriyet Gazetesi* (5 March 2000), p. 4.

18  Sungu Çapan, 'Realite'ye Zorlu Yolcuk', *Cumhuriyet Gazetesi* (3 March 2000), p. 13.

19  Berat Günçıkan, 'Hayatı Ters Işıkta Yakalamak', *Cumhuriyet Dergi* (6 June 1999), pp. 1, 10–12.

20  Gönül Dönmez-Colin, *Cinemas of the Other: A Personal Journey with Filmmakers from the Middle East and Central Asia* (Bristol, 2006), p. 135.

21  Ibid., p. 133.

22  Ibid., p. 134.

23  Ibid., p. 136.

24  Ibid.

25  *Yeni Politika* (29 April 1995).

26  Olkan Özyurt, 'Oskar Temsilcisi Yasaklandı', *Radikal Gazetesi* (3 March 2002).

27  Human Rights Report of Turkey (September 2003): www.tihv.org.tr/.

28  Öz, personal interview.

29  Agah Özgüç, personal interview (Antalya, October 2007).

30  Öz, personal interview.

31  www.turkishdailynews.com.tr/archives.php?id=13700.

32  Burcu Günüşen, 'Fotoğraf: Bir Vahşetin İmgesi', *Cumhuriyet* (23 October 2001), p. 13.

33  Atilla Dorsay, *Sinemamızda Çöküş ve Rönesans Yılları: Türk Sineması, 1990–2004* (Istanbul, 2004), p. 74.

34  Dersim, named Tunceli since 1936, is the site of the rebellions of 1937–8.

35  Öz, personal interview.

36  Ibid.

37  Özgüç, personal interview.

38  Janet Barış, 'Türk Sinemasında Ermeni Sanatçıların Ayak İzleri', *Yeni Film*, XIII (2007), pp. 56–8.

39  Özgüç, personal interview.

40  Gül Erçetin, 'İzleyici İçin Film Yapıyorum' [interview with Giritlioğlu], *Cumhuriyet Gazetesi* (16 February 1999).

41  Dönmez-Colin, *Cinemas of the Other*, p. 137.

42  Kevin Robinson and Asu Aksoy, 'Deep Nation: Turkish Cinema Culture', in *Cinema and Nation*, ed. Mette Hjort and Scott Mackenzie (London and New York, 2000), p. 218.

## 4  Yılmaz Güney

1   *Kavgayı, bir yaprağın üzerine yazmak isterdim
    sonbahar gelsin yaprak dökülsün diye*

*Öfkeyi, bir bulutun üzerine yazmak isterdim*
*yağmur yağsın bulut yok olsun diye*
*Nefreti, karların üzerine yazmak isterdim*
*güneş açsın karlar erisin diye*
*. . . Ve dostluğu ve sevgiyi, yeni doğmuş*
*tüm bebeklerin yüreğine yazmak isterdim*
*onlarla birlikte büyüsün bütün dünyayı sarsın diye*
from a poem by Yılmaz Güney called 'Sevgive Dostluk / Love and Friendship',
www.antoloji/siir/siir/siir_SQL@asp?sair=2152tsiir=47794+order=oto.

2   Yılmaz Güney, *Sürü* (Istanbul, 1994), p. 25.

3   Alfreda Benge, 'Güney, Turkey and the West: An Interview', *Race and Class*,
    XXVI/3 (1985), pp. 31–46.

4   Atilla Dorsay, 'Yılmaz Güney'in Sinemasına Genel Bir Bakış', *Milliyet Sanat
    Dergisi* (15 September 1984), p. 15.

5   Gönül Dönmez-Colin, '*Umut / The Hope*', in Gönül Dönmez-Colin, ed., *The
    Cinema of North Africa and the Middle East* (London, 2007), pp. 40–49.

6   Atilla Dorsay, '*Umut*' [September 1970], in Atilla Dorsay, *Sinemamızın Umut
    Yılları 1970–80 Arası Türk Sinemasına Bakışlar* (Istanbul, 1989), p. 52.

7   Nijat Özön, *Karagözden Sinemaya: Türk Sineması ve Sorunları*, vol. II (Istanbul,
    1995), pp. 204–5.

8   Ibid.

9   Linda Hutcheon, 'Circling the Downspout of Empire', in I. Adam and H. Tiffin,
    eds, *Past the Last Post: Theorizing Post-Colonialism and Post-Modernism*
    (Calgary, 1990), pp. 167–89.

10  Stephen Slemon, 'Magic Realism as Post-Colonial Discourse', *Canadian
    Literature*, CXVI (1988), pp. 9–24.

11  Yılmaz Güney, *Sürü* (Istanbul, 1994), p. 26.

12  Agah Özgüç, *Bütün Filmleriyle Yılmaz Güney* (Istanbul, 1990), pp. 11–12.

13  '*Umut*'un Düşmanları', *Devrim*, LIV (27 October 1970); quoted in Nijat Özön,
    *Karagözden Sinemaya Türk Sinemasının Sorunları* (Ankara, 1995), p. 327.

14  Roy Armes, *Third World Filmmaking and the West* (London, 1987), p. 276.

15  Controversy regarding the incident is still not resolved in Turkey; certain groups
    attribute the murder to the 'violent' disposition of Güney, while others consider it
    a conspiracy staged by reactionary elements. Evidence points out that a scuffle *did*
    take place, although, in all likelihood, the death of the judge occurred by accident.

16  Yılmaz Güney, *Yol* (Istanbul, 1994), pp. 13–15.

17  Transcription of the interview with Jurgen Rothik in 1983 for Spanish State
    Television, quoted in Güney, *Yol*, p. 291.

18  Ibid., pp. 301–2.

19  Dorsay, '*Umut*'.

20  Roy Armes, *Third World Filmmaking and the West*, p. 275; quoted in Gönül
    Dönmez-Colin, *Women, Islam and Cinema* (London, 2004), p. 52.

21  Atıf Yılmaz, personal interview (Istanbul, 2003).

22  Ali Özgentürk, personal interview (Istanbul, 2003).

23  Dennis Giles and Haluk Şahin, 'Yílmaz Güney: Revolutionary Cinema in Turkey',
    *Jump Cut*, XXVII (July 1982), pp. 35–7.

24 Güney, *Yol*, pp. 13–15.

25 Özgüç, *Bütün Filmleriyle*, p. 14.

26 Murat Belge in Ahmet Karaman, *Yılmaz Güney Çiviyazıları* (Istanbul, 1999), p. 431.

## 5 Gender, Sexuality and Morals in Transition

1 From Zeki Ökten's *Çinliler Geliyor / Chinese are Coming* (2007), a modern comedy that takes place in a provincial town.

2 Laura Mulvey, 'Visual Pleasure and Narrative Cinema, *Screen*, XVI/3 (1975), pp. 6–18.

3 Arus Yumul, 'Türk Sinemasında Aşk ve Ahlak', *Türk Film Araştırmalarında Yeni Yönelimler*, Sinema Dizisi 2, ed. Deniz Derman (Istanbul, 2001), pp. 47–54.

4 Gönül Dönmez-Colin, *Cinemas of the Other: A Personal Journey with Filmmakers from the Middle East and Central Asia* (Bristol, 2006), p. 143.

5 Seçil Büker, 'The Film Does Not End with an Ecstatic Kiss', in Deniz Kandiyoti and Ayşe Saktanber, eds, *Fragments of Culture: The Everyday of Modern Turkey* (London and New York, 2002), p. 159.

6 Gönül Dönmez-Colin, *Women, Islam and Cinema* (London, 2004), p. 35.

7 Dr Erol Göka quoted in Fetay Soykan, *Türk Sinemasında Kadın, 1920–1990* (Izmir, 1993), p. 65.

8 Erksan's female Hamlet is not an original one. In 1921 Danish star of silent cinema Asta Nielsen played Prince Hamlet, confessing only on her deathbed that she was actually Princess Hamlet.

9 Soykan, *Türk Sinemasında Kadın, 1920–1990*, p. 69.

10 Atıf Yılmaz, personal interview (April 2003).

11 Dönmez-Colin, *Women, Islam and Cinema*, pp. 132–4.

12 Asuman Suner, *Hayalet Ev: Yeni Türk Sinemasında Aidiyet, Kimlik ve Bellek* (Istanbul, 2006).

13 Agah Özgüç, personal interview (Antalya, October 2007).

14 Berna Moran, *Türk Romanına Eleştirel Bir Bakış* (Istanbul, 2002), p. 156; quoted in Aylin Sayın, '*Vurun Kahpeye*: Birbirinden Farklı Uyarlamalari', *Yeni Film*, XXX (October–December 2003), p. 41.

15 Sayın, '*Vurun Kahpeye*: Birbirinden Farklı Uyarlamalari, pp. 41–4.

16 Alev Çınar, *Modernity, Islam and Secularism in Turkey* (Minneapolis, MN and London, 2005), p. 31.

17 Selim Eyüboğlu, 'Bir Memleket Metaforu Olarak Kadın', in *Türk Film Araştırmalarında Yeni Yönelimler* Sinema Dizisi 1, ed. Deniz Derman (Istanbul, 2001), pp. 37–45.

18 Feriha Eriş Özgül, 'Bilge Olgaç ve Sinemasında Kadın – Interview', unpublished MA thesis, University of Ankara, 1993, p. 73; quoted in Semire Ruken Öztürk, *Sinemanın 'Dişil' Yüzü:Türkiye'de Kadın Yönetmenler* (Ankara, 2003), p. 81.

19 Öztürk, *Sinemanın 'Dişil' Yüzü*, p. 86.

20 Özgüç, personal interview.

21 Ibid.

22  Ibid.
23  One such cinema on the main street of Beyoğlu and another in a back street near the offices of the production companies have survived and still operate today. The latter, Dilbazlar cinema, was the locale of some scenes in Tayfun Pirselimoğlu's 2002 feature, *Hiçbiryerde / Innowhereland*.
24  'Tabuları Yıkmak İstemiyorum' / 'I Don't Want to Break the Taboos', *Cumhuriyet Gazetesi* (1–7 January 1993).
25  Eyüboğlu, 'Bir Memleket Metaforu Olarak Kadın', p. 41.
26  Jacques Lacan, 'The Mirror Stage', in Anthony Easthope, ed., *Contemporary Film Theory* (Harlow, 1993), p. 39.
27  Eyüboğlu, 'Bir Memleket Metaforu Olarak Kadın', p. 42.
28  Asuman Suner, 'Sinemada Bir Karşı Söylem Olarak Eşcinsellik', *Beyaz Perde*, VII (May 1990), pp. 47–8.
29  Gönül Dönmez-Colin, 'The Capital, The Banlieu and Two Girls: An Interview with Kutluğ Ataman', *Osian's Cinemaya: The Asian Film Quarterly*, I/2 (2006), pp. 17–19.
30  Esra Aliçavuşoğlu, 'Gerçek Masallar Anlatmak İstiyorum', interview in *Cumhuriyet* (9 February 1999).
31  Aydın Üstünel and Fulya Canşen, 'Azınlık İçinde Bir Azınlık', interview in *Cumhuriyet Dergi* (25 April 1999), pp. 2–3.
32  Filiz Çiçek, 'Lola and Bilidikid', *Scope*, IV (February 2006).
33  Ibid.
34  Dönmez-Colin, *Cinemas of the Other*, p. 125.
35  Dönmez-Colin, *Women, Islam and Cinema*, pp. 66–7.
36  Semih Kaplanoğlu, personal interview (Istanbul, April 2007).
37  Abdullah Oğuz, personal interview (Montreal, September 2007).
38  Handan İpekçi, personal interview (Antalya, October 2007).
39  Doğan Yılmaz, '*Barda*', *Yeni Film*, XIII (April 2007), pp. 20–23.

## 6  A Modern Identity or Identity in a Modern World

1  Asuman Suner, 'Horror of a Different Kind: Dissonant Voices of the New Turkish Cinema', *Screen*, ILV/4 (Winter 2004), p. 307.
2  Derviş Zaim, 'Your Focus is Your Truth: Turkish Cinema, "Alluvionic" Filmmakers and International Acceptance', in M. Christensen and N. Erdoşan, eds, *Shifting Landscapes: Media and Film in European Context* (Cambridge, forthcoming).
3  Duygu Durgun, 'Gerilla tarzı film üretimiyle 'yoksulluğun estetiği' [interview], *Cumhuriyet Gazetei* (December 1996), p. 12.
4  'Dursun, Mahsun ve Biz', *Cumhuriyet Dergi*, DXXVI (21 April 1996), pp. 12–14.
5  Some Turkish critics have confused 'Mahsun' with 'Mahzun'. The latter means 'sad and downcast' (Ottoman–Turkish dictionary). Zaim confirmed the irony intended in the use of 'Mahsun', adding 'his family name "Süpertitiz" (very fastidious) also contributes to the irony' (11 June 2007, by email).
6  Sungu Çapan, 'Gerçek, çoğu kez hayali aşar', *Cumhuriyet Gazetesi* (22 November 1996).

7  Gönül Dönmez-Colin, '*Tabutta Rövaşata / Somersault in a Coffin*', *Cinemaya: The Asian Film Quarterly*, XXXVII (July–September 1997), pp. 24–5.
8  Asuman Suner, *Hayalet Ev: Yeni Türk Sinemasında Aidiyet, Kimlik ve Bellek* (Istanbul, 2006), p. 245.
9  Sungu Çapan, 'Gerçek, çoğu kez hayali aşar', *Cumhuriyet Gazetesi* (22 November 1996).
10  Marcia Landy, *Cinematic Uses of the Past* (Minneapolis, MN, and London, 1996), pp. 2–9.
11  Derviş Zaim, personal interview (Istanbul, April 2007).
12  Erdal *Atabek* 'Filler Çimeni Nasıl Ezer?', *Cumhuriyet* (12 January 2001), p. 13.
13  Elif Genco, '*Çamur,* Bır Kıbrıs Metaforu', *Yeni Film*, IV (January–March 2004), pp. 4–11.
14  The idea that Islam forbids human depiction is open to debate according to Zaim: 'Certain Muslim theologians claim there is no such Islamic proscription. Different Islamic countries approach the matter in different ways, which implies that the prohibitions largely depend on the personal convictions of the ruling authorities. For various cultural and religious reasons, Turks were first introduced to the Western (European Renaissance) painting tradition only in the eighteenth century.'
15  For an insightful reading of *Las Meninas*, see Michel Foucault, *The Order of Things* (New York, 1973), pp. 3–16.
16  Zaim, personal interview (Istanbul, 2007).
17  Ibid.
18  Press conference for *Clouds of May* (Berlin, 1997).
19  Nuri Bilge Ceylan, 'Ordinary Stories of Ordinary People', *Cinemaya: The Asian Film Quarterly*, XLIII (Spring 1999), pp. 22–3. Ceylan repeats this passage during an interview with French critic Michel Ciment, 'Nuri Bilge Ceylan: les variations sur un thème me plaisent . . .', *Positif*, CDLXXXII (April 2001).
20  Güldal Kizildemir, 'Pazar Sohbeti: Kasaba'lı Anlam Avcısı' (interview), *Radikal* (21 December 1997).
21  Hikmet Temel Akarsu, 'Taşra Kasabasında Sıkışıp Kalmak', *Radikal* (27 July 2007).
22  Tuna Erdem, 'Kişisel Bir Anlatı', *Gazete Pazar* (21 December 1997).
23  Gönül Dönmez-Colin, 'New Turkish Cinema – Individual Tales of Common Concerns', *Asian Cinema*, XIV/1 (Spring–Summer 2003), pp. 138–45.
24  Fredric Jameson, *Postmodernism; or, The Cultural Logic of Late Capitalism* (London and New York, 1991), pp. 280–81.
25  Suner, 'Horror of a Different Kind', p. 312.
26  Hasan Akbulut, *Nuri Bilge Ceylan Sinemasını Okumak: Anlatı, Zaman, Mekan,* (Istanbul, 2005), p. 20.
27  Gönül Dönmez-Colin, 'Mrinal Sen: "Rambling Thoughts" on Unforgettable Masters, Lost Friends, Enigmatic Ruins and Life', *Asian Cinema*, XII/1 (2001), pp. 129–39.
28  A. O. Scott, 'He Makes Movies Oddly Like Life; Everyday Mysteries in the Turkish Film, *Clouds of May*', *New York Times* (7 April 2001).
29  Jean-Sébastien Chauvin, 'L'oeuf d'Ali', *Cahiers du cinéma*, DLV (March 2001).
30  Jacques Mandelbaum, 'Passage de generations sous une ciel de printemps', *Le Monde* (21 March 2001).

31 Emile Breton, 'Un Tchekhov turc', *L'Humanité* (21 March 2001).

32 Here Algan is referring to the wave of urban *angst* stories of the post-1980 coup years, discussed in chapter One.

33 Necla Algan, 'Türk Sineması'nda tematik açıdan bir kırılma noktası', *Yeni Sinema Dergisi* (Fall–Winter 2003–4).

34 Aslı Selçuk, '*Uzak* Dünya Turunda' [interview], *Cumhuriyet Gazetesi* (11 January 2004).

35 Suner, 'Horror of a Different Kind', p. 314.

36 Gönül Dönmez-Colin, *Women, Islam and Cinema* (London, 2004), pp. 64–5.

37 Zeki Demirkubuz, 'The Art of Story Telling', *Cinemaya; The Asian Film Quarterly*, XLIII (Spring 1999), pp. 20–21.

38 Gönül Dönmez-Colin, 'New Turkish Cinema – Individual Tales of Common Concerns', *Asian Cinema*, XVI/1 (2003), pp. 140–41.

39 Fredric Jameson, 'A Note on the Specificity of Newer Turkish Cinema', paper read at the conference *Arada/Between: Ten Contemporary Turkish Films*, Duke University (20 September 2004).

40 Dönmez-Colin, 'New Turkish Cinema', p. 141.

41 Dönmez-Colin, *Women, Islam and Cinema*, p. 66.

42 Dönmez-Colin, 'New Turkish Cinema', p. 141.

43 Susan Hayward on French New Wave in *Cinema Studies: Key Concepts* (Oxford, 2000), p. 148.

44 Nihal Bengisu Karaca, interview in Semire R. Öztürk, ed., *Kader: Zeki Demirkubuz* (Ankara, 2006), pp. 48–9 [first published in *Yeni İnsan, Yeni Sinema*, XII (May–June 2002), pp. 160–61].

45 Olaf Möller, 'Prison as Metaphor is the Guiding Light of this Turkish Director's Austere, Literary Vision', *Film Comment* (March–April 2003), pp. 20–21.

46 Susan Sontag, 'Novel into Film', *Vanity Fair* (September 1983).

47 Fatih Özgüven, 'Ayak Kokusu', *Radikal Gazetesi* (25 December 2002).

48 Alev Çınar, *Modernity, Islam and Secularism in Turkey* (Minneapolis, MN and London, 2005), p. 8.

49 Secular national daily *Milliyet*, in a five-part series entitled 'Sects, Religious Communities and the 22 July [elections]', discussed some of the Islamic sects that play an active role in Turkish politics (10 July 2007).

50 'Turkey's Religious Sects: Sheiks, Lies and Videotape', *Economist* (11 January 2007).

51 '*Takva*' Antalya'da Tartışma Yarattı' (22 October 2006): www.sinema.com/makale/6-4370/takva-antalya-da-tartisma-yaratti (accessed 31 December 2007).

52 Çınar, *Modernity, Islam and Secularism in Turkey*, p. 8.

## Afterword

1 Deniz Yavuz, 'Projelerde Son Durum', *Haftalık Antrakt Sinema*, XVIII/26 (6– 12 April 2007).

2 What Agah Özgüç calls *bunalım* films, personal interview (Antalya, October 2007).

3 Yavuz, 'Projelerde Son Durum'.

4   Olkan Özyurt, 'Sinemada Bir Yaman Çelişki', *Radikal-çevirimci* (21 January 2007).

5   Agah Özgüç, personal interview.

6   Özyurt, 'Sinemada Bir Yaman Çelişki'.

7   'The Son of the Man Who Saves the World': www.ntvmsnbc.com/news.

8   Fatih Özgüven, *Radikal* (8 February 2007), www.radikal.com.tr/haber.php? haberno=212433.

9   Orhan Pamuk, 'Who Do You Write for?', *Herald Tribune* (29–30 July 2006).

10  Jonathan Rosenbaum in Alan Williams, ed., *Film and Nationalism* (New Brunswick, NJ, 2002), pp. 217–29.

11  Pamuk, 'Who Do You Write For?'.

12  Handan İpekçi, personal interview (Antalya, 20 October 2007).

13  Derviş Zaim, 'Your Focus is Your Truth: Turkish Cinema, "Alluvionic" Filmmakers and International Acceptance', in M. Christensen and N. Erdoğan, eds, *Shifting Landscapes: Media and Film in European Context* (Cambridge, forthcoming).

14  Aydın Sayman, 'Sayın Başbakana Açık Mektup', www.sonsuzkare.com/ makale.aspx?y=id=20+sayi=10 (accessed 7 November 2007).

15  Jale Onanç, producer, personal interview (Istanbul, 7 November 2007).

16  İpekçi, personal interview.

17  Ahmet Boyacıoğlu, 'Serbest Kürsü', *Empire* (August 2007).

18  Burak Göral, 'Türk Sineması Gelişiyor(mu?)', *Empire* (September 2007), pp. 42–3.

19  Burçak Evren, 'Başımsız ya da Genç Sinemacılarla Nereye Kadar?', *Sonsuzkare*, www.sonsuzkare.com/makale.aspx?y_id=3+sayi=4.

20  Özgüç, personal interview.

21  Gökçe Uygun and Nihan İnal, 'Yeşilçam'ın yeniden canlanışı' [interviews on the 93rd anniversary of Turkish cinema], *Cumhuriyet Gazetesi* (4 January 2007).

22  Nazlı Topçuoğlu, 'AVM'lerle yayılan zincir sinemalar semtlerde perde kapattırıyor', *Referans* (27–28 October 2007), p. 12.

23  Zaim, 'Your Focus is Your Truth'.

# Bibliography

Abisel, Nilgün, *Türk Sineması Üzerine Yazılar* (Ankara, 1994)

Aça, Mehmet, and Hüseyin Durgut, *Küreselleşen Dünya Türk Kimliği* (Istanbul, 2004)

Akad, Lütfi, *Işıkla Karanlık Arasında* (Istanbul, 2004)

Akbulut, Hasan, *Nuri Bilge Ceylan Sinemasını Okumak* (Istanbul, 2005)

Akerman, Chantal, *Identification Papers* (New York, 1995)

Aksoy, Asu, and Nabi Avcı, 'Spreading Turkish Identity', *InterMedia*, XX/4–5 (August–September 1992)

Alter, Robert, *Imagined Cities: Urban Experience and the Language of the Novel* (New York, 2005)

Anderson, Benedict, *Imagined Communities* (London and New York, 2006)

Armes, Roy, *Third World Film Making and the West* (Berkeley, CA, 1987)

Atak, M., 'Her Kadının Gönlünde Bir Faşist Yatar', *Cumhuriyet Dergi* [Seçkin Yaşar'la Söyleşi] (29 October 1992)

Ayça, Engin, 'Yeşilçam'ın Masal Büyüsü', *Cumhuriyet Dergi* (8 October 2000)

Barış, Janet, 'Türk Sinemasında Ermeni Sanatçıların Ayak İzleri', *Yeni Film*, XIII (2007), pp. 56–8

Basutçu, Mehmet, ed., *Le Cinéma turc* (Paris, 1996)

Beck, Ulrich, *Risk, Society: Towards a New Modernity* (London, 1992)

Belton, John, ed., *Movies and Mass Culture* (New Brunswick, NJ, 1996)

Benge, Alfreda, 'Güney, Turkey and the West: An Interview', *Race and Class*, XXVI/3 (1985)

Bernstein, Matthew, and Gaylyn Studlar, eds, *Visions of the East: Orientalism in Film* (London and New York, 1997)

Bhabha, Homi K., *The Location of Culture* (London and New York, 1994)

——, 'The World and the Home', *Social Text*, XXXI/XXXII (1992)

——, ed., *Nation and Narration* (London and New York, 1990)

Blasius, Mark, ed., *Sexual Identities, Queer Politics* (Princeton, NJ, 2001)

Bondanella, Peter, *Italian Cinema: Neorealism to the Present* (New York, 1982)

Bourdieu, Pierre, *Language and Symbolic Power* (Cambridge, MA, 1991)

——, and Luc Boltanski, 'Formal Qualifications and Occupational Hierarchies: The

Relationship Between the Production System and the Reproduction System', trans. R. Nice, in E. J. King, ed., *Reorganizing Education: Management and Participation for Change* (London and Beverly Hills, CA, 1977)

Burçolu, Nedret Kuran, *Multiculturalism: Identity and Otherness / Multiculturalisme: identité et altérité* (Istanbul, 1997)

Butcher, Melissa, *Transnational Television, Cultural Identity and Change* (New Delhi, Thousand Oaks and London, 2003)

Ceylan, Nuri Bilge, *Uzak* (Istanbul, 2004)

Chomsky, Noam, *Middle East Illusions: Peace, Security and Terror* (New Delhi, 2003)

Curle, Howard, and Stephen Snyder, eds, *Vittoria De Sica: Contemporary Perspectives* (Toronto, 2000)

Çağlar, Keyder, *Istanbul between the Global and Local* (Oxford, 1999)

Çınar, Alev, *Modernity, Islam and Secularism in Turkey* (Minneapolis, MN and London, 2005)

——, 'Istanbul'u Nasıl Satmalı?', *Istanbul*, III (1992), pp. 80–85

Daldal, Aslı, *1960 Darbesi ve Türk Sinemasında Toplumsal Gerçekçilik* (Istanbul, 2005)

——, *Art Politics and Society: Social Realism in Italian and Turkish Cinemas* (Istanbul, 2003)

Derman, Deniz, ed., *Türk Film Araştırmalarında Yeni Yönelimler*, vols 1–4 (Istanbul, 2001–4)

Derrida, Jacques, *The Other Heading: Reflections on Today's Europe*, trans. P. Brault and M. B. Nass, (Bloomington, IN, 1992)

Dirlik, Arif, 'The Post-colonial Aura: Third World Criticism in the Age of Global Capitalism', *Critical Inquiry*, XX (Winter 1994)

Dorsay, Atilla, 'Back from Near Oblivion: Turkish Cinema Gets a New Lease on Life', trans. Lale Can, *Film Comment*, XXXIV/6 (2004), pp. 11–12

——, *Sinemamızda Çöküş ve Rönesans Yılları: Türk Sineması, 1990–2004* (Istanbul, 2004)

——, *Sinemamızın Umut Yılları. 1970–80 Arası Türk Sinemasına Bakışlar* (Istanbul, 1989)

——, 'An Overview of Turkish Cinema from its Origins to the Present Day', in Günsel Renda and C. Max Kortepeter, eds, *The Transformation of Turkish Culture: The Atatürk Legacy* (Princeton, NJ, 1986), pp. 113–27

——, 'Yılmaz Güney' in Sinemasına Genel Bir Bakış', *Milliyet Sanat Dergisi* (15 September 1984)

Downing, John D. H., ed., *Film and Politics in the Third World* (New York, 1987)

Dönmez-Colin, Gönül, 'Cinemas of Islam', in Andrew Rippin, ed., *The Islamic World* (London, forthcoming)

——, ed., *The Cinema of North Africa and the Middle East* (London, 2007)

——, *Cinemas of the Other: A Personal Journey with Filmmakers from the Middle East and Central Asia* (Bristol, 2006)

——, *Women, Islam and Cinema* (London, 2004)

——, 'New Turkish Cinema – Individual Tales of Common Concerns', *Asian Cinema*, XVI/1 (2003), pp. 138–45

——, 'Cours après le billet vert', *Le Monde diplomatique* (October 2000), p. 30

——, 'Journey to the Sun' interview, *Film & Televisie. Video*, CDXCV (October, 1999), p. 13

——, 'The Journey Must Go On', interview with Yeşim Ustaoğlu, *Cinemaya: The Asian Film Quarterly*, XLIV (Summer 1999), pp. 4–6

——, 'Dans les bidonvilles d'Istanbul: Le Bandit: Un film de Yavuz Turgul', *Le Monde Diplomatique* (9 July 1997)

——, 'Auf Der Suche Nach Vielfalt', in Bogdan Grbic et al., eds, *Die Siebte Kunst Auf Dem Pulverfass: Balkan Film* (Graz, 1996)

——, 'Ali Özgentürk: A Journey into the Self', *Cinemaya: The Asian Film Quarterly*, XXXIII (Summer 1996), pp. 42–5

——, 'Personal Stories Need Not Be Autobiographical', interview with Yeşim Ustaoğlu, *Cinemaya: The Asian Film Quarterly*, XXX (Autumn 1995), pp. 30, 32

——, 'Iz / Traces', *Cinemaya: The Asian Film Quarterly*, XXX (Autumn 1995), p. 31

——, 'Reflections of a Culture in Conflict – Turkish Cinema of the Nineties', *Blimp* (15 September 1994)

——, 'Mavi Sürgün / The Blue Exile', *Cinemaya: The Asian Film Quarterly*, XXII (Winter 1993–4), pp. 24–5

——, 'Contre l'heritage de Kemal Atatürk: Cinéma et morale Islamiste', *Le Monde Diplomatique* (October 1993)

——, 'Vertical Images of Dichotomy', *Cinemaya: The Asian Film Quarterly*, XXI (Autumn 1993), pp. 55–7

——, 'Cinema turc; reflets d'une culture duale', *Cinébulles*, XIII/3 (1993)

*Düşünce Özgürlüğü ve Türkiye* (Istanbul, 1995)

Elsaesser, Thomas, 'Double Occupancy and Small Adjustments: Space, Place and Policy in the New European Cinema since the 1990s', in *European Cinema: Face to Face with Hollywood* (Amsterdam, 2005), pp. 108–30

Erdoğan, Nezih, 'Violent Images: Hybridity and Excess in *The Man Who Saved the World*', in Karen Ross, Deniz Derman and Nevena Dakovic, eds, *Mediated Identities* (Istanbul, 2001), p. 116

——, 'Narratives of Resistance: National Identity and Ambivalence in the Turkish Melodrama between 1965 and 1975', *Screen*, XXXIII/3 (1998), pp. 259–71.

Evren, Burçak, *Sigmund Weinberg* (Istanbul, 1995)

——, *Türk Sinemasında Yeni Konumlar* (İstanbul, 1990)

Gabriel, Teshom H., *Third Cinema in the Third World: The Aesthetics of Liberation* (Ann Arbor, MI, 1982)

Gledhill, Christine, 'The Melodramatic Field: An Investigation', in Christine Gledhill, ed., *Home Is Where The Hearth Is* (London, 1987)

Göktürk, Deniz, 'Turkish Delight – German Fright: Unsettling Oppositions in Transnational Cinema', in Karen Ross and Deniz Derman, eds, *Mapping the Margins: Identity Politics and the Media*.

——, and Nezih Erdoğan, 'Turkish Cinema', in Oliver Leaman, ed., *Companion Encyclopedia of Middle Eastern and North African Film* (London and New York, 2001)

Gramsci, Antonio, *Selections from the Prison Notebooks* (London, 1971)

Güçhan, Gülseren, *Toplumsal Değişme ve Türk Sineması* (Ankara, 1992)

Günçıkan, Berat, *Murat Belge: Linç Kültürünün Tarihsel Kökeni* (Istanbul, 2006)

Guneratne, Antony R., and Wimal Dissanayake, eds, *Rethinking Third Cinema* (New York and London, 2003)

Güney, Yılmaz, *Yol* (Istanbul, 1994)

——, *Sürü* (Istanbul, (1994)

——, *Arkadaş* (Istanbul, 1975)

Hillman, Roger, '*Lola and Billy the Kid* (1999): A Turkish Director's Western Showdown in Berlin', *Post Script: Essays in Film and Humanities, Special Issue: Transnational Cinema*, XXV/ 2 (Winter–Spring 2006)

Hutcheon, Linda, 'Circling the Downspout of Empire', in I. Adam and H. Tiffin, eds, *Past, the Last Post: Theorizing Post-Colonialism and Post-Modernism* (Calgary, 1990), pp. 167–89

Irigaray, Luce, *This Sex Which is Not One*, trans. Catherine Porter (Ithaca, NY, 1985)

Işın, Engin F., 'Democracy, Citizenship and the City', in *Democracy, Citizenship and the Global City* (London and New York, 2000)

İçduygu, Ahmet, and Özlem Kaygusuz, 'The Politics of Citizenship by Drawing Borders: Foreign Policy and the Construction of National Citizenship Identity in Turkey', *Middle Eastern Studies*, XL/6 (2004)

Jameson, Fredric, *The Geopolitical Aesthetic: Cinema and Space in the World System* (Bloomington, IN and London, 1992)

——, *Postmodernism; or, The Cultural Logic of Late Capitalism* (London and New York, 1991)

——, 'Third World Literature in the Era of Multinational Capitalism', *Social Text*, XV (1986)

Jayawardena, Kumari, *Feminism and Nationalism in the Third World* (London, 1986)

Kandiyoti, Deniz, and Ayşe Saktanber, eds, *Fragments of Culture: The Everyday of Modern Turkey* (London, 2002)

Kaplan, E. Ann, *Looking for the Other: Feminism, Film and the Imperial Gaze* (New York and London, 1996)

Kara, Mesut, *Yeşilçam'da Unutulmayan Yüzler* (Istanbul, 1999)

Karanfil, Gökçen, 'Becoming Undone: Contesting Nationalisms in Contemporary Turkish Popular Cinema' *National Identities*, VIII/1 (March 2006), pp. 61–75

Kavolis, Vytautas, 'The Logics of Selfhood and Modes of Order: Civilizational Structures for Individual Identities', in Roland Robertson and Burkart Holzner, eds, *Identity and Authority: Explorations in Theory and Society* (Oxford and New York, 1980)

Kayalı, Kurtuluş, *Metin Erksan Sinemasını Okumayı Denemek* (Ankara, 2004)

Kinzer, Stephen, *Crescent & Star: Turkey between Two Worlds* (New York, 2001)

Kırel, Serpil, *Yeşilçam Öykü Sinemasi* (Istanbul, 2005)

Landy, Marcia, *Cinematic Uses of the Past* (Minneapolis, MN and London, 1996)

Leaman, Oliver, ed., *The Companion Encyclopedia of Middle Eastern and North African Film* (London and New York, 2001)

Livaneli, Zülfü, *Mutluluk* (Istanbul, 2005)

Maktav, Hilmi, 'Vatan Millet Cinema', *Birikim*, CCVII (July 2006)

Malouf, Amin, *In the Name of Identity: Violence and the Need to Belong* (New York, 2001)

——, *On Identity* (London, 2000)

Mango, Andrew, *The Turks Today* (London, 2004)

Marks, Laura U., *The Skin of Film: Intercultural Cinema, Embodiment and the Senses* (Durham, NC and London, 2000)

Monceau, Nicolas, 'Nuri Bilge Ceylan, vue intimes d'Istanbul', *Le Monde* (18–19 May 2003), p. 21

Mulvey, Laura, 'Visual Pleasure and Narrative Cinema, *Screen*, XVI/3 (1975)

——, *Visual and Other Pleasures* (Bloomington, IN, 1989)

Naficy, Hamid, *An Accented Cinema: Diasporic and Exilic Filmmaking* (Princeton, NJ, 2001)

——, ed., *Home, Exile, Homeland: Film, Media and the Politics of Place* (London and New York, 1999)

——, *The Making of Exile Cultures: Iranian Television in Los Angeles* (Minneapolis, MN, 1993)

Nelson, Hilde Lindemann, *Damaged Identities, Narrative Repair* (Ithaca, NY, 2001)

Onaran, Alim Şerif, *Türk Sineması*, vols I and II (Istanbul, 1994)

Onaran, Oğuz, Abisel, Nilgün, Köker, Levent and Eser Köker, *Türk Sinemasında Demokrasi Kavramının Gelişmesi* (Ankara, 1994).

Özbek, Meral, *Popüler Kültür ve Orhan Gencebay Arabeski* (İstanbul, 1994)

Özgüç, Agah, *Türk Filmleri Sözlüğü* (Istanbul, 1998)

——, 'Film Karelerinde Yaşayan Eski Istanbul', *Cumhuriyet Dergi*, CDXIV (27 February 1994), p. 17

——, *Bir Sinema Günlüğünden Aykırı Notlar* (Istanbul, 1992)

——, *Bütün Filmleriyle Yılmaz Güney* (Istanbul, 1990)

——, *Türk Sinemasında Cinselliğin Tarihi* (Istanbul, 1988)

Özön, Nihat, *Karagözden Sinemaya: Türk Sineması ve Sorunları*, vols I and II (Ankara, 1995)

——, *Sinema Uygulayımı Sanatı Tarihi* (Istanbul, 1985)

Öztürk, Mehmet, 'Türk Sinemasında Gecekondular', *European Journal of Turkish Studies*, Thematic Issue, I (2004); available at www.ejts.org/document94.html (accessed 5 February 2008).

——, *Sine-masal Kentler* (İstanbul, 2002)

Öztürk, Semire Ruken, ed., *Kader: Zeki Demirkubuz* (Ankara, 2006)

——, *Sinemanın Dişil Yüzü* (Istanbul, 2003)

Pamuk, Orhan, 'My First Passport: What Does it Mean to Belong to a Country?', *New Yorker* (16 April 2007)

——, *The Black Book* (New York, 2006)

——, 'Who do You Write for?', *Herald Tribune* (29–30 July 2006)

——, *Istanbul: Memories of a City* (London, 2005)

Robinson, Kevin, and Asu Aksoy, 'Deep Nation: Turkish Cinema Culture', in Mette Hjort and Scott Mackenzie, eds, *Cinema and Nation* (London and New York, 2000)

Rosenbaum, Jonathan, 'A "Global" (Postnational) Future?: Multinational Pest Control – Does American Cinema Still Exist?', in Alan Williams, ed., *Film and Nationalism* (New Brunswick, NJ, and London, 2002)

Said, Edward W., *Orientalism* (New York, 1978)

——, *Culture and Imperialism* (New York, 1992)

Saktanber, Ayşe, *Living Islam: Women, Religion and the Politicization of Culture in Turkey* (London and New York, 2002)

Scognamillo, Giovani, *Türk Sinema Tarihi* (İstanbul, 1998)

Shohat, Ella, and Robert Stam, eds, *Multiculturalism, Postcoloniality and Transnational Media* (New York, 2003)

——, *Unthinking Eurocentrism: Multiculturalism and the Media* (London, 1994)

Slemon, Stephen, 'Magic Realism as Post-Colonial Discourse', *Canadian Literature*, CXVI (1988)

Sontag, Susan, 'Novel into Film', *Vanity Fair* (September 1983)

Soykan, Fetay. *Türk Sinemasında Kadın, 1920–1990* (Izmir, 1993)

Spivak, Gayatri Chakravorty, *A Critique of Postcolonial Reason: Toward a History of the Vanishing Present* (Cambridge and London, 1999)

Stam, Robert, *Subversive Pleasures: Bakhtin, Cultural Criticism, and Film*, (Baltimore, MD, 1989)

——, *Reflexivity in Film and Literature* (New York, 1992)

Stokes, M., 'Beloved Istanbul: Realism and Transnational Imaginary in Turkish Popular Culture', in W. Armbrust, ed., *Mass Mediations: New Approaches to Popular Culture in the Middle East and Beyond* (Berkeley, CA, 2000), pp. 224–42

Suner, Asuman, *Hayalet Ev: Yeni Türk Sinemasında Aidiyet, Kimlik ve Bellek* (Istanbul, 2006)

——, 'Horror of a Different Kind: Dissonant Voices of the New Turkish Cinema', *Screen*, XLV/4 (Winter 2004), pp. 305–23

——, 'Masum ve Mahsun: 1990'lar Korku Sineması', in Deniz Derman, ed., *Türk Film Araştırmalarında Yeni Yönelimler*, vol. IV (Istanbul, 2004)

——, *Araf: The Saint of Incipient Insanities* (Istanbul, 2003)

Şafak, Elif, *The Bastard of Istanbul* (London and New York, 2007)

Şahin, Haluk, 'Yeni İletişim Ortamı ve Kimliğimiz', *Varlık Dergisi*, MIX (October 1991)

Şen, Abdurrahman, *Cemre: Kültür, Sanat ve Edebiyat Üzerine Politik Yazılar* (Istanbul, 1990)

Tanilli, Server, *İslam Öağımıza Yanıt Verebilir mi?* (Istanbul, 1993)

Thoraval, Yves, *Les Cinemas du Orient, Ian, Egypt, Turquie* (Paris 2000)

Türk, İbrahim, *Düşlerden Düşüncelere Söyleşiler* (Istanbul, 2001)

Türkali, Vedat, *Yeşilçam Dedikleri Türkiye* (Istanbul, 2001)

——, *Tüm Yazıları Konuşmaları* (Istanbul, 2001)

van Bruinessen, Martin, 'Race, Culture, Nation and Identity Politics in Turkey: Some Comments', paper presented at the 'Mica Ertegün Annual Turkish Studies Workshop on Continuity and Change: Shifting State Ideologies from Late Ottoman to Early Republican Turkey, 1890–1930', Department of Near Eastern Studies, Princeton University (24–6 April 1997)

Velioğlu, Özgür, *İnançların Türk Sinemasına Yansıması: Şamanism, Gök-Tanrı, Animizm, Naturalism, Totemizm, İslamiyet İnançları Açısından* (Istanbul, 2005)

Vidler, Anthony, *The Architectural Uncanny* (Boston, MA, 1992)

——, *Warped Space: Art, Architecture and Anxiety in Modern Culture* (Cambridge, 2000)

Williams, Alan, ed., *Film and Nationalism* (New Brunswick, NJ and London, 2002)

Yavuz, Hakan M., *Islamic Political Identity in Turkey* (New York, 2003)

# Acknowledgements

I would like to thank Michael Leaman for all his editorial guidance; producers Mehmet Altıoklar and Jale Onanç, Özen Film's chairman Mehmet Soyarslan, filmmakers Mustafa Altıoklar, Reis Çelik, Kudret Güneş, Semih Kaplanoğlu, Kazım Öz, Ali Özgentürk and Derviş Zaim and the director of TURSAK (Turkish Foundation of Cinema and Audiovisual Culture), Engin Yiğitgil, for their generosity with their time and expertise; Istanbul International and Antalya Golden Orange Film Festivals for making it possible to view so many Turkish films; the Kurdish Institute in Paris for opening their Yılmaz Güney files; Professor Oliver Leaman for his continuous support and my life-partner Andre Colin for his patience and his invaluable emotional and intellectual encouragement during the realization of this project.

This book is based on independent research. It did not receive any form of financial assistance from governmental or non-governmental organizations, academic or non-academic institutions. The opinions expressed belong to the author.

# Index